# THE FALL OF MUSSOLINI

# THE FALL OF
# MUSSOLINI

## ITALY, THE ITALIANS,
### AND THE
## SECOND WORLD WAR

PHILIP MORGAN

**OXFORD**
UNIVERSITY PRESS

# OXFORD
## UNIVERSITY PRESS

Great Clarendon Street, Oxford OX2 6DP

Oxford University Press is a department of the University of Oxford.
It furthers the University's objective of excellence in research, scholarship,
and education by publishing worldwide in

Oxford  New York

Auckland  Cape Town  Dar es Salaam  Hong Kong  Karachi
Kuala Lumpur  Madrid  Melbourne  Mexico City  Nairobi
New Delhi  Shanghai  Taipei  Toronto

With offices in

Argentina  Austria  Brazil  Chile  Czech Republic  France  Greece
Guatemala  Hungary  Italy  Japan  Poland  Portugal  Singapore
South Korea  Switzerland  Thailand  Turkey  Ukraine  Vietnam

Oxford is a registered trade mark of Oxford University Press
in the UK and in certain other countries

Published in the United States
by Oxford University Press Inc., New York

© Philip Morgan 2007

The moral rights of the author have been asserted
Database right Oxford University Press (maker)

First published 2007

British Library Cataloguing in Publication Data

Data available

Library of Congress Cataloging in Publication Data
Data available

Typeset by SPI Publisher Services, Pondicherry, India
Printed in Great Britain
on acid-free paper by
Biddles Ltd, King's Lynn, Norfolk

ISBN 978-0-19-280247-7

1 3 5 7 9 10 8 6 4 2

*The book is dedicated with love to my wife, Glen,*
*and to my daughter, Ellen, who both think that I am*
*becoming like my father, the silent witness of this book.*

# Preface

My father fought in the British army against the Italians and Germans in North Africa, and again in the long Italian campaign of 1943 to 1945. My mother and I could never understand how a man with such big and clumsy hands could have made his way through the lower ranks to be a sergeant in a bomb disposal unit. He was always reticent about his war experiences in North Africa and Italy, even when he knew that I was writing this book and was beginning to crowd him about it. He remembered, or allowed himself to remember, sifting with other soldiers through the silk shirts left in the wardrobe of the abandoned villa of a Fascist leader on the Adriatic coast, and how some of his fellow soldiers speculated and bartered their way to useless occupation currency fortunes before demobilization. In strictly rationed disclosures, he gave me some sense of a war fought against boredom and inertia, interspersed with periods of intense danger and activity, and of things going wrong, militarily and logistically. He apparently ended up fighting with the American forces during the Italian campaign. Was this deliberate, or was he simply put on the wrong ship, or landed in the wrong place?

He certainly said very little about Italy and the Italians, and this is surprising in view of what the war did to my father. Coming from a large working-class mining family in South Wales, for whom England was a foreign country, he demobilized to a marriage with my mother, a London-born Land Army 'girl', a short stint with a radio components factory (those hands again), and then emergency training to become a school teacher in the new towns just north of London. The whole itinerary was an individual case of the war's unintended enabling and transforming impact on people's lives. The war made people mobile, largely against their will and desires, in both a spatial and mind-opening sense. For conscripts like my father, it unearthed and tested people's capacities, and opened up new opportunities.

My father's reticence about his role in wartime Italy as foreign invader-occupier-liberator, belies the rhetorical question asked about the East German political police in another context, 'Why are some things easier to remember the *more* time has passed since they occurred?'[1] The longer time went on, the more silent my father became, as he decided not to reveal his Italian war. I wondered whether the personal testimonies which do exist have covered up some experiences, while uncovering others, making these witnesses as silent as my father. Although he did not want to talk about it, I at least came to realize that part of many Italians' experience of the war would have been how they reacted to invading and occupying forces which included my father.

Two summers ago, my wife and I were on holiday walking in the wooded hills of the Langhe, south of Turin in north-western Italy. I was certainly not on a field trip researching for this book, though I probably should have been. But we could not help noticing that the war memorials in the villages we passed through commemorated those who died in the 'war of liberation' between 1943 and 1945, but made no mention of the casualties of the 'Fascist' war of 1940 to 1943. In a small isolated chapel, we did come across a modest sign and photograph on the wall, recording the death of a young priest at the hands of the 'Nazi-Fascists' in 1944. It had no more than a generic indication of the circumstances in which he was killed, and the reasons for which he died.

We had hardly discovered anything new. But it is clearly important how people remember wars, because of what it reveals or disguises about the values and culture of post-war society and those who survived. 'Life is not what one lived, but what one remembers and how one remembers it in order to recount it,' says Gabriel Garcia Márquez,[2] whose novels are all about the making of historical and cultural myths. The Langhe village monuments to the war need deciphering and contextualizing. Who put up the monuments, or decided on the inscriptions, the local town council, the local partisans association? Whose selective commemoration were they? If it was the ex-partisans, then they belonged to an organization committed to protecting a certain collective memory of a certain war. I wondered how those locals felt whose sons had died fighting the Fascist wars of 1940 to 1943. A public commemoration might well be imposing one kind of memory on another. And when were they erected or inscribed? How soon after the war? I wondered how geographically specific this sort of remembrance was. If I went on a walking holiday in Tuscany, would I find the same monuments, the same inscriptions?

This chance holiday encounter with commemorations of the country's recent past, opened up wider questions. Did Italians deliberately choose to forget that Fascist war, to become oblivious to it? Or are we dealing rather with contested memories and commemoration? There will be much more on historical memory and reminiscence in the book, and it will, I hope, be interesting to follow how a historian of archive documents such as myself deals with a different order of documentation in popular history, the oral and written testimonies of ordinary Italians. It is worth adding, at this point, that all the translations from Italian language sources are my own.

P.J.M.

# Acknowledgements

I would like to thank all my editors at Oxford University Press, especially the one at the beginning, Catherine Clarke, and the one at the end, Luciana O'Flaherty, for the interest and attention they have given to the book and its author.

# Contents

# List of Illustrations

# List of Maps

# Abbreviations

| | |
|---|---|
| CLN | Comitato di Liberazione Nazionale (Committee of National Liberation: regional, provincial, and local anti-Fascist groups) |
| CLNAI | Comitato di Liberazione Nazionale per Alta Italia (Committee of National Liberation for Northern Italy: organization coordinating the anti-Fascist Resistance in German-occupied Italy) |
| CVL | Corpo Volontario della Libertà (Voluntary Freedom Corps: the Resistance army) |
| Decima Mas | Decima Flottiglia Motoscafi Antisommergibili (Tenth Motor Torpedo Boat Squadron; later, a RSI police force) |
| EDES | National Republican Greek League (non-communist Greek resistance movement) |
| ELAS | National People's Liberation Army (communist-dominated Greek resistance movement) |
| GAP | Gruppi di Azione Patriottica (Patriotic Action Groups: urban resistance groups) |
| GNR | Guardia Nazionale Repubblicana (Republican National Guard: RSI police force) |
| IMI | *internati militari italiani* (Italian military internees) |
| MSI | *Movimento Sociale Italiano* (Italian Social Movement: neo-Fascist party) |
| PCI | *Partito Comunista Italiano* (Italian Communist Party) |
| PFR | *Partito Fascista Repubblicano* (Republican Fascist Party) |
| PWB | Pyschological Warfare Bureau (Information and 'cultural' branch of Allied Military Government) |
| RSI | Repubblica Sociale Italiana (Italian Social Republic) |
| SAF | Servizi Ausiliari Femminili (Women's Auxiliary Service of the RSI) |
| UNPA | Unione Nazionale Protezione Antiaerea (National Union for Anti-aircraft Protection: voluntary organization for civilian air raids defence) |
| Waffen-SS | Armed SS (German SS fighting troops) |

Map 1. Modern Italy

Map 2. The military war in Italy: the armistice and German defensive lines

# Introduction: Remembering the Second World War in Italy

M OST continental European countries, with the exception of the neutrals Sweden and Switzerland, have lived through one or all of the experiences of fascist dictatorship, and war, defeat, and foreign occupation. Even though West European countries had not become fascist before the outbreak of war, they suffered military defeat and Nazi German occupation. Some people collaborated with the occupier, some resisted, and the reasons for collaboration and resistance varied greatly. In other Nazi-occupied countries, as in Italy, during and after liberation, the resisters and the people took sometimes bloody revenge on those who collaborated with the Nazis. One of the most encouraging signs of recent Italian writing on the war is its willingness to catch up with the more nuanced understandings of 'collaboration' and 'resistance' and of the grey zones between collaboration and resistance, which have emerged in historical studies of, say, wartime occupied France and the Netherlands.[1] Since war, invasion, and occupation were a European and not a uniquely Italian experience, it is as well to remember that Italy's governments and people had to confront and deal with broadly similar challenges to those faced in other belligerent countries.

Governments at war, whether democratic, fascist, or communist, had to find ways of mobilizing, allocating, and making good the shortfalls in finite supplies of human and material resources, and in doing so, secure and maintain a kind of internal political and social truce, based on a popular acceptance or perception of shared misery, of equality of sacrifice. This put a real premium on political leadership, and on the inevitably closer relationships in war between government, political leaders, and their peoples. The people's continuing trust and confidence in their leaders, perhaps the most important component of civilian morale and reflected in their commitment, or not, to the war effort, was crucial to surviving and winning the war and, indeed, to the very validation, or not, of each country's political system.

Again, this was a war where many, perhaps even most, civilians in Europe became combatants or victims of war, which, leaving aside organized genocidal killings, was largely a result of widespread enemy air bombardment of civilian as well as military targets. There were more civilian than military casualties overall during the Second World War, though this was not actually the case in Italy, as far as one can tell, since there are no agreed figures for the number of Italians who died during the war. Estimates for the total number of military and civilian dead between 1940 and 1945 veer between just over 300,000 and about 450,000,[2] and it is likely that civilian dead, including those who died or went missing in the partisan war, Allied bombing raids, and in reprisals and deportations, amounted to about half of those who were killed in military action.

The air bombing by all belligerents was, quite literally, meant to terrorize enemy countries into surrender. It generally proved to be inaccurate, and the practice of area- or carpet-bombing (wiping out everything in the proximity of a target in the hope that the target itself might actually take a hit) increased the destructive range and impact of bombing campaigns. Perhaps 64,000 Italians were killed in Allied wartime bombing raids, over two-thirds of whom died after Italy had officially changed sides, the result of the bombing of German-occupied northern and central Italy between September 1943 and April 1945. This was about the same figure as the UK, and both sets of casualties were way below the 600,000–700,000 killed in bombing Germany; but it was bad enough.

The war's destructive impacts were direct and immediate, and often a deeply demoralizing and divisive experience for peoples at war. Governments and leaders strained to keep their populations united behind the war effort. We cannot assume that the evacuations to the countryside of bombed-out urban families, whether it occurred in Britain, Germany, or Italy, were necessarily an opportunity to demonstrate social cohesiveness and bonding, or as the Nazis' propaganda had it, a practical exercise in cementing the *Volksgemeinschaft* (people's community).[3]

There is, sometimes, a danger in making exceptional the Italian experience of the war, or in making the Italians' experience of it stereotypically Italian, as with the view that evacuation procedures in Italy's industrial cities were somehow peculiarly incompetent and improvised in a characteristically Italian way. Mussolini himself put Italy's lost war down to almost congenital deficiencies in Italians' will and temperament, and blamed Italy's collapse on the intractable human material which had resisted twenty years of Fascist remoulding. Evacuation in wartime Italy was sometimes inept and chaotic, but probably no more so than the outcome of the British government's initial unreadiness to meet the consequences of the bombing of civilians.

But there were aspects of Italy's war which arguably made it unique. Italy's Fascist dictator, Benito Mussolini, fell from power not once but twice, first in July 1943, and again in April 1945. It happened, of course, to Napoleon and France in 1814–15—imagine it happening in Nazi Germany. Once the king had dismissed Mussolini as prime minister in July 1943, his transitional government was unable to carry out its (totally unrealistic) plan for Italy's safe and painless exit from the war. This failure meant both a prolongation of the war in Italy itself and the Nazi German restoration of Mussolini to nominal power in the north Italian Social Republic. The outcome was an aggravation of the civil war between Italians, the 'war within the war' which characterized the period from autumn 1943 to spring 1945. Not that the civil war aspect of responses to Nazi occupation was specifically Italian; as the historian Mark Mazower has gloomily remarked, 'In those countries that endured Nazi occupation, the war years are coming to be seen, not just as a struggle between enemy powers, but as a civil war in which societies fractured along class, ethnic or ideological lines and any semblance of national cohesion vanished.'[4]

What was experienced in Italy, and nowhere else, was the interim period of the so-called Forty-Five Days, between the first fall of Mussolini on 25 July 1943 and the eventual armistice between Italy and the Allied powers announced on 8 September 1943. It should become clearer in the course of this book that the real watershed wartime event for Italy and Italians was probably not so much the first fall of Mussolini in July 1943 as the armistice of September 1943, the consequences of which forced Italians to confront their relationship to the state and its institutions and their understanding of what the Italian nation actually was. The armistice precipitated the Nazi German occupation of northern and central Italy, as the Allies made their unexpectedly slow and painful military conquest of the country from the south. This meant that Italy, for a particularly lengthy period, was a country still at war and being invaded and divided by not one but two occupying armies. It is usual, and perhaps still justified, to speak of northern Italy being 'occupied' by the Germans and 'liberated' by the Allies from the south. While it would be wrong to equate the Nazi and Allied occupation regimes in terms of malevolence, dual occupation once again compromised and complicated Italians' sense of nationhood and knowing where they belonged, and who they were to fight.

The war was a defining point in ordinary Italians' lives, as it was for many people of that generation. It had an inescapable and extraordinary impact on the Italians, forcing them into making choices, including, of course, choosing not to choose, even if only as a strategy for survival, and into becoming participants in, as well as observers of, great events. Since the war affected so many people, it becomes especially important to establish how the war in Italy has been remembered since 1945. Memories of the war, and particularly of the armed resistance to German occupation between 1943 and 1945, not only shaped how Italians saw themselves and their new democratic system of government after the war but also conditioned how the history of the war has been written.

It is important, then, for this introduction to start at the end, rather than the beginning, with a look at how the war was remembered in the post-war period. Providing some of this context now will, I hope, make intelligible the events of the war in Italy dealt with in a more chronological manner in the chapters which follow. What I have to say about the Italian people's attitudes and responses to the war and the Fascist regime should be measured against, or rather located in, this context.

Initially, the tendency was to remember the war by forgetting it, or remembering only part of it. The needs and demands of reconstruction after such a physically destructive and morally divisive war were so great that it seemed that national recovery itself would be threatened by dwelling too much on the war. The mood of national reconciliation was also official and governmental, something welcomed and promoted by the anti-Fascist parties which had emerged during and as a result of the armed resistance to German occupation. It was exemplified in the amnesty announced in June 1946 by the Communist Minister of Justice Palmiro Togliatti, even-handedly extended to ex-Fascists and anti-Fascists for crimes committed during the war and liberation of the country.

There was much to be gained from forgetting and forgiving in the initial post-war period, and not only in terms of internal pacification. Italy had changed sides in 1943, leaving the Axis alliance with Nazi Germany to fight against Germany alongside the Allies. The country's uncertain international status as an ex-enemy ally would affect how punitive any post-war settlement was to be. Italy's post-war governments had every interest in portraying a country united, not divided, in its common struggle with the Allies against Nazi Germany. Italy's immediate post-war anti-Fascist governments, which included the socialist and communist left, resisted attempts by Yugoslavia, for instance, to extradite Italian 'war criminals' for their actions in invading and occupying the Soviet Union and the Balkans during the war, and did so, as an article in the socialist national newspaper *Avanti!* very significantly put it, out of 'love of country and love of forgetting'.[5] To this day, no Italian has been tried for war crimes.

So the memory which emerged in the early post-war years was the reassuring one that the overwhelming majority of Italians were anti-Fascist, and had resisted both German occupation and the exiguous minority of Italians who had collaborated with the occupier and supported the Fascist Republic, Nazi Germany's client state in northern Italy. This became a consoling judgement on the twenty years of Fascism in Italy as a whole, as well as a judgement on the war. It was far from 'telling ourselves the truth' about Fascism and the war, which the Italian film director Vittorio De Sica claimed for the neo-realist films made about the war, after the war.[6]

But the deliberate forgetfulness was understandable, indeed even justifiable, at the time. The same obliviousness occurred in every West European country emerging from fascism and Nazi occupation after the war, and for much the same reasons. Everybody was interested in forgetting what had happened during the war, or in telling themselves what they wanted to hear about their behaviour during it. The French Resistance leader and head of the post-war French government, Charles de Gaulle, muffled the memory of Vichy France's wartime collaboration with Hitler by creating the idea of a country and people unified around him in their resistance to Nazi tyranny. The Dutch had less difficulty in doing this, since there was no equivalent in the wartime Netherlands of a collaborating Dutch government. But people needed to forget the uncomfortable fact that a very high proportion of Dutch Jews had been deported to the Nazi death camps in Eastern Europe, something which could only have happened with a degree of cooperation from Dutch officials and people. One could say that the initial post-war forgetting of the war in Italy prevented, or postponed, Italians assuming some kind of collective awareness of and responsibility for Fascism. It camouflaged both the involvement of Italians in the Fascist regime of the 1920s and 1930s, and the divided personal, political, and national loyalties expressed by people during the war itself. But that was the point of not remembering.

Remembering the war as the time when the nation resisted and drove out the Nazi occupier also served the function of dignifying and validating the fresh start after 1945 of a democratic parliamentary republic. The republican constitution of 1948 was seen as the outcome of the united and concerted efforts to create a new democratic Italy from the ruins of the old Fascist Italy, by the anti-Fascist political parties which drew their strength and will to act from the popular, patriotic anti-Fascist resistance against the Nazi occupier and their Fascist allies between 1943 and 1945. It is quite justified to argue now that the anti-Fascist resistance could not bear the weight of being the consensual founding and legitimating myth of a democratic and republican Italy. The Resistance did not, in fact, involve the majority of Italians, north or south. It perhaps would not, therefore, have been a sufficiently collective experience to engage fully the memories and pride of the nation, post-war, in its newly fledged democratic system. But again, that was the point and function of the Resistance myth. Myths in modern societies are made up of words, symbols, and images which convey a set of visionary beliefs aiming to engage and mobilize people's psychological energies and emotions behind political action, and behind political systems. They have played, and continue to play, a really significant role in legitimating modern nation-states and their governments. A myth does not have to be true in order to convince people of the aura, meaning, and significance attached to historical events. Mythologizing a partial experience as a universal experience served its purpose of making credible and valuable the transition of the country from a Fascist dictatorship to a parliamentary democracy.

The wartime and immediate post-war unity of anti-Fascist forces broke up in Italy in 1947 and 1948, as it did elsewhere in liberated Europe, with the passing of the war into the cold war and the hardening of the post-war division of Europe into Western and Eastern blocs. After the 1948 elections, politics in Italy took on the cold war mould. Governments were dominated by the Christian Democrats and held together by anti-communism, while the Italian Communist Party (Partito Comunista Italiano, PCI) and the socialist left were excluded from government. The Christian Democrats both contributed to and drew on the cold war divisions across Italy and Europe by denigrating the communist contribution to the wartime armed resistance, as a way of discrediting the PCI's democratic and national credentials. In a 'trial of the Resistance', ex-communist partisans were investigated, tried, and convicted for violent crimes committed not only during and after liberation in April 1945, but also during the war itself. A largely unpurged judiciary which had made its career under the Fascist regime enacted a kind of revenge on those forces which had initially wanted to rid the state bureaucracy of its 'Fascists'. The judges applied anti-subversive Fascist laws which remained on the books against the men who fought against fascism in its home-grown and Nazi forms.

It was from the late 1940s that the Resistance myth became largely one sustained by the Italian left. Precisely because it was excluded from government, the PCI needed its resistance role to continue to justify its place in democratic national politics. The golden years of the Resistance myth were, in fact, after the easing of cold war tensions from the early 1960s into the 1970s, with the Socialist Party, if not the communists, entering centre-left national government coalitions, the PCI enjoying actual power in new elected regional administrations and approaching a compromise with the Christian Democrats. The contestation of the Resistance myth of their fathers came from further on the left, the New Left stimulated by student and worker agitation of the late 1960s, for whom the orthodox communist and socialist left had betrayed the resistance and its revolutionary goals and possibilities.

In the early 1990s, there occurred what appeared to be the crisis and collapse of Italy's post-war political system. With the 'first' Republic apparently gone, its legitimating myth of the anti-Fascist Resistance has taken further hard knocks, too. Often, this has taken the form of a sanitized, conflict-free, nostalgic, heritage industry version of popular history, appropriate enough, perhaps, for a consumerist society where history is a commodity and an entertainment like any other. This kind of history conveys a recent past as smooth and free of problems as the one based on a certain unifying myth of the Resistance.

Interestingly, public monuments marking and remembering the war were often close to authentic popular memories of the war. This must be because many of the monuments to the war were not official, or created to denote an officially endorsed public memory. It is really quite significant that there is still no national monument to resistance to German Nazi occupation of Italy between 1943 and 1945, and that the national monuments of the war are located on Italy's contested north-eastern frontier. These are the national museum on the site of the German concentration camp of La Risiera di San Sabba, at Trieste, and the site of the mass killings of Italians by Yugoslav partisans in deep ditches (*foibe*) at Basovizza, also near Trieste. The Italian state has not been concerned, then, to commemorate the Resistance. It might also be said that it has discouraged public memory of the Resistance, since Fascism and the war were not made part of the school curriculum until the 1960s. Their inclusion was unpopular with the teachers required to teach them, because many of them belonged to the largely unpurged state personnel inherited by the Republic from the Fascist period, and were obliged to historicize themselves.

Streets and squares have been renamed after Resistance martyrs, and public monuments to the Resistance have been erected by local and regional authorities in areas like Emilia-Romagna, where the Resistance was particularly strong and active and had lasting popular and political resonances. Small-scale monuments, typically plaques or inscribed stones, have been created at or near the sites of German atrocities against civilians, or the execution of partisans, often a matter of family or local community initiative, and to that extent, therefore, private memories. Such private commemoration has, apparently, been something traditionally undertaken by Italians. It seems to be an entirely appropriate and authentic way to mark the war, since resistance was, in the main, made up of unorganized, individual actions, the outcome of individual choices and dilemmas.

The day of liberation from German occupation, 25 April, has been marked by annual public ceremonies. Although the usual public and political dignitaries have attended, addressed, and been seen at such occasions, they were, and are, organized by the national ex-partisans' associations, groups who are naturally anxious to keep alive a particular view of the war. These annual ceremonies have changed in character, tone, and resonance over time, often reflecting what the current political situation was. Now, in contemporary Italy's post-Fascist climate, the ceremonies commemorating liberation are almost defiant in remembering the exploits and achievements of a popular anti-Fascist and anti-Nazi movement.

It is something of a marketplace in commemorations of the war. For a long time, there have been in existence equivalent associations of Fascist Republican ex-combatants and their families, which under recent governments led by Silvio Berlusconi, have been given a kind of parity with the ex-partisans. Sponsored by a National Alliance politician and backed by the Berlusconi government in which the Alliance was a coalition partner, a bill brought before the Italian parliament in January 2006 gave the same combatant status to the 200,000 soldiers of the wartime Fascist Republic as that already held by regular armed forces personnel and wartime resistance partisans. The really contentious clause of the bill was the one which included the Fascist militias, the real equivalents on the Fascist side of the partisans and the men who fought the partisans alongside the Germans in a bitter civil war. For the bill's supporters, it recognizes the war service of those who had 'remained faithful to the fatherland even though they knew the war was lost'. For its opponents, it is 'a disgrace with which an attempt is being made to rewrite history'.[7] The introduction of the bill indicates a more general trend, that the celebration of liberation has to compete with other official commemorations of the war years.

The battleground of memories was, and is, evident, too, behind the more specific and local remembrance of the war. The anniversary of the German massacre of civilians at Guardistallo, near the Tuscan city of Pisa, has been marked by speeches by local politicians and academics singing the praises of the partisans who operated in the area. The oral testimonies gathered from survivors of the massacre show a very mixed and divided response to the role of the partisans, some memories actually blaming the massacre on the presence and activity of the partisans. These divided recollections of the same event were clear, also, in the interviews given to Allied investigators of the massacre shortly after the area was liberated. Suppressed or neglected popular memories are now in the open and a matter of historical investigation. Their use by historians ensures that forgetting does not become amnesia.

There is, then, continuing and unresolved conflict among Italians over Italy's Fascist and wartime past. It is important to read what follows with some awareness of why Italy's history is so controversial, and why that history still apparently matters to how Italians see themselves more than sixty years after the end of the Second World War. This book offers a reconstruction and a re-evaluation of the history of Italy and Italians during the war years. As far as this is possible for any historian to do, it is based on how Italians actually were during the war, rather than what they imagined or wanted themselves to be. The book pivots around Mussolini's first fall from power in July 1943 and the armistice of September 1943. Chapter 1 concentrates on the dramatic, and at the time surprisingly undramatic, story of July 1943, which is practically all high politics, or at least 'high' personalities, since this was the limited political sphere where Mussolini's fate was decided. The book then moves backwards to the Fascist war of 1940 to 1943, where the impact of the war on people's lives assumes crucial importance in explaining the events of July 1943 (Chapters 2 and 3). It then moves forward to consider the interregnum leading to the announcement of the armistice with the Allies and Italy's official changing of sides, in September 1943, a story, again, of high politics, and irresponsible high politics, at that (Chapters 4 and 5). The book concludes with a treatment of the repercussions of the first fall of Mussolini and the Fascist regime in the midst of its own war, felt in foreign invasion and occupation, and civil war (Chapters 6–8).

Mussolini himself practically disappears from the story after Chapter 1, making a dramatic and final reappearance right at the end of the book, with his death in April 1945. This is deliberate and authentic. Particularly after his return to Italy as head of the Fascist Republic in late 1943, he was a political cipher. Engaged in largely routine desk work at his government offices on the shores of Lake Garda, he sometimes railed ineffectually against the German exploitation and dismemberment of his country and Hitler's reluctance to allow even a nominal independence to the Republic.

The other reason for keeping Mussolini in the background, which was actually where he was, is that the book intends to be as bottom-up as it can be. What might appear as a sudden lurch from high politics to the ground level of Italians' wartime existence, is, again, deliberate. The book looks, to the extent that this is possible, at how people responded to and coped with the extraordinary pressures of wartime living, and the invasion, occupation, and division of their country by warring foreign powers. It tries to take in the competing demands made on popular resources and loyalties in different parts of Italy by the Fascist Republic and the other 'Italies' located in the monarchical south and the northern anti-Fascist resistance movements. It also includes the experiences of Italians outside Italy, in the dispersed 'Italies' of those interned in Germany or elsewhere, or fighting and occupying in Italian armies on foreign soil. The book, then, is a kind of monument to the divided memories of Italy's war.

# I

# The First Fall of Mussolini, July 1943

I N the early hours of 25 July 1943, after a sitting which lasted for over nine hours, a vote was taken at the final meeting of the Fascist Grand Council. Nineteen of the twenty-six high-ranking Fascists attending the Grand Council voted for a motion which led eventually to the removal of Mussolini as the head of the Italian government. When Mussolini met the king for a slightly earlier than normal audience on the afternoon of 25 July, Victor Emmanuel III told him that there was to be a new government under Marshal Pietro Badoglio. Not only was Mussolini dismissed as head of government; the king had him arrested by a waiting group of *carabinieri* (military policemen) within the palace grounds, and taken away to a *carabinieri* barracks in Rome in a windowless military ambulance. There were two coups, in other words, a Fascist and a monarchist one, and the royal coup superseded and overtook the Fascist coup, on 25 July 1943.

When the vote was completed, Mussolini's melodramatic parting shot to the Council was, 'You have provoked the crisis of the regime.'[1] In the absence of a stenographer and any official record of the meeting, words to this effect, anyway, appear in several, though by no means all, of the inevitably self-serving accounts written up for posterity by the protagonists of the meeting. Mussolini was right, he was always right, but only in retrospect.

Assuming he actually said this, it seems likely that Mussolini simply wanted to have the last word (yet again), and to intimidate and warn those Council members who had voted against him. There was nothing in Mussolini's demeanour and conduct at the meeting to suggest that the dictator had suddenly realized and acknowledged the significance of the vote. The same might be said of some of the Fascist leaders who had voted for the motion put before the meeting by Dino Grandi. This was the way Fascism ended, not with a bang but with a confused whimper.

Mussolini had no reason to think that he could not handle the meeting. The Fascist Grand Council was the main collegial organ of the Fascist regime, bringing together some of the top leaders who held national government, Fascist Party, and syndical-corporative positions. But Mussolini had successfully transformed it into yet another instrument of personal dictatorship. It could discuss all major matters of Fascist Party and government policy, and initially controlled the Party's organization and cadres until Mussolini took these into his own hands, as head of government. The Council could nominate candidates to fill vacant ministerial posts, and keep an updated list of likely candidates to succeed Mussolini as head of government, as well as discuss the succession to the throne. Because of this, it could have been the Fascist 'constitutional' body which ensured the continuation of the Fascist regime beyond the lifetime or political span of Mussolini.

However, Mussolini called and presided over its meetings, set its agendas, and nominated its members. Some of those who voted for Grandi's motion were there not by virtue of offices they held, but because of Mussolini's personal co-option. He never allowed the Council to take seriously its right to designate his successor. Such an omission was of some significance in July 1943, since it left unchallenged the king's right as head of state to appoint and dismiss the head of government, Mussolini. It was never Mussolini's practice to take votes, nor even to consult the Council on all major policy issues and decisions. The Council's penultimate meeting was nearly four years earlier, in September 1939, when Mussolini presumably felt he needed some kind of collective endorsement of his personally painful and embarrassing decision for 'non-belligerency', not to join the war on the side of Nazi Germany.

The Grand Council was his body. Even if a vote, exceptionally, was taken on this occasion, it was still a purely consultative forum whose opinions Mussolini did not need, and was not required, to take into account. The fact that he had agreed to call it at all did not denote, in his mind, anyway, an actual or imminent crisis, because whether it met, or not, was ultimately an irrelevance. This meeting served some immediate purpose for him. It flushed out his opponents, or obliged them to keep silent. Either way, it was an opportunity to assert his authority over other Fascist leaders. It was, indeed, Mussolini's confidence in his personal supremacy and hold over the Fascist leadership which allowed him to approach the meeting with such certainty of its outcome. Mussolini derisively remarked to his newly appointed Chief of Police, Renzo Chierici, just before the Council meeting, that its members were 'people who live by reflected light; if you put out the light, they sink back into the darkness from which they have emerged... There is nothing they want more than to be persuaded, and it will not be difficult for me to shepherd them back into the fold—that Grandi, that Bottai, also Count Ciano.'[2]

Mussolini had long been contemptuous and distrustful of the Fascist ruling elite, assuming that it was both incompetent and corrupt, and was reluctant to delegate real responsibilities and power to it. Such contempt was cause and effect of the evolution of Mussolini's form of personal dictatorship during the 1930s. Never trusting his peers to do the job meant a ridiculous centralization of ministerial offices in his own person; the Fascist government was essentially Mussolini in dialogue with himself. His self-imposed isolation in government accentuated his sense of being the national leader who alone could realize the historical mission to make Italy a great power. Although Mussolini could only exercise nominal control over so many ministries, his subordinates, because of his titular control, never actually felt responsible for or accountable for anything; it was all a matter for the dictator. The outcome of this combination of light-touch government from above and an inbuilt evasion of responsibility from below, was that often things just did not get done.

So, when Mussolini began the Grand Council meeting with a long filibuster on military affairs, avoiding the real issues of the political responsibility for Italy's disastrous war, he was immediately vulnerable to the quite scathing attacks by Grandi and others on his dictatorial style of government and the way it had affected the preparation for and running of the war. Mussolini had been the nominal minister for all three armed forces since coming to power in 1922, except for a break between 1929 and 1933. In 1940, Mussolini had finally badgered the king to surrender to him the substance of the crown's formal constitutional position as commander-in-chief of the armed forces. Like Hitler, Mussolini believed that war was too important a matter to leave to the generals, and wanted to enter a Fascist war as the country's supreme military commander. The situation in July 1943 was that Allied forces had invaded and were conquering Sicily, and landings on the mainland seemed to be only a matter of time. Mussolini's responsibility was inescapable, and Grandi's implacable conclusion at the Grand

Council meeting that the country was militarily indefensible, appeared to be unanswerable. 'It is the dictatorship that has lost the war,' declared Grandi, adding sarcastically in the direction of Mussolini, 'In the seventeen years in which you have held the three armed forces ministries, what have you done?'[3]

It was this conviction that Mussolini's personal dictatorship had led the country to disaster which informed Grandi's motion before the Grand Council. Grandi was an old guard Fascist, who, as boss of the Fascist movement and paramilitary squads of Bologna, the central Italian city in the heartland of the original Fascism, had participated in Fascism's violent anti-socialist and insurrectionary offensives of the early 1920s. He had held a string of important government and public offices, including that of foreign minister between 1929 and 1932. When Italy entered the war in 1940, he was minister of justice and president of the Fascist 'parliament', the Chamber of Fasces and Corporations. His Fascism appeared to have been institutionalized and moderated by office. He was certainly opposed to Fascist Italy's Axis alliance with Nazi Germany, a position he had ultimately unsuccessfully defended as Italian ambassador to Britain during the 1930s. He now wanted to find a way out of the Axis war.

The resolution Grandi put to the Grand Council envisaged the immediate reactivation of the authority and functions of the state's constitutional and collegial organs, the king, the Council itself, the government Council of Ministers or cabinet, parliament, and the corporations. It also urged Mussolini to return constitutionally supreme military command of the armed forces to the king, and also called on the king to resume 'that supreme initiative of decision which our institutions attribute to him'.[4] Parts of Grandi's full resolution were somewhat equivocal. But there was no need to read between the lines to realize that the motion was calling for the end of Mussolini's dictatorship, to be replaced by collegial and collective government, and for the king to resume his constitutional powers. These were both military—specified in the motion as command of the armed forces—and political—including presumably the power to dismiss and appoint the head of government, which was not specified in the motion, but, rather, intimated in the 'supreme initiative of decision' wording.

The ambiguity of Grandi's motion lay in the references to a distinctively Fascist state organ, the Grand Council, being revived, and to 'our' (meaning Fascist) laws and 'constitution'. Did Grandi want by his motion to bring about the end of Fascism and the Fascist regime, or just the end of Mussolini's dictatorship? Did he hold out hopes of a moderate Fascist government without Mussolini which was likely, at least, to extend his own and his group's political careers? He and Giuseppe Bottai, another Grand Council member, had certainly talked before the meeting about the two scenarios, involving the king's replacement of Mussolini either by a non-Fascist government under a military man, or by a moderate non-Mussolini Fascist government. Galeazzo Ciano was Mussolini's son-in-law and another Grand Council member, who was also involved, late on, in the Grandi 'group' sessions. He reportedly fantasized with a friend over a meal on 24 July about how, once 'il pazzo' ('the madman', Mussolini) had gone, there would be a Fascist triumvirate in power: Bottai, Grandi, and himself. Bottai himself recalled seeing Grandi about a week after the Grand Council meeting, and found him very bitter about the way things had turned out, that his Council motion had not led to a reformed (in both senses) Fascist government, but rather to the 'demolition of Fascism'.[5] Bottai, again reflecting shortly after the event, claimed that the Grandi 'group' had sought to work out a solution to the country's crisis not against Fascism, but within Fascism, and would have accepted 'a de-Mussolinized Mussolini'.[6] This has something of the feel of the de-Stalinization which occurred in the Soviet Union and Sovietized Eastern Europe after Stalin's death in 1953, that you denigrate the man, the better to preserve the system.

On balance, though it is by no means certain, the Grandi group probably thought that Mussolini being succeeded by a moderate Fascist government was a workable proposition. The equivocation in some of the wording of Grandi's motion was probably deliberate. There was not only the concern to keep open as an option a Fascist succession to Mussolini. Grand Council members, who were likely to be both offended and alarmed by a direct attack on Mussolini's position, needed to be persuaded that Grandi's motion was more anodyne than it might have looked. Before the meeting, Grandi sold his motion to Tullio Cianetti, then Minister of Corporations, as being little more than getting the king to share the burden and responsibility of the war and government with Mussolini. On this basis, Cianetti gave his verbal support. Bottai, towards the end of the meeting, muddied the waters in precisely the same way, playing down the significance of the motion in an attempt to rally the waverers. Bottai's intervention happened at probably the most difficult point of the meeting for the Grandi group, with Cianetti and Giacomo Suardo wanting to withdraw their previous support for the motion, the latter in tears of shame and recrimination at the prospect of voting against Mussolini.

Bottai had done enough. When the vote was taken, there were nineteen in favour of Grandi's motion, and seven against, with Suardo abstaining and Roberto Farinacci not voting. Luigi Federzoni, the ex-Nationalist one-time minister of the interior and another of the Grandi group, suggested afterwards that the margin of the majority was down to the fact that many of the Grand Council members voting for the motion did not really understand what it meant. If this was so, then the deliberate equivocation of some of Grandi's motion had arguably done the trick. If Council members were dim enough to vote for the end of Mussolini's dictatorship without realizing that they were doing it, then this also helps to explain the lack of real drama to the meeting.

The balance of the meeting certainly ebbed and flowed. It flowed with the Grandi group up to the interval or pause in the meeting, during which Grandi solicited and won more signatures to his motion, while Mussolini and his support planned a pretty effective counter-offensive. On the resumption, the bone-headed Enzo Galbiati, national commander of the Fascist Militia, the regime's paramilitary formations, denied that there was a rupture between Fascism and the nation, which was the gist of the Grandi group's analysis of Italy's current parlous wartime situation, before the interval. Instead, according to Galbiati, there was only a split or betrayal and defeatism *within* Fascism. In a clear threat and warning to these defeatists, Galbiati roared at the Council, 'What will the battalions of Militia blackshirts camped at the gates of Rome say, when they get to know what is happening here, tonight?'[7] Mussolini intensified the pressure and raised the stakes, saying that Grandi's motion posed the question of the very existence of the Fascist regime. It did, of course, though Mussolini did not ever expect the Grand Council debate to precipitate the actual political crisis of the regime. He played what he clearly thought was one of his trump cards, and revealed another reason for his confidence that the Grand Council meeting would not lead anywhere. He felt sure that the king still liked and supported him, and that he, Mussolini, still retained the king's confidence. Turning on the Council, Mussolini challenged them, what then would their position be? 'Fate attenzione, signori!'[8]

Both Grandi and Bottai realized that Mussolini's words had really hit home, and that the Duce still seemed capable of being the 'padrone'[9] of the situation. This was the one really sticky point of the session. Ciano said later that, panicking, he feared that they would now be arrested. He, as well as at least Bottai and Grandi, had apparently packed hand grenades into their briefcases for the meeting. Grandi now passed one of his grenades under the table to another Council member, Cesare Maria De Vecchi. Federzoni had apparently decided not to arm himself for the meeting, discretion being the better part of valour, since he expected to be overwhelmed anyway if a violent confrontation occurred.

The moment of tension passed, and was, in a sense, a manufactured piece of drama. Mussolini's wife, Rachele, had urged her husband to have the lot of them arrested, as he left for the Grand Council meeting. She was right, too, but again only in retrospect. Mussolini had made no preparations for arrests nor for violence, because of the confidence he took with him into the meeting and which sustained him throughout it despite the hard knocks he received. Not least of these was the decision of his son-in-law, Ciano, to speak and vote for Grandi's motion. Those present noticed that the only evident emotion to register on Mussolini's face during the meeting, came when Ciano turned against his father-in-law. But the dictator felt that he could dominate the Council, and, failing that, continue to dominate the king. He fully expected to see the king at the next routine audience, and get royal agreement to a government reshuffle which would involve Mussolini dropping his armed forces ministries, perhaps even returning military command to the king, but leaving him as head of government. As Grandi commented on Mussolini's final words about provoking the crisis of the regime, 'he says it; but he still does not believe it, however'.[10]

Despite what would have immediately struck the meeting's participants as an inconclusive outcome, something really important had happened at the meeting. It was the moment when leading Fascists stood up to Mussolini and showed a complete lack of confidence in his leadership of the Fascist regime and of the country. It was also something more. These same Fascists now disassociated Fascism from the nation and the national interest. They were undoing what twenty years of Fascism had attempted to realize, the Fascistization of the country, so that, in Mussolini's words, 'Italian and Fascist, rather like Italian and Catholic, mean the same thing.'[11] By opposing Mussolini in the Grand Council, the Grandi group were saying that Mussolini was no longer acting in the national interest, and were making a choice between loyalty to Mussolini and loyalty to the nation. At the close of his first prepared speech to the Council, Grandi pointedly reminded Mussolini of a speech the Duce had made in 1924, when he had said, 'May all factions perish! Even our own. As long as the fatherland is preserved.'[12]

The Fascist system rested on the principle of charismatic leadership and was cohered by the myth of the infallible Duce. This unrecoverable collapse in the leader–follower relationship between Mussolini and some of his Fascist *gerarchi* (hierarchs), literally denoted a breakdown of the Fascist regime. The Council meeting was the demonstration, not the cause, of the end of these Fascist leaders' personal and political loyalty to Mussolini as Duce. We should not underestimate how difficult it was for old Fascists to break with Mussolini, when the emotional and political attachments were so deep and lasting. These were men who went back with Mussolini to the origins of Fascism. For some of them, to oppose Mussolini was to oppose themselves, to renege on what they had invested in Fascism.

Perhaps only Ciano, a younger man who belonged to a different type and generation of Fascists, was immune to the pull of a shared personal and political history. As Mussolini's son-in-law, whom Mussolini appointed foreign minister in 1936 at the ripe old age of 33, Ciano was, and was perceived to be, a nepotistic parvenu. Ciano's attachment to the dictator was familial rather than political, or rather, the familial became the political. Aspiring to be the man who succeeded Mussolini, Ciano knew that he had to remain close to the Duce. It was precisely because of his family connections that Grandi was reluctant to allow Ciano entry to his group and reluctant even for Ciano to sign his Grand Council resolution. Grandi could never bring himself to trust a man whose political fortunes were so closely tied to being married to Mussolini's daughter. He also knew, or feared, that if things went badly after the Grand Council meeting, Ciano's signature on his motion would be like a suicide note—which it was. Ciano, along with other Grand Council members who could be found, was tried and executed as a traitor by the Italian Social Republic, whose head was Mussolini, in January 1944.

The general reasons for the disaffection of some of Fascism's leaders were, of course, Mussolini's growing monopolization of power and decision making, and his contemptuous treatment of his collaborators, or rather subordinates, whose advice he did not seek, let alone take. It was, in other words, the installation of a personal dictatorship at the expense of their Fascism and their contribution to Fascism. But disaffection was not the same as breaking with Mussolini. Discontent coagulated into opposition during the war, and as a result of it.

Bottai provides an interesting individual case of a more general process. Except for four years from 1932 to 1936, he had been a government minister throughout the regime, undersecretary and then full minister of corporations up to 1932, and minister of education from 1936. Intelligent and competent, he had developed and promoted a technocratic, corporatist vision of Fascism, and retained a belief that it was possible, indeed necessary, to circulate and exchange ideas and personnel within the framework of a totalitarian system. Yet he was one of the Fascist ruling class who was most attuned to, most susceptible to, and most taken in by Mussolini, as man and myth. He believed in the force of Mussolini's dynamic and charismatic leadership and thought that Mussolini was a political genius. Bottai's deconstruction of the man and myth was poignantly expressed almost in the language of disappointed love. Coinciding with his loss of Mussolini was Bottai's rediscovery of his Catholicism, which allowed him, he thought, to show a degree of human compassion for Mussolini, while denying the dictator his respect.

The turning point for Bottai was Mussolini's sudden, spiteful, and apparently arbitrary decision in January 1941 to pack off the regime's *gerarchi* to the military fronts. Ciano, an air force pilot, was dispatched to a base in Bari, in south-eastern Italy. Although he flew a few bombing sorties over Greece, he lived the same pleasant, well-heeled, and hedonistic life in the city's best hotels which he had made for himself as foreign minister in Rome. Bottai, probably alone among the temporarily conscripted *gerarchi*, actually saw active military service on the Albanian-Greek front, the scene of Fascist Italy's most disastrous military campaign of the war, the attempted invasion of Greece in October 1940.

Mussolini's decision to empty the government and Party of their leaders was actually a calculated move to humiliate them. The entire Fascist ruling elite was, quite literally, expendable. The move showed the country, that in the eyes of the Duce, they contributed absolutely nothing to the war effort. Government could carry on perfectly well without them, a matter for Mussolini alone and the civil service, apparently a fantasy of how government would operate which Mussolini had entertained for some time. Bottai recorded how he felt about Mussolini's decision, after a frosty farewell from the dictator: 'Something, which for over twenty years was beating in my heart, suddenly stopped: a Love, a loyalty, a sense of surrender. Now, I am alone, without my leader.'[13] Thereafter, Bottai's diaries reveal an unrestrained resentment and loss of respect for the Duce. These feelings came out especially in his observations on the sessions of the Council of Ministers, or cabinet meetings, for Bottai, boring, inconsequential, unconnected affairs, and a mark of how far collegial government had degenerated as a result of Mussolini's dictatorship. Mussolini speaks, Bottai wrote snidely in January 1943, 'with the customary tone of someone revealing indisputable truths', when 'instead all his arguments are artificial and made up of lies'. Bottai concluded bitterly that Mussolini had finally lost his way: 'This man, who has accustomed us to believe that he has an appointment with destiny, no longer knows himself what his destiny is.'[14]

Mussolini's coup against his own ruling class in January 1941 was also the turning point for Grandi, who went off to Albania as well. He met and talked with Bottai on several occasions during their enforced three months' suspension from government.

Bottai had lost Mussolini and found God. He also found Ciano, in an unlikely friendship which started at the beginning of the war, strengthened during it, and eventually enabled Ciano to enter the Grandi group. Bottai socialized a lot with Ciano in Rome during the war. He came to like him, although he was well aware not only of Ciano's slick intelligence, but also of his superficiality and love of the attention and perks which came with high office, that deadly mix of laziness and ambition blighting Ciano as a man and politician. That Ciano was indiscreet and an intriguer was probably what actually charmed and attracted Bottai to Ciano's social circle; he could rely on Ciano for all the latest political gossip and felt closer to the real centres of power and influence, as a result. The two of them, when they met, certainly fed on each other's loss of respect for Mussolini. Ciano increasingly during the war talked of Mussolini as 'il testone' (big head) and even more disrespect-fully, as 'il vecchio' (the old man), used not in an affectionate or godfatherly way, but to mark down someone who was clearly past it.

The reference to Mussolini ageing was hardly incidental. Mussolini's physical decline during the war was marked. The loss of respect was undoubtedly connected to the fact that he no longer embodied in his own person the dynamic, virile, warlike presence of the new Fascist man, an essential compon-ent of the Mussolini myth as Duce. Bottai constantly recorded his sense of Mussolini's physical collapse, noting that he was 'pallid, emaciated, alone, assaulted by old age', with the features of 'an old man, like King Canute'.[15]

This was long before the most serious incidence of Mussolini's stomach illness in late 1942 and early 1943, eventually diagnosed as gastritis and a duodenal ulcer. Losing weight and with high blood pressure, Mussolini was sometimes bent double by his stomach cramps and pains, and forced to spend days at a time at home, absent from his office in Rome. The illness was also, self-evidently, psychosomatic. Mussolini's debilitating bout of illness coincided with the worst period of the war yet, for Italy, with the Allied landings and advances in North Africa, fresh and more devastating waves of Allied bombing of Italy's Northern cities, and the Axis' defeats at and after the battle of Stalingrad in the USSR. Mussolini's absence through illness paralysed government at this critical juncture of the war.

The sense of Mussolini's physical and personal, and hence political, decline were palpably felt down the chain of Fascist command. The Minister of Exchange and Currency, Raffaello Riccardi, was a minister whom Mussolini would not have seen regularly. He described to Ciano the scene of a diminished dictator being confronted with the news that Marcello Petacci, the corrupt and speculative businessman brother of Mussolini's official mistress, Clara, had been involved in a gold smuggling operation, an affair which Ciano had maliciously informed the Chief of Police about in June 1942. 'While I was speaking with the Duce,' said Riccardi, 'I had before me a humiliated man. We were no longer on the same level; I was two steps above him.'[16] Later, at the height of his illness, in November 1942, Giuseppe Gorla, the Minister of Public Works, mentioned that Mussolini had 'the look of a dead man: a cadaverously white face, with sunken eye sockets and feverish blue-encircled eyes,' who 'seems on the point of fainting from one moment to the next'.[17]

The one important Fascist boss whose lack of respect for Mussolini predated the war was Roberto Farinacci. The self-appointed spokesman of revolutionary and intransigent Fascism, he was effectively sidelined by Mussolini from national politics after a characteristically turbulent period as Fascist Party secretary in 1925–6. Having earlier plagiarized wholesale the dissertation leading to the award of his law degree, he had then made a lucrative legal and business career trading on his political contacts. He achieved a political rehabilitation of sorts when Mussolini made him a member of the Grand Council in 1934. Not that Mussolini had ever managed to rid himself of Farinacci. In his hyperactively overfamiliar and overbearing way, which always grated with Mussolini, he endlessly criticized, fulminated, and complained to Mussolini through the pages of his daily newspaper and a voluminous, private, largely one-way correspondence with Mussolini. A copy of Farinacci's plagiarized thesis lay on the files of Mussolini's personal secretariat, the perfect blackmailing tool. One wonders how often Mussolini was tempted to use it, to contain the outbursts of this uncomfortable and intemperate man. Bottai, who was hardly this irascible man's soulmate, remarked that Farinacci 'always lacked confidence in the capacity of the Duce to handle and overcome the situation'.[18]

The Fascist malcontents were effectively driven together during the 1942–3 winter by that conjuncture of Axis military reverses and worsening conditions on the home front, which made it unlikely that the war could ever be won, and increasingly likely that it would be lost. The trouble was that while these Fascists had all lost confidence in Mussolini's leadership as a result of Italy's disastrous war, they could not agree on a solution to this crisis of credibility of Mussolini and the Fascist regime. Farinacci got some of them together for a meal in Rome in November 1942, though Grandi called off. Bottai reported helplessly that there was 'nothing in common between us, only the sense of this terrible bewilderment'.[19]

This shared bewilderment, accentuated by the Allied invasion of national territory, was enough to induce them, finally, to take a first step. The immediate impetus to the calling of the Grand Council meeting emerged from a mini-'council of war'[20] called by the Fascist Party Secretary, Carlo Scorza, on 13 July 1943. This gathering included Bottai, now an ex-minister after Mussolini's final drastic government reshuffle of February 1943; Renzo Chierici, the Chief of Police; and two junior ministers at the interior and foreign ministries respectively, Umberto Albini and Giuseppe Bastianini. All three of them were old-guard Fascists and the beneficiaries of that same reshuffle. Some versions claim that Grandi and Farinacci were present as well. Scorza had found that all the top *gerarchi* were understandably turning down his invitation to go on a national speaking tour to rally the population behind the war effort, now that Sicily had been invaded. Instead, rather than have to face the country, a deputation of Fascists approached Mussolini on 16 July, and the Duce conceded the Grand Council meeting for 24 July.

Beyond the conviction that they had to do something, divisions remained. It was already clear that while for all of these Fascists the problem was Mussolini, for some of them he was also the solution. That Mussolini was the problem was evident from the decisions taken by the United States and Britain at the Casablanca conference in January 1943, on how best to press home their military successes against the Axis forces in North Africa. Their decision to deploy the now battle-hardened North African armies in an invasion of Sicily in the summer of 1943 was, in fact, a kind of compromise between rather different views on how to win the war. The US military wanted to organize a cross-channel invasion of German-occupied France from Britain and strike at Germany conventionally through western and northern Europe. The British thought that continuing the war in the Mediterranean would quickly knock Italy out of the war, a political as well as a military blow to the Axis. The Americans, in turn, always attempted to limit military operations in Italy because they diverted men and resources from the priority, a mainland invasion of Europe striking at Nazi Germany. At the end of the conference, the US President, Franklin D. Roosevelt, announced that the aim of the Allies was to secure the 'unconditional surrender' of all the Axis powers. This meant, in effect, that the Allies were committed to defeating fascism and would not negotiate with the fascist regimes and make a separate peace with them. The declaration was intended to reassure the Soviet Union, their ally engaging the Axis forces to the east.

Of those Fascist *gerarchi* who had convinced themselves over the winter of 1942–3 that Italy had to get out of the war, only Grandi had really worked out how to handle the Allied war aim of unconditional surrender. He kept the full ramifications of his plan from the Grand Council, but certainly revealed them to the king and his advisers. The plan was for the king to resume his constitutional military and political powers and replace Mussolini with a government which immediately repudiated the Axis alliance with Nazi Germany and started fighting against the Germans. Simultaneously, a royal government should approach the Allies to arrange a surrender and changing of sides, and Allied military support for Italian action against the Germans.

This was not far from the solution eventually adopted by the king in September 1943; but only after what, for Grandi, was an inordinate and damaging delay. His plan required an immediate and simultaneous Italian military attack on the former ally, Germany, and a political and diplomatic approach to the would-be new allies, Britain and the USA. Such immediate action would, in Grandi's view, have a chance of success. Militarily, it would take place before the Germans could strengthen their forces in mainland Italy. Politically, it would neutralize the Allied aim of unconditional surrender. The Allies would have to treat Italy not as a defeated enemy, but as an ally who was already fighting the common enemy, Nazi Germany.

Grandi's scheme had an implacable political logic, and it was high risk, but perhaps no more risky than any other plan to disengage Italy from the war. Ciano's 'take' on Italy's possible exit from the Axis alliance and the war, was different. At least anti-communist to the last, Ciano, foreign minister until February 1943, thought that it might be possible for Italy, once Mussolini had been ditched, to negotiate a separate peace with the Western Allies while continuing a war against the USSR. He patronized some initial approaches to the Allies, one an absurdly indirect feeler using as intermediary a Polish princess living in the Italian-occupied zone of France. Ciano's predilection for aristocratic women was well developed in Roman high society. Another rather more serious approach through the Italian ambassador in Portugal, was rejected out of hand by Britain's Italophobe Foreign Minister, Anthony Eden, in December 1942. This was because it had come from a Fascist minister and so cut across the Allied concern, evident even before the Casablanca declaration, not to negotiate with but to defeat fascism.

Both Grandi's and Ciano's views assumed that the removal of Mussolini was necessary for any disengagement from war alongside Germany, and any engagement with the Allies. Bastianini effectively replaced Ciano in February 1943, when Mussolini appointed him as undersecretary at the Foreign Ministry while becoming titular head himself. Both of Bastianini's pretty desperate solutions to Italy's crisis in early 1943 could only be realized if Mussolini stayed in power. His preferred approach was for Mussolini, who in his view was the only man capable of even attempting this, to persuade Hitler to reach either a compromise peace or a defensive military stand-off with the USSR. Either would allow the diversion of German forces to defend Italy in the Mediterranean. Shoring up the Axis position in the Mediterranean might then induce the Allies, in turn, to make a compromise peace and end the war.

Bastianini's even less realistic fall-back position was for Mussolini, again, to convince Hitler that since Italy could not militarily continue, the Germans should allow Italy to leave the Axis and the war, on the condition that Italy declared itself to be strictly neutral in the war between the Allies and Germany. This was a solution made in heaven for Italy, since it would get Italy out of the war, while avoiding both German and Allied invasion of mainland Italy, and the country, therefore, becoming a theatre of war. But it was pure fantasy to expect any of this to happen. Bastianini knew that Mussolini had even turned down a serious offer from the Vatican to mediate a peace with the USA, in May 1943.

Farinacci, like Grandi and Ciano, was prepared to contemplate the removal of Mussolini. But he approached the question of the war from a completely different angle from the others. He could accept Grandi's outburst at the Grand Council meeting that the dictatorship had lost Italy the war, but only in the sense that the dictatorship had not been dictatorial enough. He thought that the fortunes of war could be reversed once Fascist Italy intensified, rather than loosened, the Axis alliance with Nazi Germany. This meant accepting overall German military command of Axis forces in Italy, and a Fascist Party dictatorship replacing Mussolini's personal dictatorship. A regime of hard men would have to supplant a regime of 'women and priests'.[21] Only such a properly Fascist and totalitarian dictatorship, which Farinacci imagined was how the Nazis organized Germany, was capable of controlling and mobilizing Italy's human and material resources for the Axis war effort. Farinacci spoke to Scorza, the national Fascist Party Secretary, who essentially felt the same way about making Mussolini 'the prisoner'[22] of the Fascist Party and of moving him to the sidelines as a kind of honorary figurehead.

Farinacci, while putting his weight behind the calling of the Grand Council, single-mindedly took his pro-German and pro-Axis stance to the actual meeting. He put his own motion to the meeting, which significantly made no mention of political decision making returning to the king and, unlike Grandi's motion, pointedly included the Fascist Party as one of the constitutional organs to be reactivated. Scorza's own motion, introduced at the last minute, made similar noises in a less specific and more muffled way. Farinacci refused to vote for any motion but his own. But neither his nor Scorza's motions were voted on, after Grandi's motion was carried by nineteen votes to seven.

In the midst of all this rather frenzied politicking in early 1943, two men took a realistic and consistent stance. One was Mussolini, the other was Hitler. Mussolini was open to Foreign Ministry suggestions that Hitler should be persuaded to come to some defensive cessation of fighting on the Russian front, which would enable the full commitment of Axis forces to fighting Italy's war in the Mediterranean. He had had this idea for some time. He was less happy about broaching it directly with Hitler at their intermittent wartime personal summits, because he knew that he would be exposed to one of Hitler's interminable and relentless monologues in a language he could only imperfectly follow, and because he knew that Hitler would say 'no'. Mussolini allowed his foreign ministers to raise it with Hitler and their Nazi German counterpart, Joachim Ribbentrop. Ciano did so at one such meeting in December 1942. Hitler's response was, as usual, utterly consistent. Making peace with Bolshevism was, for Nazism, 'the squaring of the circle and . . . impossible'.[23]

At the final meeting of the two fascist dictators before the Grand Council, at Feltre, in north-eastern Italy, in July 1943, Mussolini had, as usual, let Hitler dominate the conversation. During a break, Mussolini was confronted by his diplomatic and military staff: Dino Alfieri, Italian ambassador to Germany; Bastianini; and General Vittorio Ambrosio, head of the Italian armed forces high command, who in a quite explicit fashion which reflected their desperation, demanded to know why Mussolini was not attempting to persuade Hitler to let Italy out of the war. Alfieri described Mussolini's reply as pathetic, but it was not. It was extremely clear-sighted and realistic about the prospects for Fascist Italy. Mussolini said:

> Let's think about the possibility of detaching ourselves from Germany. It's very simple; one day, at a given time, we announce it on the radio to the enemy. What will happen? The British and Americans will justifiably demand that we surrender. Are we ready to destroy at a stroke twenty years of Fascism? To cancel out the achievements which we have worked so long and so hard to realize? To acknowledge military and political defeat, our first? To vanish from the international stage? It is easy to talk about a separate peace. But what would Hitler do? Do you really think that he would allow us to have any freedom of action?[24]

Mussolini realized very well what was at stake, Fascism in Italy, and that was why he could neither see nor allow any alternative to continuing to fight the war at Nazi Germany's side. The Allies would never negotiate a separate peace with Mussolini and would make his removal and that of the Fascist regime a condition for any such negotiations. Hitler would never allow Italy to leave the Axis voluntarily, even for neutrality, and would fight Germany's war in Italy, if need be. To leave the Axis was not only to deny Fascism; it was the end of Fascism.

It is difficult to describe the Grandi group who took on Mussolini in the Grand Council meeting as a conspiracy. Everybody who mattered—Mussolini, the king, Scorza, Farinacci (and through him the Germans)—had been informed and kept up to date on the drafting of Grandi's motion to the Grand Council—by Grandi himself. Perhaps it is not surprising, then, that Grandi was apparently taken unawares by what happened after the Grand Council meeting. What occurred had been organized and prepared for with some degree of secrecy. The king, of course, was crucial to the successful outcome of Grandi's plan. After the Grand Council vote, Grandi expected the king to exercise his constitutional powers and either receive the resignation of Mussolini or dismiss him. This, in fact, was probably the only connection between the two coups.

The practical aspects of the royal coup had been planned earlier. But the king apparently only made the decision to activate the plan a few days before the Grand Council meeting. Nothing could go ahead without the king's order; the king just took longer than anyone else to come to a decision.

Some of the army generals had decided that Italy had to be extricated from its disastrous war at about the same critical juncture of the war, the winter of 1942–3, which had precipitated the decision of some prominent Fascists. Like some of the Fascists, it took the generals a little time to work out whether Mussolini's presence or absence was necessary to the process of leaving the war. The key figure here was Ambrosio, one-time commander of Italian forces in Italian-occupied ex-Yugoslavia, then chief of staff of the army, and from February 1943 chief of the general staff of the armed forces—nominally, then, Italy's top military figure.

Ambrosio initially hedged his bets. He attempted to anticipate Mussolini's removal by planning to repatriate as many Italian troops serving abroad as was possible, in order to head off any German or Fascist reaction to Mussolini's dismissal. If the Germans realized what he was planning to do, then it might well provoke the German occupation of Italy and lead to fighting between German and Italian forces, which he understandably wanted to avoid. So, he also pressurized Mussolini to persuade Hitler that the only options available to Germany were either to reinforce Italy to an extent which would make Italy defensible against Allied attack, or to allow Italian withdrawal from the war. The abortive Feltre meeting between Hitler and Mussolini in mid-July 1943, finally convinced Ambrosio that Mussolini was the problem, not the solution, and had to be removed. Mussolini's 'pathetic' response to his and the other's ultimatum showed that there was no hope of Mussolini ever being instrumental in bringing about Italy's exit from the war. Ambrosio returned to Rome ready to put into effect the arrangements for the dictator's arrest.

Feltre was probably what decided things for the king, as well. But the decision had been an unconscionable time coming. Victor Emmanuel had, after all, put up with twenty years of Mussolini and the steady erosion of the monarch's constitutional position as head of state and supreme military commander. The fact that he had done so was the source of Mussolini's confidence during the Grand Council meeting, whatever its outcome. The king had submitted to being a political cipher during the 1930s and had even accepted Mussolini's decisions which he did not like, including the Axis alliance with Germany and Italy's entry to the war. He had done this because he was naturally reticent and timid, because he actually rather liked and admired Mussolini, and because his strict interpretation of his constitutional role required him to respond to the politicians, not have them respond to his initiatives.

He was always concerned about the future of the monarchy as an institution, and felt pessimistic about its prospects, whatever happened. If Italy won the war, then Mussolini would probably have the confidence to finish off the monarchy. If Italy lost the war, then the monarchy would have to pay for its collusion with Fascism. Doing nothing, initiating nothing, opposing nothing, at least gave Mussolini no excuses to move against the monarchy. The king's stance of constitutional inertia was probably the only position that he was temperamentally capable of reaching.

So, at the worst point of the war, it was a sign of the king actually being active, in his understanding of the word, that he began in early 1943 to make himself available for audiences with all and sundry. The pattern of these interviews was unvarying. Whether it was a dissident Fascist like Grandi or an ageing conservative anti-Fascist politician like Ivanoe Bonomi, the king listened, made little or no comment, and told them to 'trust their king'. Such reserve and inscrutability drove Ciano, who was incapable of either, to distraction. Of his own meeting with the king in June 1943, Ciano remarked, 'After spending an hour and a half with him, you leave knowing less than you did before of his intentions.'[25]

The man on whom so much depended seemed to be constantly stone-walling, or deciding not to decide. Grandi managed to extract from one such meeting that the king would welcome some initiative from a constitutional organ of state which would give him a pretext to act or, rather, something to respond to. Such a hint probably encouraged Grandi to press ahead with a Grand Council meeting, the point of which he was always sceptical about, given Mussolini's domination of that body.

So it was; the Grand Council debate and vote served their purpose and enabled the royal coup to proceed. Mussolini on 25 July 1943 paid in full for twenty years of cohabitation with a man and an institution who and which remained, despite wear and tear, an alternative focus of national loyalty and authority, not least for the armed forces. The king's arrest of Mussolini represented the culmination of a wider process whereby during the war national fellow-travelling institutions of the Italian establishment detached themselves from the Fascist regime and Mussolini.

Mussolini's first fall from power in July 1943 occurred with minimal fuss and drama; it scarcely seemed to happen at all. Why was there no reaction to the downfall of the dictator, no attempt to stop or reverse it? There is certainly no sense of Mussolini being resigned to losing power. 'I concede power to nobody,' growled Mussolini to Grandi when the latter had shown him his Grand Council resolution just before the meeting.[26] Mussolini went to the audience with the king on 25 July as if it was a routine affair, and obviously expected to emerge from it as he had entered it, as head of government. The feeling of resignation, the depression, the inertia, the sense of being swept away by events, hit Mussolini after the arrest and were caused by it, so unexpected had it been. We have, here, then, the basic reason why there was no Fascist reaction to Mussolini's fall. So secure did Mussolini feel about the outcome of the Grand Council and of his audience with the king, that he did not need to prepare for, nor threaten, violence and repression. There was no crisis of the Fascist regime which required the Fascist Militia to mobilize to defend the Revolution.

There were other mitigating factors. According to the same friend and confidant of Ciano's who had dined with him on the day before the Council meeting, the frantic response to the Grand Council vote of Alessandro Pavolini, Minister of Popular Culture until the February 1943 reshuffe, was 'Get the machine guns! Take to the hills, and resist!'[27] But what exactly was there for Fascists to resist in the Grand Council vote? Not many Fascists would have seen the situation as starkly as Pavolini apparently did, especially when some of those members voting for Grandi's motion probably had no real sense of its significance. The Grand Council was taken by Fascists to be the supreme decision-making organ of the regime. Were they meant to countermand a vote taken by their own collegial body? At the very least, the lack of clarity surrounding the meaning of the vote and what would happen as a consequence, stalled any concerted Fascist reaction to it.

The king's arrest of Mussolini was a different matter, of course. But by this point, the *carabinieri* and the military had taken the pre-emptive measures which made a Fascist reaction unlikely to succeed or even to happen.

Crucially, the king had *arrested* Mussolini and swiftly imprisoned him; Mussolini was in no position to communicate with and mobilize anybody. When Scorza wandered off to the *carabinieri* headquarters to find out why Mussolini had not returned from his audience with the king, he was promptly arrested, as was Galbiati, the Militia commander. Troops and policemen were ordered to take other precautions against a counter-coup. They took control of the city's key installations, including its communications centres, and surrounded Fascist Party and Militia headquarters. According to Grandi, Galbiati had ordered mobilization of the Militia a few hours before Mussolini's audience with the king on the afternoon of 25 July. There was a newly formed 'M' division, trained by the Germans for internal security, stationed quite near Rome, though it was unclear whether it could concentrate its forces quickly enough for another 'March on Rome'. Galbiati's orders, anyway, were intercepted by the Interior Ministry and never arrived. Lacking any initial incentive or order to react, both Party and Militia now found it impossible to react.

Whether the Fascist Party and Militia would have reacted to any call to arms is a moot point; 25 July was a Sunday, after all. Hitler later derisively condemned a Fascist Party which had melted away like snow in the sun at the time of Mussolini's fall. This was probably unfair, since even he anticipated that Fascists would 'come over to us'[28] once the Germans had intervened quickly and decisively, which he expected and wanted. The lack of any immediate German response is the final explanation of why Mussolini's arrest went unchallenged.

The Nazi leadership in Germany appeared to have been singularly ill-informed by their representatives in Italy about what was happening around 25 July. This confusion, again, delayed a reaction. Largely because they were being briefed by Farinacci, the Germans believed that the Grand Council meeting would focus on Farinacci's not Grandi's motion, and that its outcome was likely to be, therefore, a tightening of the Axis alliance and more totalitarian policies and controls in Italy. Hitler thought initially that Mussolini had resigned, not been dismissed and arrested, and had no idea where Mussolini was. This was important, because resistance would be best organized round the Duce or some other comparable figure. Farinacci was shuttled out to Germany very quickly. But he, quite simply, blew his chances of being the leader of any counter-reaction by repeating to an incredulous and irritated Hitler his Grand Council criticism of Mussolini's lack of dictatorial verve.

Even before Mussolini's arrest was confirmed, Hitler regarded his dismissal as open treachery. He considered sending a German division to occupy Rome which would 'arrest the whole government, the king and the whole bunch right away'.[29] A day later, on 26 July, the idea of a German-led coup against the king's new government restoring the Fascist Party to power was still alive, but already receding. Hitler wanted to send to Italy 'politically reliable units', 'crack formations that are politically close to fascism', to act as 'a magnet to gather the people together' and reconstitute 'the Fascist backbone' of the country.[30] These would come from army group 'South' in the USSR. But—more delay—this transfer would require other troops to be shifted around the Russian front or a shortening of the front itself. Since this would have been very difficult, Hitler eventually had to settle for a rather more drawn-out general reinforcement of German forces in Italy, as advised by his generals. This was one of those rare occasions when Hitler's and the Nazi leadership's political intuition and priority gave way to military advice and considerations.

Hitler's will to act quickly, and especially his anxiety to locate and rescue Mussolini, were indicative of how important Mussolini's fall was, or was felt to be. This was fascism's first serious political defeat for twenty years. The fear was that the overthrow of the first fascist and the first totalitarian, Mussolini, would precipitate the general collapse of fascism. For the Jew who did not leave Germany, Victor Klemperer, the one glimmer of hope in his dark existence, in November 1942, was the 'cold, sober certainty' that 'Italy was going to break away in the next few weeks and then everything would come to an end very quickly.'[31] Even though the wish was clearly father to the thought, Klemperer retained a kind of nostalgia for this brief hiatus of hope, recalling in January 1944 how 'on the day of the news of Mussolini's fall, someone . . . said: "we don't really need to turn up in the morning now" '.[32] Anti-Fascists and opponents of both fascist regimes probably entertained the same warm thoughts about 25 July 1943.

The Nazis themselves felt the draught. Josef Goebbels, the Nazi Propaganda Minister, thought that Mussolini's removal had given 'world fascism such a heavy blow' that it would even threaten the hold of Nazism in Germany by encouraging 'subversive elements' there to attempt the same thing as the king.[33] German police reports on reaction to Mussolini's fall similarly reflected on the contagion from Italy of the idea which was 'very widespread', that 'the form of government in the Reich, which was

considered immutable, could also suddenly change in Germany as well'.[34]
Hitler's public response to Mussolini's fall was delayed until 10 September
1943 and was as much a response to the armistice between Italy and the
Allies declared a few days before. In his radio broadcast to the German
people, Hitler castigated Italy's 'treachery', which served as a warning to the
Nazi Party and German people that there could be no repeat in Germany.

But the Nazis' concern for their own position in Germany could only have
been momentary. Most Nazi leaders and, if police reports are to be believed,
most German people discounted Fascist Italy's contribution to the Axis war
effort and expected Italy to collapse soon militarily, anyway. The Germans had
been planning for some time to reinforce their presence in Italy and control
both Italy and its military and economic resources. German military command
of all Axis forces in Italy was one of the demands they brought to the meeting
between Hitler and Mussolini at Feltre, just before the Grand Council meeting. Although Mussolini's removal was a surprise, it was immediately assumed
that it was a first step towards Italy leaving the war. The failing will of the
Italians to fight on was well known to Germany. It was unlikely to weaken the
German will to resist, rather the opposite.

Hitler was understandably more concerned about the international repercussions of Mussolini's fall. As in Italy itself, Axis defeats in the USSR in early
1943 had increased the restiveness of Germany's other minor allies and satellites
in Eastern Europe, all of which had contributed national armies to the
anti-Bolshevik crusade. Encouraged by Bastianini, the governments in
Hungary, Romania, and Bulgaria had misguidedly begun to look to Mussolini
as the man who could lead them out of the Axis and out of the war. That
restiveness could only grow, now that Mussolini's removal by the king clearly
presaged an Italian exit from the Axis war. Why else would the king overthrow
Mussolini?

The effects of Mussolini's fall, on the assumption that it was bound to mean
Italy's secession from the Axis, rippled through the rest of neutral and Nazi-
occupied Europe. The neutral countries started to bend their neutrality away
from the Axis as a result of what they interpreted as its serious weakening.
Barely two weeks after Mussolini's fall, Sweden terminated the agreement
which allowed German troops transit across the country to occupied Norway.
Internal resistance to Nazi occupation across northern, western, and south-
eastern Europe was emboldened by Mussolini's removal. One can scarcely
ignore the other internal and external reasons for the strikes and popular

agitation in Nazi Germany's 'model' protectorate, Denmark. But their timing was, again, hardly two weeks after the events of 25 July.

Mussolini's fall could only weaken the Axis in the short term, if the Nazis failed to react to its impact; and react they certainly did. Hitler, right from the start, was determined to recoup the shattered prestige of international fascism. Later than intended, in the autumn of 1943, he restored Mussolini and a Fascist regime in German-occupied northern and central Italy, well realizing that a Mussolini-led government was the one guarantee of the Axis surviving. Increased resistance across occupied Europe invited increased Nazi German repression and controls, which in some areas, changed the status of countries in the wartime Nazi New Order. Denmark, as a result of the events of the summer of 1943, passed from self-government to direct emergency Nazi rule. Hungary's efforts to manoeuvre its way out of the Axis were ended by Germany's invasion of its ally in March 1944 and the imposition of a pro-German and then Hungarian fascist government. In a sequence of unintended cause and effect, Mussolini's fall had, if only temporarily, appeared to strengthen rather than weaken Nazi Germany and its hold on Europe. Fascism had fallen in one country, but had been reinforced in the others.

Britain had favoured attacking Italy, the weak point of the Axis alliance, as much for the political and psychological as for the military gains in the Allied war on fascism. Hitler's prompt initiative to restore Mussolini and Fascism in Italy was his attempt to reverse those gains. But there can be no doubt that Mussolini's fall helped to align the more sceptical USA behind Britain's wish to move on to the invasion of mainland Italy. As Hitler knew, 'The English will take advantage of this, the Russians will cheer, the English will land'.[35] Mussolini's unexpected removal in July 1943 made a complete Italian military collapse appear imminent. A mainland invasion would speedily remove Italy from the war, either by military defeat or by the king's government offering to surrender. Once Italy had surrendered, it was possible to grasp final Allied victory against Nazi Germany. It would not, of course, turn out to be as tidy as this. But a major consequence of Mussolini's fall was that it made certain an Allied invasion of mainland Italy.

# 2

# Fascist Italy at War, 1940–1943: Propaganda and Reality

ITALY'S 'Fascist' war, from June 1940 to July 1943, used to be something of a blank in the country's historical consciousness. Most writing—and certainly most written-up memoirs—has tended to give more attention and significance to the events of 1943 to 1945 than to the events of 1940 to 1943. There are good reasons for giving preferential treatment to how the country left the Second World War, ahead of how Italy entered and fought a Fascist war. For the country as a whole, the years 1940 to 1943 were ones of almost continuous military defeat, a national humiliation felt by all Italians.

One might want to exclude from this general sense of national shame those anti-Fascists inside and outside the country who took a longer and a different view of the war. They consciously adopted their own brand of the revolutionary defeatism which the Russian Bolshevik leader Lenin applied to his country when it went to war in 1914. Taking contradictory reassurance from the maxim, much deployed by the Marxist socialist left, that the worse things are, the better things are, some Italian anti-Fascists expected, or hoped, that war would bring about the crisis and collapse of the Fascist regime.

But even among these optimistic pessimists, for whom the outbreak of war was a release from their own sense of political impotence, a feeling of injured patriotism prevailed. Piero Calamandrei was a leading democratic anti-Fascist throughout the years of the Fascist regime, a university professor and jurist who, as a member of the post-war Constituent Assembly, was instrumental in pulling together the 1948 Constitution of the Italian Republic. For him, Fascism was like an occupying foreign power, and so, writing in his wartime diary, he could welcome the British forces' victories against the Italian army in North Africa early in 1941, 'as if the victors were us'. Yet, Italy's disastrous defeats in Greece and Albania, preceding and coinciding with those in Libya, provoked in him 'an uncontainable anguish'. Italy now seemed to be on the brink not only of losing its colonies in Africa, but also of losing its national independence, 'the product of the Risorgimento', the late nineteenth-century process of national political and territorial unification.[1] Of course, the point for Calamandrei, a democratic interventionist and volunteer in the First World War, was that the Fascist nation was never his, which justified his wartime stance as a 'patriotic traitor'. But his private pain expressed the patriotic dilemma of those who opposed the Fascist regime, which in the earlier, different circumstances of a Fascist military victory in Ethiopia in 1936, had led some anti-Fascists to rally behind a national war directed by Fascism.

A country which met military defeat, especially calamitous after successful minor imperialistic ventures in East Africa and years of Fascist martial rhetoric and preparation, would not easily find a way of expressing and remembering such a defeat. This partly explains the muted commemoration of the war of 1940 to 1943 on public monuments after 1945. It was best, and natural, to forget, or rather to highlight, the positive and affirmative message of the events of 1943 to 1945, when the nation led to ruin and defeat by Fascism had remade itself in the glorious resistance to and liberation from Nazi occupation.

One is struck by the conscious or unconscious relegation of the war of 1940 to 1943 to a kind of collective oblivion. Something of this can be observed from the interviews conducted by a team of historians in the 1980s among the inhabitants of a small unnamed town in the Appennine mountains of southern central Italy. The team had consulted the available contemporary written sources, from the reports of the local *podestà*, or Fascist mayor, and of the military police force, the *carabinieri*, who operated most extensively in the typical Italy of small towns servicing rural hinterlands, to the local Catholic priest's regular monthly bulletin for his parishioners, and the censored letters passing, and not passing, to and from local conscripted soldiers on the military fronts. These written sources all pointed in the same direction and to the same conclusion, that this local community's morale and cohesion were being steadily undermined by the cumulative material and psychological effects of the war in the course of 1942 and early 1943. Yet the oral testimonies told a different story, and people's memories centred on the experience of the communal miseries suffered under German occupation from September 1943: 'In the people's recollections, the war starts with the enemy at home, with the terror which is total. The onset of every difficulty and every worry, even of a material nature, is made to coincide with this.'[2]

Another good reason for blanking out the years 1940 to 1943 was the uncomfortable fact that there was practically no anti-Fascist or popular involvement in the first fall of Mussolini in July 1943. Mussolini's departure was the outcome of a coup, or two overlapping coups, planned and executed by a few members of the Fascist establishment and a few members of a conservative monarchical Fascist fellow-travelling establishment. Again, an unfavourable contrast could be drawn with the events of 1943 to 1945, or how they were sublimated post-war, when a popular resistance movement was responsible for the second and definitive fall of Mussolini and the defeat of his Nazi masters. An argument has been made, however, for the emergence of a mass anti-Fascist opposition in the country in late 1942 and early 1943, which was when, therefore, a democratic and Republican Italy starts. The connections between the emergence of an undoubted mass discontent with Mussolini and the Fascist regime by late 1942, and the coup(s) overthrowing Mussolini in July 1943, were probably less direct and less transparent than this retrospectively reassuring line of argument would indicate.

There were, it seems to me, both external and internal explanations for the elitist rather than the popular overthrow of Mussolini in July 1943. The British and US governments and military did not appear to be seriously interested in fomenting and supporting internal organized popular resistance as a way of undermining and overthrowing the Fascist regime. For one thing, Allied bombing raids on Italian cities were doing a pretty effective job in demoralizing the Italian population, as intended. Also, the Allied governments did not want to make any hostages to fortune in order to encourage popular resistance. They did not want to offer political promises about the country's future which they later might not want to honour. For very much the same reason, Hitler was suspicious of those people in German-conquered and occupied Europe who wanted to collaborate with the Nazis in the devising and implementation of any Nazi New Order. His reluctance to accept a proffered collaboration extended to the natural allies of the Nazi occupier, the local fascists, whose nationalism he regarded as an obstacle to a racially reordered Europe.

It was certainly the case that some very effective Allied propaganda transmitted to Italy and Italians by 'Radio London', condemned Mussolini as the man solely responsible for taking Italy into a disastrous war. The distinction made between the Fascist dictator and his misled and miserable people, in effect indicated that things would automatically get better for the Italians if, or once, Mussolini had gone. But it was a far cry from this to encouraging internal resistance and sabotage, which the Allies did, and continued to do, in Nazi-occupied Europe. The principle of unconditional surrender operated here, too. Italy was not an occupied country, as France was, but an enemy power, who could expect to receive Allied forces as invaders, not as liberators.

When Mussolini and the Fascist regime fell in July 1943 to a monarchist coup, the Allies knew that the Badoglio government would make some kind of an approach to them for a separate peace. The success of the royal conspiracy and the new royal government's survival beyond the arrest of Mussolini, showed what the Allies had banked on all along, that no popular initiative was necessary to push Italy out of the war. The most Eisenhower expected was that on the declaration of the armistice, the king and the Italian armed forces would, if necessary, call on the people to help them expel the Germans from the country.

Badoglio's government making an appeal to the people was out of the question. This provides us with one of the internal explanations for the non-involvement of anti-Fascist or popular forces in the first fall of Mussolini. The monarchist coup against Mussolini intended to exclude any such participation. The aim was not simply to keep its planning as secret as possible, but primarily to ensure a socially and politically conservative succession to Mussolini and Fascism.

The anti-Fascist movements themselves were hardly in any position to force the pace of change. By late 1942, they were beginning to organize again in Italy. But only the Italian Communist Party, the PCI, which had attempted to keep a clandestine presence in Italy throughout the years of the Fascist regime, showed any will or capacity to exploit workers' anti-war feelings. By the time of Mussolini's first fall, anti-Fascism was not organizationally strong enough to shake the Fascist regime, whose extensive repressive apparatus remained largely intact. After July 1943, the Badoglio government kept it intact to contain and limit the revival of anti-Fascist forces.

While it was not the Italian people who overthrew Mussolini in July 1943, their sense of disaffection and alienation from the Fascist regime as a result of the war, was very evident and widespread from as early as the summer of 1942. The evidence for this comes from the regime's own sources of information on the public mood, especially the police, the informers working for the political sections of the police, and the censors of wartime correspondence. These are clearly compromised sources, the content of which reflected the concerns of the agents filing the reports as much as those they were reporting on. But the unvarnished expressions of popular attitudes and feelings can be extracted from them. The policeman investigating and repressing anti-Fascist behaviour would have to reveal that such behaviour existed, and in some detail. The army of informers who occupied the nooks and crannies of Italian life passed on verbatim the conversations and banter of the milieux they had penetrated—often the drinkers, smokers, and gossips who gathered in the same piazza in the same city on each and every day and who obviously formed part of the social group of the informer himself. Many of the voluminous number of wartime letters exchanged between servicemen and their families, wives, lovers, fiancées, girlfriends, even their ex-school-teachers, the parish priest, the political secretary of the local Fascist Party organization, were either never delivered or were received with huge blanks in them, after censorship by the underemployed members of the intellectual proletariat recruited to read them. But censorship could not negate the attitudes, feelings, grievances, and discontents of the people who had expressed them.

The fact that the Fascist regime invested so much energy in gathering information on the people it ruled, did not mean that it swayed and bent to the public mood. The totalitarian task was to mould and reshape popular attitudes, not be governed by them. When police reports in 1939–40 noted that, in general, the Italian people were not particularly enthusiastic about entering the war, nor about the Axis alliance with Nazi Germany, Mussolini's response was not to convert the non-belligerency of 1939 into a genuine neutrality and keep out of war altogether. He could hardly be a Fascist and not want war. If his people were apparently unready for war, then the Fascist response could only be war, as the supreme test of national will. Italy would become a warrior nation, through war.

Mussolini wanted a real, fighting war, though he realized it would have to be a short one, given that, at the moment, Italy lacked the resources and capacity to sustain a long one. It was to be an 'Italian' or 'parallel' war, fought alongside Nazi Germany but pursuing specifically Italian objectives, which boiled down to control of the Mediterranean. In his mind, anyway, it was also to be an offensive war. He was the driving force behind the offensives against France in June 1940, from Italian East Africa into British Somalia in August, from Libya into Egypt in September, and from Albania into Greece in October. These were the dictator's decisions, pushed through against the defensive inclinations and technical objections of his armed forces chiefs, including Badoglio. He decided to enter the war at the last and, therefore, the best moment, at the point when rapid and dramatic Nazi military successes in northern and western Europe seemed to indicate that the war would soon be over and result in a definite victory for the Axis.

The decision to fight at this point of the conflict was probably what reconciled most of the country to war. This was dangerous, in terms of Mussolini's relationship as Duce with the Italian people and in terms of Italians' support for the war effort. Everybody, starting with Musssolini, expected the war to be short and to be victorious. In fact, it became prolonged and its outcome increasingly uncertain. As the war lengthened, it heightened demands on the Italian people. They had come to understand and accept Mussolini's infallibility and genius as Duce as being political rather than military. He was a brilliant leader because he intuitively knew when it was the right time to act. In this case, he had pulled off the best political trick of all, joining the war at the point when Italy could expect to secure maximum gain from minimum pain. In his own people's eyes, Mussolini's reputation as a leader, the aura or myth of infallibility, was bound to be shaken by a lengthening war, because it demonstrated not Mussolini's political genius but his political miscalculation.

Mussolini had, and kept to, an understandably simplistic view of public opinion during the war, which reflected both his dictatorial and totalitarian temperament and his underlying contempt for the Italian people. He thought that the popular mood in wartime would always vary with the military situation; it would be optimistic when Italy and the Axis were winning, pessimistic when they were losing. The popularity of the war among Italians hardly mattered to Mussolini, as a result. The public was fickle, its mood could not be trusted and need not be taken account of. This was another huge hostage to fortune, because it automatically excluded defeat as an option, or a possibility; all that mattered was final victory.

Mussolini's patronizing view of his people and of the fortunes of war was partly justified. Especially in the North African desert, the military campaigns were forwards and backwards affairs. The initial Italian conquest of British Somalia in August 1940 and Graziani's tentative advances into Egypt in September were more than reversed in late 1940 and early 1941. British counter-offensives led to the Italian withdrawal from the Libyan region of Cyrenaica and the capture of 130,000 Italian prisoners of war, and to the loss of Italy's short-lived East African empire. The situation in North Africa was retrieved and, in turn, reversed, in the course of summer 1942 by Axis forces nominally under Italian command but actually commanded by the German general Erwin Rommel. A British counter-attack from El Alamein in October 1942 and Anglo-American landings in Morocco and Algeria a month later, opened up a two-front war in North Africa, leading to the definitive defeat of Axis forces there in May 1943.

The irresponsibly planned invasion of Greece in October 1940 saw Italian forces pushed back into Albania by the Greeks. It took a long time to stabilize the front before the Italians, as in North Africa, were bailed out by the Germans, who invaded and conquered both Yugoslavia and Greece in spring 1941. About 60,000 Italian troops fought in the USSR from August 1941, rising in the Axis summer offensives of 1942 to about 230,000 men, who were then caught out by the Russians' winter counter-offensives in December 1942 and January 1943.

The extraordinary dispersal of Italian military forces across various fighting fronts probably meant Italy's military effectiveness was diluted in all of them. Italy's involvement in the USSR, particularly, absorbed men and equipment which would have been better deployed in North Africa. But the fact that Italian forces were fighting in so many places where the military situation shifted so dramatically, gave Mussolini and the regime some justification for asserting that although some battles were being lost, the same could not necessarily be said for the war.

If we are to believe the trends which emerged cumulatively from police and informers' reports, people's spirits did improve in the course of 1941 and 1942, as Italian reverses in the Balkans and North Africa were made good largely because of German military intervention in Italian theatres of war. This change of mood seemed to confirm Mussolini's cynical intuitiveness about fluctuations in popular opinion during the war. In probably the only instance after the declaration of war in June 1940, a Mussolini wartime speech actually managed to match and catch an improving popular outlook. 'Soon it will be spring,' he announced in both a cheery and a corny way in late February 1941, 'and with that season, our season, good times will come'.[3] He was right, on this occasion. But, very significantly, he was to be proved wrong in continuing to assume that there was an automatic connection between the variable popular mood and the variable fortunes of war.

A *carabinieri* report of May 1942, while lamenting what it judged to be the current scepticism and resignation of the Italian people, appeared to endorse the Mussolini view on public opinion. The present greyness in the popular mood, concluded the report, was a 'state of mind with all the characteristics of contingency and is extremely sensitive to any external stimulus, both in a positive and negative sense'.[4] In other words, a grey dawn would soon become a golden sunset. One can hardly ask for a better example of how *some* reports of the police were stroked into a shape which would ultimately please and reassure their masters. But in the summer of 1942, the military situation of the Axis was improving; there were fresh and successful offensives in both North Africa and the USSR. Despite the optimistic gloss put on the report, it was actually registering a depression in the popular mood, which was confirmed in other reports at the same time. The poor mood coincided with a military situation which should have been raising depressed spirits.

It is usual to locate the demoralization of the Italian home front in the dreadful winter of 1942–3, in the coincidence of a number of negative factors, including the serious military reverses in the USSR and North Africa, literally the turnaround point of the war, and intensified Allied bombing of Italian cities. However, the persistent low spirits of the Italian people in the summer of 1942 indicated that the popular mood was becoming detached from the ebb and flow of the military campaigns. What was happening on the military fronts was not necessarily determining the morale of the home front. It showed that a general war weariness had set in before that terrible winter of 1942–3.

The war which began in June 1940 was certainly launched as a Fascist war. In his speech to the nation announcing the declaration of war, Mussolini spoke of it as being a war against 'the plutocratic and reactionary democracies', a war of 'poor and numerous working peoples against the profiteers who ferociously hold on to their monopoly of all the riches and all the wealth of the world'.[5] This was, then, in Fascist terms, a just war, since it was to bring about an international redistribution of territory and resources, a conquest of essential 'living space' for the territorially and materially confined peoples of Fascist Italy and Nazi Germany. A war portrayed in this way also represented the classic fascist sublimation of internal social tensions and divisions in international conflict. 'Yes, you workers, this is, above all, your war, as well as the war of all Italians . . . for the glory of your country and for the well-being of the working masses.'[6] The redistribution of territory and resources internationally by war would allow the extension of material prosperity to all Italians, and so bring into being a regime of greater social justice internally. The war, in Mussolini's words, would be another decisive step towards the 'reduction of social distances'[7] in Italy itself.

Since Italy was, relatively speaking, a poor country struggling to become a rich country, the war would be won because the Italian people had been forged by Fascism into warriors who would fight with superior faith, spirit, and will, to their enemies, corrupted and impoverished as they were by the prevailing materialism of their societies. Depicting the war in these iconoclastic terms, as a clash of rival civilizations, made even more sense once the USSR and the USA had entered the war in 1941. In Fascist propaganda, what cemented the unholy enemy alliance of Britain, the USA, and the Soviet Union were their materialistic cultures, the concern with material abundance and the satisfaction of material needs alone, whether this was pursued in the mode of individualistic capitalism or that of collectivist communism. It was a war of man against machine, 'flesh confronting steel',[8] a Fascist soul nation defying and overcoming a soulless materialism. There was a serious and self-evident problem for the regime in all this talk of the war being won by spirit and will. It made the morale of the people and of the armed forces absolutely crucial for the winning of the war, and so placed an enormous burden on the regime's capacity to sustain popular morale at a level which would enable people to continue supporting the war effort.

But potentially, anyway, this was impressive and resonant propaganda. Glorifying the Italians' superior will, character, and temperament made a virtue of necessity and rationalized away the technological and material military superiority of Italy's powerful enemies; a poverty of means would be compensated for by a wealth of spirit. Propaganda usually works, or works most effectively, when it confirms or reinforces existing attitudes and opinions, when there are already well-rooted sentiments on which to build. The wartime propaganda portraying Italy as fighting a war for international and internal social justice, replicated over two decades of pre-Fascist Nationalist and then Fascist depictions of Italy as a 'proletarian' nation struggling for its rights against the 'plutocratic' nations. The invasion and conquest of Ethiopia in 1935–6 united most Italians against the one country seriously applying League of Nations' economic sanctions on Italy, which was Britain, contemptuously portrayed as the overfed, over-indulgent country of five meals a day.

Making the poverty of Italians the country's defining virtue and morality was bound to signify something for a poor people being taken to war. The regime's wartime propaganda themes were certainly resonant in some expressions of popular patriotism during the early years of the war, both among those who were conscripted and those who remained at home. This was an infantry sergeant's history lesson for his mother from the French front in June 1940: 'Rome fought against all the barbarities of the world to achieve its greatness and independence, and won; now, it is fighting against the democracies for the freedom of peoples, and it will win.'[9] Naturally, this letter would have passed through the censor, because of its conventional imperialist, international class war, and clash of civilizations vocabulary.

There are echoes of the war being 'the best days of your life' in the patriotic sense of anticipation and adventure expressed by a volunteer officer bound for the Greek war: 'it's really magical, this word "front"! It means everything: privations, holocausts, bloody battles, heroic acts, triumphs.'[10] Even more revealing were the rather more forced traditionally self-sacrificing sentiments of a student conscript, the son of a local artisan, which were suitably spiced up with Fascism's 'I don't give a damn'[11] mentality. 'I hate the comfortable life!' he wrote in March 1941, and went on, 'the sacrifices, the discomforts and the privations don't lower my morale, but arouse in me a redoubled certainty of an expected victory'. This letter, along with another one from a local soldier in Libya at the same time, who said that 'we are ready for anything, arms in hand, to break a chain of injustices', was published in the Catholic parish bulletin and so reached a wider audience. The parish priest's own homilies on the patriotic sacrifices of these local young men, simply repeated almost verbatim the Fascist reasons for war, which were to gain 'work for a people with many workmen . . . and to ensure finally a long period of peace with justice for Italy'.[12] More poignant were these words of rectitude and certainty which appeared in a letter from someone in Florence to an Italian living and working in the United States, the Italians' 'second fatherland'[13] and the country of however many meals a day one wanted: 'Italy will win because we deserve it.'[14]

The tone and content of these initial popular feelings about the war, commonly expressed throughout 1940 and 1941, were evidently to change as the war lengthened. Our patriotic parish priest very honestly aired in his church bulletin the concerns of his parishioners, which he admitted he could not really adequately address. The sacrifices willingly borne, even invited, in 1940–1, were now in July 1942 (note the date of the bulletin), very much resented and a cause of growing anxiety about the prolongation of the war: 'but God, what's He doing?...Why so many tests, so many sacrifices, so much grief? What's the Pope doing? Why doesn't he bring the war to an end?'[15]

When the letters from the military fronts of 1942 and early 1943 complained about the superior equipment and weaponry of enemy troops and the non-availability and malfunctioning of their own, it was clear that the battle of civilizations had been lost in the minds as well as the bodies of Italy's soldiers. They rather prosaically concluded that men had demonstrably not been able to prevail against machines, and blamed the technological and supply gap on the incompetence and unpreparedness of the military command and the Fascist regime. What a difference being defeated made. This was the catch of the regime's wartime propaganda, and perhaps, indeed, of all propaganda; it raised expectations which the real war could not concretely deliver. What happened to soldiers and their families who had been told that they were poor in means but strong in spirit, once it became palpably clear from their own humiliating experience of warfare that the war was being won by armies of inferior peoples with superior means?

It was probably the case that the only Italian servicemen to resist such general demoralization by the end of the Fascist war, and who continued to behave as if they had internalized the Fascist rationale for war, were rather special and specialized military units. What characterized them was the fact that they were made up of volunteers, rather than conscripts, and attempted to make the volunteer spirit the essential component of their cohesiveness and sense of purpose as military forces. The army disliked and was disorientated by volunteers, whose gung-ho fanaticism and sense of being special apparently made them difficult to train and discipline in a regular way. It was only, in the end, political intervention which allowed them to operate at all.

Raising the minimum age of recruitment to 18 years was the army's way of discouraging and stemming the volunteering of young men or old boys from the Fascist Party's umbrella youth organization, the Italian Youth of the Lictors (Gioventù Italiana del Littorio, GIL). The army seemed only too happy to include most of the 20,000 or so GIL members who were organized in their own battalions, in the temporary partial demobilization of the Italian army ordered by Mussolini in October 1940. But Fascist Party pressure and Mussolini's direct endorsement finally enabled the raising of a small force of about 2,000 19 year olds. These young men had initially belonged to a volunteer battalion of Young Fascists (Giovani Fascisti), the Fascist youth organization for 18 to 21 year olds, which had managed during the 1930s to recapture something of the violent and aggressive élan of the original Fascist paramilitary squadrist formations of the early 1920s. They were sent to fight in North Africa in July 1941. This was more than could be said for the 80,000 young men who doubled the university student population between 1939–40 and 1942–3, knowing that being a student would enable them to postpone military service until they were 26 years old. The suddenly overwhelming desire to study presumably said something about the will to war of the Fascist generation who entered their Fascist war in 1940.

The other volunteer formation was the Folgore division of parachutists. It became very conscious of its status as an elite force because of its special and militarily glamorous function, and rigorous recruitment procedures and training, which in themselves developed a strong *esprit de corps* in those who were selected for the force. They were never able to execute the military operations for which they trained. Their airborne landing on the island of Corfu, as part of the Greek campaign, was put off because too many of them were being injured or killed during training exercises as a result of defectively manufactured parachutes. An airborne invasion of the British Mediterranean island of Malta was planned, but eventually cancelled. This political and military decision made by those above had very serious consequences not only for the protection of convoys sailing from the Italian mainland to supply and reinforce Italian forces in Libya, but also for the protection of Italian cities which were bombed from bases on the island.

So the Folgore were deployed for the first and only time as parachutists rather like extras for the recent Hollywood film of *Captain Corelli's Mandolin*, landing ceremonially on the Greek island of Cefalonia in the spring of 1941 after the armistice had been signed to end the fighting with the Greeks. Thereafter, the Folgore saw actual military action as an infantry not a para-chutist division, in North Africa, and most of them were killed or captured at El Alamein in 1942. They lived on, more propagandistically than militarily effective, as the Italian press's 'holocaust division',[16] reputedly Italy's most ferociously committed and destructive fighting force, its remnants reassembled and fighting to the point of final surrender in North Africa in May 1943. Their activities were deliberately glamorized by the regime as a model and example to others of the fanatical never-say-die fighting spirit which would save the Axis in North Africa. It was hardly surprising that the division's survivors and new recruits rallied to Mussolini's Salò Republic in 1943, and were similarly showcased as the exemplars of the nihilistic backs-to-the-wall mentality of an embattled Fascism.

There is a wider significance in the trajectory of the Folgore from one Fascist war to another in 1943. A young Fascist soldier on the north-eastern Italian frontier wrote to his girlfriend fresh from participating in military operations against communist partisans in occupied Slovenia, very late on in Italy's Fascist war, in May 1943. Perhaps predictably, his anger and frustration at fighting a very nasty partisan war were directed inwards at that 'sea of people' back in Italy who had lost the national will to fight. 'Perhaps the spirit of the entire Italian people has gone putrid. Nobody in Italy seems to realize that we are fighting in a great struggle for life or death; no one has even the slightest sense of honour, we're behaving like idiots.'[17] ('We're behaving like shits' would be a better rendering of the insult the young Fascist actually used, 'facciamo schifo'.) The resentment of the soldier at the defeatism of the home front, which he held responsible for his own predicament at the fighting front, became a common refrain in the letters of some troops as the war lengthened, especially among those who could be identified, or identified themselves, as still believing in a Fascist war. This was the sectarian, intransigent, embittered language of civil war, of soldiers wanting to avenge themselves on the defeatist Italians back home who had 'betrayed' them, sentiments some of them carried into their involvement with the Fascist Republic between 1943 and 1945.

The fatal hostages-to-fortune flaws of wartime propaganda were evident also in Mussolini's attempts to get the Italian people to fight a Fascist war properly by hating their enemies. Trying to make something out of military defeat and civilian suffering, Mussolini urged the Italians to stop being sentimental and start hating the peoples who were inflicting the defeats and making their daily lives intolerable. In a speech at Rome in February 1941, he argued that the events in Greece should accentuate the country's hatred of the enemy, 'that cold, conscious, implacable hatred, the hatred embedded in every heart, spreading in every household, which is indispensable for victory.'[18] The injunction to hate was repeated by Mussolini in perhaps the worst ever wartime speech by any national leader in terms of the impact it had on the people who heard it, in December 1942, after some of the most devastating Allied bombing raids of the war. 'You don't make war without hating the enemy,' said Mussolini. 'You don't make war without hating the enemy from morning until night, in all the hours of day and night, without propagating this hatred and making it the inner essence of your being.'[19]

The Fascistized Italian press at least took him at his word. After the Allied bombing of Sardinia in June 1943, the *Corriere della Sera* cried revenge: 'For every disembowelled Sardinian child, a disembowelled enemy child.'[20] Allied bombing was an atrocity, 'gangsterism'; photographs in the newspapers concentrated on showing wounded and dead children lying in the ruins of bombed-out cities. This was a dangerous and counterproductive thing to do. It might have been realistic propaganda, an incitement to hate. But it showed the enemy that the bombing campaign was working, and it also showed the Italians that the bombing campaign was working and what was really happening to their fellow citizens.

The Italians themselves rarely seemed to accept this propaganda of hate. They were almost terrorized by Allied bombing. But what they expressed on the basis of their own experience of the bombings was not a hatred of the American 'gangsters' dropping the bombs. Instead, they were shocked, incredulous, and angry at what was perceived to be the total inadequacy of the authorities' preparation and response. People's letters were full of criticisms of the poor performance of the Italian air force and of the country's anti-aircraft defences, which left cities defenceless against bombing attacks. They also spoke of air raid sirens either not sounding before raids, which caught people unawares, or sounding continuously, false alarms which forced people in and out of shelters. The public and private shelters were regarded as death traps, poorly constructed and maintained, and always dangerously overcrowded.

The Sicilian cities of Palermo and Catania were bombed throughout the war. Like most cities on the island and in the south, they were always in the range of Allied bombers and they took a particularly intense battering before and during the Allied invasion of Sicily in June and July 1943. When the bombings started and were still a dramatic novelty, people in Palermo, and in the other bombed cities, naturally tended to exaggerate the destructive impact of the raids on lives and property. The imagining of destruction was part of the frisson and terror which the early bombings induced. But later, police reporting to their superiors in Rome and shocked residents writing to friends and family elsewhere in Italy, almost exactly coincided in their descriptions of a bombed-out city on its knees, recording in prosaic, concrete, eyewitness terms the breakdown of public services and utilities. The city in early 1943 had long since given up on being adequately defended against bombing raids. It was by this point not even being defended against their consequences. Fires burnt themselves out; survivors cleared and scavenged through the rubble, unaided and unguided. In a report which we know reached Mussolini's desk on the eve of the Grand Council meeting, the police chief of Catania succinctly summarized the situation in the city: 'without flour and without water, 30,000 people who crowd into unsafe shelters are subjected, day and night, to incessant terrifying naval and air bombardment which is transforming the city into a heap of ruins'.[21]

There was the same basic convergence in eyewitness and informers' reports on the institutional breakdown exposed by the bombing of Milan in October 1942. Here the sense of outrage and incredulity was heightened by the experience of it being, uniquely for Milan, an attack made in daylight in the afternoon. A resident soon after evacuated to enjoy the mountain air north of Milan, wrote: 'just imagine, they gave the alarm when the planes were already over the centre of the city, and at an altitude of 200 metres [656.2 feet] they were able to bomb and machine gun far and wide very much as they wanted, making the city look like a burning funeral pyre. So, it was our fault, too'. The public authorities' response did not materialize. 'Absolute deficiency of firemen and transport,' commented the informer; 'also inadequate were the teams trained to excavate and clear debris. The population are furious... about the complete lack of any services and because the authorities have shown that they are absolutely unprepared to undertake any useful and timely intervention.'[22]

People tended, then, to blame their wartime troubles not on the bombers, but on the incompetence and lack of concern of their leaders, who had taken them to war and failed to provide even a basic national security. In many cases, blaming the government was entirely justified. Preparation for civil defence had been superficial and inadequate. This was an amazing lack of foresight, when Italian military and popular strategists alike shared the near-universal inter-war perception that the bomber would always get through. Future wars, it was commonly thought, would be decided by the power of bombing from the air. The failure to recognize that there might be a need for air defence was what appeared most striking and culpable. Badoglio had apparently even turned down the idea of using lottery funding for anti-aircraft installations, and it was not because he believed that the taxpayer should be responsible for such a basic element of national defence. One can only assume that the lack of adequate preparation of defence against air attack was another good reason for Mussolini wanting and expecting a short war. Certainly, a victorious short war would make the lack of preparation irrelevant. This was certainly how Mussolini rationalized things in a meeting of the Supreme Defence Commission in 1940. The defence of Italian cities would, in effect, be unnecessary, since the Axis would pre-empt the need by winning the war and bombing the enemy itself into submission.

Another reason for the lack of attention to anti-aircraft protection and civil defence was the belief that the best way to defend urban populations from air attack was, in fact, for them to evacuate the cities. Forced into the countryside, urban industrial workers could replace the labour of a con-scripted agricultural workforce. The war would also, in this way, push forward one of the Fascist regime's long-running policies to 'ruralize' and, hence, reshape Italians, by moving them from the cosmopolitan and morally corrupting environment of city life to breathe the pure and virtuous Fascist air of the countryside.

Some provincial prefectures, following central guidelines, certainly worked out evacuation plans before the war and tried to implement them during the war itself. Pesarò, for instance, was to receive evacuees from towns like Pola and Fiume across the Adriatic in Italian and Italian-occupied Yugoslavia, according to a national evacuation plan, and in a local deal between prefectures, also took in refugees from the Ligurian industrial port city of Genoa, to which many men from Pesarò had migrated, for work. But, as we shall see, it was difficult to manage these plans in practice, when the process of evacuation was largely spontaneous and disorderly, and often took the form of people commuting between their temporary countryside residence and their workplace in the cities.

In 1940, there were, apparently, 230 anti-aircraft batteries in existence, defending ports and airfields but not the cities. In the course of the war, these were reinforced by some German-equipped and German-staffed installations. But it was far from adequate. The capital city, Rome, was first bombed only on 19 July 1943. But Rome was uniquely defended by the presence of the Pope, and no other Italian city could expect the divine protection enjoyed by the Eternal City. The civil defence organization, UNPA, was underfunded and voluntarily, that is Fascist Party run, from the start. In 1939, at the outbreak of the Second (though not yet Italy's) World War, there were around 4,000 air raid shelters in Italy, both public and private residence-based, covering, if that is the word, about 300,000 people. In the major northern industrial city of Turin, with a population of about 600,000, there were by the end of 1943, public shelters with a capacity of about 25,000 people, while private and factory shelters catered for another 150,000. Arrangements in some city residential areas amounted to little more than a pile of sand in a ground floor recess or basement, which was exactly how Mussolini thought things should be done in that same Supreme Defence Commission meeting. His answer to the problem of an air raid warning system, by the way, was rather like expecting people to detect a fire in their homes by smelling the smoke. When a raid was coming, Mussolini thought you could always rely on those people with the sharpest hearing to inform the rest, presumably by shrieking loudly enough above the rumble of the bombers for the others to hear.

If we realize, once again, that propaganda probably has the least effect when going against the grain of people's existing attitudes, then it was unlikely that the regime could ever get Italians to hate the Americans who were bombing them. For many Italians, especially from the south and the islands, the USA was their first, let alone their second, fatherland, still the land of migration, opportunity, and the second chance. The consumerism and materialism of US culture, so derided in Fascist wartime propaganda, was precisely what attracted many Italians to the USA, or the idea of the USA. If anything, the stock of the USA was enhanced during and as a result of the war, as defeated Italian soldiers acknowledged to themselves and others that such material abundance, expressed in better provisions, better equipment, and better weapons, was enabling the Allies to win the war.

As interesting was the regime's apparent inability to get Italians to enter into the spirit of Fascism's anti-Bolshevik crusade and hate the Russians. Mussolini's decision to send Italian troops to participate in the Nazi German invasion of the Soviet Union in the summer of 1941, at least made sense in terms of Fascism's mythical origins as the political force which had saved

1. Not yet stuck in the mud: Italian troops in the Soviet Union, probably autumn 1941.

2. The anti-Bolshevik crusade: Italian troops destroying a monument to Lenin in the Soviet Union, August 1941.

Italy from Bolshevism immediately after the First World War. The decision might even have reflected Mussolini's relief that the Axis had finally returned to its anti-communist track after the ideologically problematic hiatus of the Nazi-Soviet Pact of 1939 to 1941—the Hitler-Stalin agreement which had so stupefied Mussolini and the Fascists when it was made. An Italian presence in the USSR would be Mussolini's way of affirming that Hitler, at last, was fighting Nazism's proper war in the proper place. Within eighteen months, Mussolini would only be wishing that Hitler could stop the fighting in the USSR. Anyway, committing 60,000 troops to the initial Russian campaign was not what Hitler actually wanted nor expected. Later, however, he asked for more Italian troops to be sent to Russia in 1942. Italian involvement did not obviously square up with what remained of the idea of the parallel war and the pursuit of Italy's own living space in the Mediterranean. In fact, the one undermined the other: military involvement in the USSR absorbed men and resources rather desperately needed in the Mediterranean theatre.

The fact was that Italian participation in the Russian war seemed to be just a case of being there, and did not appear to serve or secure any vital national strategic and territorial interest. This might be one reason, at least, why Italian veterans of the Russian campaigns were so embittered by their experiences: they did not feel that they had much to fight for or defend. Certainly, in these Italian soldiers' records of their encounters, the Russians did not live down to the stereotypical propaganda depiction of a barbarous and uncivilized people. It was obvious that the censors had to work really hard on the correspondence to and from the Soviet Union. Both the tone and content of the censored letters from the Russian front suggest that the soldiers' discovery of the basic humanity of their enemy was something of a shock.

Much of the soldiers' scorn in the letters was kept back for their officers, as cold and distant as the terrain in which they were fighting, and their Axis allies, the Germans, and the continuing incompetence and lack of preparation of their political and military leaders. The question of winter boots became something of a cause célèbre. At least the military commanders got it right in insisting that the Italian troops should be equipped in boots like the Russian ones, made of fur and animal skin. But the first Italian army in Russia mainly did without them in the 1941–2 winter, and suffered more frostbite than casualties, as a result. The army's requisitioning department simply did not provide for the manufacture of the kind of boots the *in situ* military commanders wanted. By the time the second and much larger Italian army entered the terrible winter of 1942–3, the army had managed to locate the skins, in Romania, but were so slow in making and sending the boots that they did not arrive until early in December 1942. The winter boots fiasco imprinted itself on the memory of the 40-year-old Italian woman who volunteered to nurse with the Red Cross in the USSR. She remembered 'those poor boys who came to us in dreadful condition . . . They had black, frozen feet, as if charred, which fell to bits . . . I can really say that I, too, went to war, in the true sense of the word.'[23]

After the battle of Stalingrad in late 1942–early 1943, the Italian army was brought up to the front line, to hold it and cover the German retreat. The Italians were forced into their own disorganized and frantic retreat. An army of some 140,000 men broke up, lacking a functioning command structure, transport, communications, medical aid, and air support. Around 80,000 Italian troops died. The soldiers in their letters brought together and contrasted in the same account, their feelings about the allies and the officers who abandoned them, and the Russians who had helped them to survive a terrible experience. 'A thousand kilometres [620 miles] on foot was what our beloved German comrades made us do because they didn't want us to make use of the trains,' wrote a soldier in March 1943, who bitterly reflected on Germany's betrayal of them: 'this was how the dead whom we left on the Don were rewarded.'[24] Clearly now resting with his feet up, another soldier recorded his impressions of the past three months of fighting and retreat, concluding that it was the Russians who had provided him with what he had been missing about home:

> we have received the most friendly treatment from the Russians, who are our enemies; while we can find nothing to praise about our Italian military commanders, and we cannot say anything good about our German comrades, who take every opportunity to find a way to make clear their contempt for us . . . The Russians have helped us in every way they can during the retreat. They have put us up, given us food to eat, deloused us, washed us, given up their beds to us. And all this not out of fear, but out of a pure sense of hospitality and of humanity. To see the kindness with which sometimes the ordinary women welcomed me, that really moved me and made me think of my own dear parents.[25]

The Italian newspapers barely mentioned what the army was experiencing in Russia in 1942–3. The censor would have made sure that nothing of the preceding letter would have reached its intended audience. But in the spring of 1943, the remnants of the army were repatriated. Thousands of exhausted soldiers were turning up on Italy's Alpine borders and starting to give first-hand, uncensored word-of-mouth accounts to the Catholic welfare volunteers who looked after them and to their families, neighbours, and friends on their arrival home. The censor would have intervened again, but the contents of this letter showed how hearsay would have spread the news of the Russian war beyond those directly involved because they had sons and fathers in the USSR. A woman wrote from Castell'Arquato, in the northern province of Piacenza, in April 1943, that she had heard about someone who had just returned from Russia saying enthusiastic things about the humanity of the Russian people. This exposed something which was the conclusion of the letter writer and would have been the conclusion of the returning soldier, that 'all the propaganda being put out' was 'a continual pack of lies'.

Her reflection that 'if they're left in Russia any longer, they'll all come back Bolsheviks',[26] was hardly given or to be taken literally, but it was a pardonable exaggeration. Many officers and men who were returning veterans of the Italian army in Russia found their way into resistance movements to the German occupation of north and central Italy after September 1943. It seems impossible not to connect their becoming partisans to what they experienced in the USSR in 1942–3. They hated the Germans, as the ex-allies—now invaders and occupiers—who had left them to die in Russia. They already knew from experience how the Germans behaved towards the Russians as an occupying force and what Italians could now expect from German occupation of their own country. They clearly wanted to emulate the Russian partisans, who had fought to defend their country against brutal and rapacious occupiers.

Soviet propaganda apparently distinguished between the German troops, with whom there was no possibility of contact, or quarter, and Italian troops, with whom some kind of human contact, even fraternization, was possible. The point of the 'bad guy'/'good guy' contrast was clearly to undermine and weaken the Axis alliance. There is some evidence, including the letters already mentioned, that Russian civilians acted according to the propaganda and distinguished between the two sets of troops in the way they treated them in 1943. If this was the case, then post-war memories of the Russian campaign and especially what they focused on, the 1943 retreats, converge with the contemporary accounts. It takes a human to recognize a human and during the 1942–3 campaigns, the 'good' Italian soldier met the 'good' Russian peasant. Many of the peasant soldiers in the Alpine regiments who fought in the USSR would not exactly have felt at home in Russia. But in the human and humane contact with an enemy population, they must have sensed and experienced something of the basic social solidarities which they expected of their own peasant culture and way of life in the hills and mountains of Piedmont.

Every myth, like every cliché, has or had some basis in reality and certainly becomes a reality capable of affecting the way people think and behave, and remember. There was, and is, a very pervasive myth that Italians were, and are, *brava gente*, basically decent people, even in war. However, this view of themselves is difficult to sustain in light of the experience of the Italian wartime occupation of the Balkans from the spring of 1941. What was remembered most about Russia after the war were the defeats and retreats of early 1943 and the occasions of fraternization between Italian troops and the local Russian people. These memories meant that the Italian soldiers could see themselves as being as much the victims of war as their Russian hosts. No such sublimation of experience was really ever valid in dismembered and occupied Yugoslavia. A muted recognition of this filtered into the memories of some veterans who had gone through both the Russian campaigns and Balkan occupation. Most of the Italian forces involved in the invasion of Greece also served in the Soviet Union. 'Russia', they said, 'was better than Yugoslavia, Albania or Greece',[27] better for them and for the countries they invaded and occupied.

Italian political and military control over Dalmatia and southern Slovenia, and the nominally satellite mini-states of Croatia and Montenegro, was fragile and volatile from the start. Slav resistance to Axis occupation was disruptively evident from the summer and autumn of 1941. The Italian military command rationalized its inability to cope with insurgency by managing the conflict politically, leaving Slav nationalist partisan bands alone as long as they countered and checked the communist partisan formations.

To confront the deteriorating situation, more troops were transferred to occupied Yugoslavia in 1942, men who might have been sent to North Africa instead. In 1942–3, there were two whole armies stationed in the area straddling Italy's now extended north-eastern frontier with the ex-Yugoslavia, and around half a million Italian troops occupying Yugoslav territory and parts of Greece. These men bore the brunt of an increasingly nasty anti-partisan war, as

Italian forces adopted and—in Greece at least—anticipated the violently repressive methods of their German allies against all Slav partisans and their local host populations. Excessive violence was required of Italian occupying forces, and it could be carried out with impunity. In March 1942, General Roatta, commander of the Second Army in Italian-occupied Yugoslavia, issued to his military commanders a detailed handbook on counter-insurgency, which included the infamous directive for a reprisal policy of 'not a tooth for a tooth, but a head for a tooth'. One of Roatta's commanders, General Mario Robotti, complained to his officers that 'you are not slaughtering enough people'.[28]

The same brutal practices were adopted throughout Italian-occupied Yugoslavia and Greece. In early 1943, a concerted Italian army sweep across occupied central Greece involved, in some zones, the mass rapes of girls and women. But things were particularly gruesome in Slovenia, in the summer and autumn of 1942. Around 46,000 Italian troops, rising to over 50,000 in the great anti-partisan offensives of late summer, participated in the grisly cycle of irregular warfare. Military expeditions to clear an area of partisan activity and round up partisans and those who fed and sheltered them, willingly or not, expected and invited local resistance, provoking reprisals, hostage taking and hostage killing, the summary execution of captured or wounded partisans, the burning of villages, and, in some cases, the shooting of entire village populations. About 25,000 Slovene men and women were captured and deported to concentration camps in Italy and the Adriatic islands. The only limitation on the internment policy was the finite capacity of the camps. General Robotti personally selected and imprisoned as hostages ten local dignitaries in the Slovenian capital of Ljubljana during the winter of 1942–3. Their lives would be forfeit in the event of any partisan attacks in the city. He oversaw a quite deliberate policy to isolate the partisans from the local people, and to terrorize and subjugate the Slav population, even if it meant taking over a wasteland. Italian control, said Roatta, had to be achieved 'at whatever cost . . . even if all Slovenes have to be shot and all of Slovenia destroyed'.[29]

It is obviously difficult to distinguish how Italian soldiers felt at the time about what they had to do, from their post-war memories of their actions, which were understated, as you might expect. A military chaplain serving with a Sardinian regiment involved in anti-partisan operations in Croatia could at least provide a contemporary rationale for military action against civilian populations, which must have struck a chord with his previous service in Italy's East African colonies. 'By destroying everything,' he wrote, 'we remove the rebels' means of survival; by terrifying these people even more than the rebels are capable of doing because they have less means than we do, we will make them bend towards us.' This was straight from the Roatta manual on counter-insurgency. The chaplain was not someone who was on the edge of such activities. He compassionately and realistically acknowledged the consequences for both victims and perpetrators.

> The state in which we left that most unfortunate of places! We abandoned it to a crowd of old men without sons, of women without husbands, of children without fathers, all powerless people, most of them deprived even of their homes, which had been burnt out, and completely lacking any means of subsistence . . . everything had been plundered and destroyed; we left them to die of hunger.

This was written of a raid which took place in July 1942. Later, he was not only present at, but obliged to get involved in, the reprisal killings of civilians by Italian troops in a Croatian village. Here, the compassion was for those soldiers who 'grumbled that it was not their job, that they had no way of knowing that these people were guilty'.[30] The chaplain's advice and reassurance to the executioners on the spot was that they had to go ahead with the shootings, that the killings were ultimately not their responsibility. Continuing in a way which was both chilling and concerned, the chaplain emphasized to the men that the important thing was to shoot the villagers efficiently, so that they would not die suffering too much. What strikes you, in retrospect, about this dreadful scene, was that this dual harassment and intimidation of peasant communities, this squeezing of civilian populations between the two competing coercive forces of the partisan band and the occupying army, was re-enacted later in the Italy of 1943 to 1945.

This is a rather gratuitous reflection on what was to come. It becomes more legitimate when one realizes that some of the Italian soldiers terrorizing civilians in occupied Yugoslavia would, after the dissolution of the Italian armies following the September 1943 armistice, join Slav partisan groups and resistance formations in Italy itself. One could provocatively say that they carried on terrorizing civilians, albeit on the opposite and 'right' side. An Italian veteran commented to the historian Claudio Pavone, in words which were part confession, part justification: 'I had been to Yugoslavia, and I too had burned villages, shot hostages, raped women. When my eyes were opened, what could I do? I became a partisan.'[31] Of course, one detects here the way in which memory softens the unpalatable past. But the sense that the Resistance redeemed the atrocities of occupation might not have been just memory's easing of a bad conscience. It would depend on when his eyes were opened. There was a kind of tacit retrospective acknowledgement in the recollections of the Balkan veterans that the Yugoslav partisans were both more honourable and more savvy than they were at the time. Some Italian soldiers remembered that, while they normally shot captured partisans, captured Italian soldiers, but not their officers, were usually freed by the partisans and given the choice of joining them or returning, humiliated but alive, to their units, stripped of their arms, clothing, and boots. Would the opening of eyes have occurred here? Certainly, these soldiers were faced with a choice, and it was not, at this point, anyway, a matter of life or death. They would live, whatever the choice made.

Anti-partisan and counter-insurgency warfare was hardly moral, since it did not discriminate between fighters and civilians. The people who lived in the same area as where the partisans operated, were as guilty as them. Understandably selective memories expressed, however, a relative morality for the post-war, if only partially for the war experience itself. We know, for instance, that in Slovenia, most expeditions against civilian populations were undertaken by troops of the regular army. But in many personal accounts of the war in Yugoslavia, ex-soldiers said that the Germans behaved far worse than the Italians. As for the behaviour of the Italians, the feeling was that the perpetrators of atrocities against civilians and partisans were not regular army soldiers like themselves, but rather the Fascist Militia often attached to serving army divisions. The really nasty work, in other words, was carried out by fanatical, ideologically committed volunteers, whose Fascism made them into the psychopaths capable of murdering non-combatant civilians.

It may well be the case that, as oral historians tell us, memories of the past are of limited use in reconstructing what happened, but they, nevertheless, reveal a person's mentality or culture. None of this is particularly reassuring in the instance of the veterans of the Balkan wars. The interviews conducted with a group of them exposed a latent racism or xenophobia which might not have been so latent forty years earlier. Most scorn was directed at the Albanians, seen as backward and primitive in a way which would not have been out of place if expressed by an Italian soldier or official in one of Italy's East African colonies in the late 1930s and early 1940s. One man, who was from the far north (Bergamo), even compared the Greeks to the Italians of the south, Italy's own 'backward' people, and claimed that these were views he had bantered over with Greeks during his war service in their country. The Slavs were perhaps not as bad as Albanians, but were 'Arabs', 'Muslims'.

One veteran compressed his memories of the Yugoslav experience in this way: 'After Russia, they sent me to Yugoslavia, against those Slavs ... that was tough! Worse than Russia ... I was at an altitude of 1,000 to 1,500 metres, right on the border carrying out round-ups ... Then, the Yugoslavs lived the same life as the partisans against the *repubblichini* [the men of the Fascist Salò Republic].'[32] What does one make of this surreal combination of muted, probably real time, judgements and those filtered through and made analogous to the next big experience, the Resistance in Italy and the civil war between resisters and Fascists in 1943–5? The memory clearly shows an empathy towards the Yugoslav partisans, and by extension, the Italian partisans, which may or may not have been real at the time. But the toughness and worseness of the anti-partisan war he admitted to participating in, are sublimated into the physical discomfort, no doubt considerable, of having to be a soldier in such high mountainous altitudes.

Not all of these ex-soldiers joined the Yugoslav partisans, if confronted with the choice, though some of them evidently did. One of the veterans who was most explicit in describing a specific atrocity and feeling shamed by it, apparently refused to join the Slav partisan bands after the September 1943 armistice, along with his immediate comrades. His reasons for doing so might, of course, have had nothing to do with the politics of the choice, one way or the other. He might simply have assumed that the war was over, for him and his fellow soldiers, and that he was likely to be able to return home for good. He miscalculated, along with thousands of others, and ended up in a railway truck being transported to an internment camp in Germany.

Few of these survivors, naturally enough, thought that they had room for making any choices at all, since they were simply soldiers carrying out orders. However, it seems likely that Italian military atrocities against civilians in the Balkans during the war were not only a matter of soldiers obeying orders, or being reassured that it was necessary for them to do so by a military chaplain. Those military commanders and officers actually giving the orders seemed to have internalized Fascism's imperialist mentality with its contempt for native peoples. But, again, action against civilians might well have been seen by those in command as militarily necessary, and the inevitable working out of an implacable military, rather than ideological or cultural, logic. What seems clear was that the Italian military command had a definite strategy of controlling occupied territory by terrorizing the local population, and implemented it. The strategy involved treating its victims as inferiors, and, in this sense, was a matter of waging a Fascist war, not just any war. As for the soldiers on the ground, they were caught up in a self-justifying spiral of vicious violence and counter-violence, where they could be seen simultaneously as both victims and perpetrators. 'Reprisals' were, after all, not the start of things. They were a 'legitimate' response to the violence of the enemy. Their choices were ones determined by the choices of the others, and, so, unavoidable. This line of reasoning is, admittedly, perhaps no more than a sophisticated version of the 'only obeying orders' theme.

During 1942, the war became unpopular in Italy not just because it was not yet over militarily, but primarily because of the impact on people's lives of food shortages and Allied bombings of Italian cities. People justifiably blamed the government for causing and worsening food shortages, and they blamed the government for not adequately preparing for and respond- ing to Allied bombings. The Fascist regime failed to pass the only test it wanted to be judged by, which was war. It failed to do the things it was ideologically primed to do: win the fighting war, and organize and mobilize the people in support of the war effort. Above all, the Fascist regime failed the ultimate test of the validity of any governmental system at war, which was to secure and maintain a social truce or equilibrium coming from a sense of an equality of sacrifice among the people. Italians were divided, not united, by the experience of war. Many of them came to feel that they were unjustifi- ably paying a higher personal cost for the war than others. As a result, their commitment to the national, collective cause dipped, and the war became a matter of personal rather than national survival, literally every man and woman looking out for themselves. The Italian people's wartime abandon- ment of the public for the private good, was the real sign of the redundancy of Fascism, which was premised on raising and mobilizing a national con- sciousness and for over twenty years had invaded the private sphere in the name of its version or vision of the collective welfare. What Fascism had done to create a Fascist nation can be measured in the police and informers' reports on how people in Milan, Turin, and other heavily bombed north Italian cities reacted to the first Allied bombing raid on Rome in July 1943. There was not a trace of commiseration or solidarity, but an almost obscene gratification that the capital city, the seat of government, of course, had finally suffered what they, in the 'real' Italy, had been suffering for years.

Food was what Italy produced, and the organization and regulation of food production had been a feature of Fascist Italy's autarkic or self-sufficient war economy since the late 1930s. Then, the regime had set up an obligatory requisitioning scheme for cereals and other agricultural foodstuffs and raw materials. These official stockpiles, or *ammassi*, were intended to remove essential foodstuffs from the market economy and guarantee regular supplies at stable and fair prices for both producers and consumers. The *ammassi* continued to operate during the war, and so it is difficult to see how things could go wrong with the food supply.

Food supply was, of course, a crucial area for every country at war. It was especially vital for a relatively poor and low-consumption society like Italy's, since a far higher proportion of people's incomes in Italy went on basic food items than, for instance, in Britain and the USA. We have already seen how the Fascist regime made a virtue of Italy's relative poverty. Certainly, Mussolini himself expected the Italian people to be capable of enduring more shortages and deprivation precisely because of their already existing low levels of consumption. They were used to hardship, and could put up with more. The problem was that low consumption was Italy's national weakness as much as its national strength. Once food became short and more highly priced as a result, ordinary working-class Italians were unable to maintain their already quite low levels of food consumption. Many of them started to suffer from malnutrition. Italians on higher incomes, who had always lived way above subsistence levels, now found themselves spending as much as half of their incomes on food, a proportion as high as that in working-class families before the war. Many middle-class Italians were dipping into and even exhausting their savings, in order to try to maintain their usual consumption of food.

There is evidence not so much of people starving in Italy during the war, as of hunger, malnutrition, and poor diet. A university professor at Trieste, Luzzatto Fegiz, acting as a consultant on food matters for the Ministry of Agriculture, produced a series of quite devastating surveys of Italians' eating patterns in the course of 1942 and early 1943, so devastating that he was eventually sacked for producing such unpalatable results. In his spring and summer 1942 survey of around 300 families in fifteen provinces, he found that while agricultural families, naturally enough, were still eating satisfactorily, only 2 per cent of urban families—both middle- and working-class—were eating sufficiently or more than sufficiently. Extrapolated nationally, his survey findings were that perhaps up to fourteen million Italians were going hungry. His late 1942–early 1943 sample showed that a greater number of urban middle-class families were eating rather better than before, but that they were spending far more in order to do so. Some people were spending a quarter of all that they spent, on buying food on the black market. The effect of the black market on poor families was highlighted in Fegiz's May 1943 report. Prices had trebled, and nutrition was in some cases a third below the physiological minimum.

The repercussions of a highly priced scarce food supply were felt throughout Italian society and the economy. Industrial workers were not able to eat at or above the calorific norm, even when the already inadequate food rations were increased for men doing heavy industrial work. Their productivity and sociability were affected. They were more easily and quickly tired in the workplace, and were irritable and exhausted at home. A hungry tiredness began to creep into offices, as much as in the factories. A female clerk in Milan in 1942 said that 'in our office, there's a general feebleness around; several hours before closing work is practically suspended. The men smoke furiously.'[33]

Hunger also had anxiety-inducing psychological effects, as people wondered how they were going to cope. The all-too-precise accounting for her loss of weight had an obsessive feel to it in this letter of a woman living in Bologna, written in May 1942: 'Since rationing I have lost 20 kg [44.1 lb] in weight. Some, maybe, from the lack of food and fats, some from the work, and some from the anxiety and distress to which we are subjected.'[34] People stayed away from work, debilitated by malnutrition. Absenteeism became customary, with workers, especially female workers, taking time off to search for food. The practice became so prevalent that in March 1943 unexplained work absences beyond a certain span were treated as desertion. Persistent absentees could expect to be tried by a military tribunal and were liable to up to six months' imprisonment. The money fines for individuals buying black market goods were heavy, about the equivalent of three weeks' wages for an industrial worker. These penalties did not seem to deter the female textile workers of Biella, a wool town in the mountains north of Turin, who skipped work to bike down into the valleys for food, initially at weekends and then on any day when they needed food. And why not? The reasons for continuing to take these long bike rides seemed more compelling than those inhibiting this essential bit of exercise. By early 1943, they were being paid up to 25 lire a day, which bought 1 kg (2.2 lb) of rice on the black market, when the official price was ten times lower. Their official food rations, when they were actually distributed, offered 1,000 calories a day, an amount which could only lead to malnourishment. In the absenteeism and low productivity of workers, we have the perfect illustration of how the impacts of the war led to the private superseding the public. People's time and energy were spent in locating food for themselves and their families, time and energy not expended on manufacturing weapons, equipment, clothing for the armies on the military fronts.

In effect, the daily search for food and the black market which both prolonged and satiated the search, operated like a massive sponge.[35] It soaked up people's time, energy, and money, absorbing resources needed for the war effort. The middle classes stopped saving and money which they usually channelled into public loans to the government to help finance the war, now went on food and—an incongruous phenomenon this—on a general spending spree. Inflation made holding on to money appear useless. It was better to spend on things now when they were in financial reach and available, since in a short while, they might be too expensive or unavailable. The busy streets, the full restaurants, theatres, and cinemas of some Italian towns and cities for at least some of the time, were hardly a self-confident popular declaration of business as usual. The bustle was, instead, the sign of a rather desperate and hopeless abandonment to living for today, on what people had today and possibly would not have tomorrow. Only perhaps in the capital, Rome, was the normal excess of big city life really normal. Protected from Allied bombing by the Pope's residence, it was as if the war had never come. There was not the faintest whiff of shortages in the wartime diaries of Bottai, Ciano, and the rest, cruising the restaurants and clubs of the city to agonize together over the regime's and Mussolini's future in late 1942 and early 1943. 'People are barely aware of the war' in Rome, wrote a top Foreign Ministry official and resident as late as mid-March 1943. 'Foodstuffs are very much more plentiful this year ... theatres and cinemas packed with people. Nobody seems aware of the looming threat of invasion.'[36]

High food prices especially taxed the relatively fixed incomes of industrial workers and lower-middle- and middle-class white-collared private and public sector employees. These urban middle-class folk were the backbone of the Fascist regime's popular support, Fascism's natural nationalistic class constituency. Their loss of confidence in Mussolini and the regime as a result of the socio-economic effects of the war on their standard of living, was a particularly dangerous and telling development. The war seemed to be shredding these people's incomes and way of life, making things difficult all round. It became increasingly hard to secure and retain maids in middle-class urban households. 'Before agreeing to work for you,' remembered one middle-class matron, 'they asked if you had enough provisions in the house, and whether they could be guaranteed to be fed above the ration levels.'[37]

It is difficult to feel much sympathy for bourgeois families who could not survive without a maid, and one can hardly blame the maids for making the most of being in demand. But one gets a better sense of the difference wartime conditions were making to perceptions of class and status, and to the middle classes' changing perception of their apparently established place in society, from a rather sad letter written in late spring 1942. It listed the travails of a patriotic middle-class Italian family, this one living in Sestri Levante, a resort and dormitory town on the Ligurian coast near Genoa.

> I would never have thought that I would be living this anxious, nervous, and totally prosaic existence, the point of which, the continual day and night problem of which, is one thing, and always the same thing: food. You sit down at table and eat in silence the meal which has cost you so much sweat, not so much in earning the money for it, as in finding the food for it, paying for it and cooking it in the least bad way possible. Our countryside looks beautiful, promising roses and garlands for the peasant and, alas, thorns aplenty for us poor consumers. The serving woman, at the end of the month, tells me some story and takes off to her place, where it appears there is no lack of, rather an abundance of, bread, *focaccia*, all the various flours which exist, including those on her ration card . . . I can well believe it, since she is the daughter of peasants, which means today's rich people, along with the shopkeepers. And so here I am . . . humiliated to the point of seeing my own serving woman leave my house for the want of bread! Be brave, we'll try to keep clinging on to the rock of life . . . until we see victory's dawn.[38]

Again, it is hard to see how the world can come to an end when the servant leaves. But there is almost everything here, in this one letter. The meaning of life was reduced to the daily obsessive search for food. There was the sense of a comfortable, ordered social universe being destabilized by war, of social upheaval and inversion, where the servant was better-off than the mistress, the countryside a better place to be than the town. There was the urban consumer's resentment at being exploited by the wartime nouveaux riches, the peasants and the shopkeepers. There was the final, pathetic maudlin burst of patriotism, pathetic in our terms, because this person's self-sacrifice for the nation amounted to the social humiliation of being unable to hang on to one's servants. Less histrionically, but perhaps just as banally, we can see how the worsening wartime food situation was translated into daily personal mini-dramas, preventing normal social interaction and social solidarity, from this letter of March 1942. It was written by a man in Turin to his nephew in France, recording the effects of the reduction in the bread ration: 'Every so often Anna Maria calls by to ask for the charity of a piece of bread, and most times we don't have any ourselves and cannot give her any.'[39]

The continual inflation in food prices for Italian consumers during the war was, of course, a matter of demand constantly outstripping supply. There were certainly falls in agricultural production in Italy during the war, partly caused by lower productivity, with the other demands of the war economy squeezing the supply of fertilizers and fuel to the agricultural sector. It was difficult to make up the shortfall with imports, given that Italy was at war with the major global grain exporters, and Nazi Germany usually managed to monopolize grain supplies from the Axis-occupied territories. There were also greater wartime calls on Italian agricultural production, such as supplying the many and far-flung military fronts and the empire, for as long as that lasted.

The Italian consumer was also pushed further down the queue by the increasing need to prioritize export of agricultural produce, especially fruit and vegetables, and agricultural labour, to its Axis ally, Nazi Germany. These exports were to offset essential German supplies of fuel and industrial raw materials for the Italian war industries. What turned out to be a net extraction of resources from Italy to Germany, was one more sign, among many, of Fascist Italy's subordination to Nazi Germany in the Axis. It became a matter of considerable popular comment and resentment in 1942–3. Italian consumers believed that the Fascist government was deliberately forcing them to go without in order to feed their ally, yet another example of the way Italians were fighting Germany's war.

But although falls in agricultural production were real enough, they were not sufficiently serious in themselves to explain the food shortages and high prices in wartime Italy. The problems lay, rather, with the supply and distribution of foodstuffs, how the food reached the consumer. This was largely down to the government and how it regulated the food market, or, as important, that the government was perceived as being responsible by the people. To some extent, both the Fascist regime and the Italian public were the victims of their own false expectations that the war would be short and victorious, meaning that more extensive central food controls would be unnecessary. The rationing of what might be regarded as basic foodstuffs was applied initially in the autumn of 1940 to olive oil, butter, pasta, rice, and flour. In itself, then, this was an unwelcome surprise. It seemed to indicate that Italy was in for the long haul and worse, therefore, was to come. Because rationing was not anticipated, these early measures encouraged some panic buying of rationed foodstuffs which, in the inexorable way of things, brought about the very situation rationing was intended to prevent. The rationed goods disappeared from the shelves of the shops to be hoarded on the shelves of people's kitchens, and their scarcity drove up prices.

Rationing of the staple food product, bread, was introduced in October 1941, sixteen months into the war. The delay was important, because it meant that this basic measure was not decided on in order to anticipate or pre-empt bread shortages, but as a response to an already evident market shortfall caused by a decline in grain supplies for bread from spring 1941. From the start, then, the rationing scheme was running behind the development it was meant to be handling, and it never caught up.

The other basic flaw of the bread ration system was that the ration itself, 250 g [0.6 lb] per person per day in late 1941 and progressively reduced during 1942, was insufficient to feed a person in terms of calorific and nutritional value. The rationing scheme, generally, was not actually intended to cover all basic food needs. Inadequate food storage facilities, incompetence and graft at the *ammassi*, a transport and communications system disrupted by the effects and demands of war, combined to delay, often for weeks, the distribution of rationed goods and to reduce unpredictably the actual amounts distributed to levels below the official rates. The effect, then, of the way the system was devised and of governmental mishandling of its own scheme, was that Italians could not expect to survive on their supplies of rationed foodstuffs. A system which was not intended to guarantee a supply of basic products, and ultimately never did so, was an open invitation to the continuation of a free market in food and to the emergence of an unofficial black market during 1941. To feed themselves, Italians had to have recourse to the free market and when the supply of goods became short there, to the black market. In both arenas, the laws of supply and demand pushed prices continually upward.

Rationing was justified, self-evidently, as a measure of social justice, or as a necessary measure of social equalization. Arrigo Serpieri, the well-known Fascist agricultural expert and one-time junior Minister of Agriculture, surrounded the decision to ration sugar and coffee in the warm glow of social inclusiveness, during a public meeting in Florence in February 1940. The ration card, he said, enables the citizen to feed himself at a time of war 'without the cruel thought that what you are consuming liberally means others going hungry'.[40] Mussolini, indulging once more in his wartime anti-bourgeois rhetoric, this time at the expense of two of Italy's most prominent industrialists, put it rather more crudely and sarcastically in the Council of Ministers' meeting which decided on the bread ration in September 1941: rationing was egalitarian 'because of the way it ensures that all the Agnellis and the Doneganis have to eat like their humblest worker'.[41]

It should be as self-evident that the rationing schemes introduced by the regime were incapable of either making food generally available or of distributing food fairly and evenly. In fact, the rationing system was bound to cause inequality of treatment and inequality of sacrifice among Italian consumers, and an almost boundless resentment of one consumer for another. 'If you have money, then you eat; if you don't, then you die,' remarked a woman from Marsala, in Sicily, in December 1940.[42] She exaggerated on the effect, but not on the principle, of the regime's defective rationing scheme. Everybody complained about the shortages and the high prices, and everybody thought that everyone else was better off than them.

In some provinces, the *ammassi* operated reasonably efficiently, in others less so. Where they malfunctioned, they became a part of the problem of food supply rather than its resolution. Mussolini blamed the decision to ration bread from October 1941 on those farmers who were not consigning their quotas of grain to the *ammassi*. In the northern region of Lombardy, apparently, consignments were almost totalitarian. But in Sicily, consignments were barely a quarter of what was required.

One of the issues was pricing policy. There was often a disproportionate difference between the prices paid to the farmers for their grain and the official wholesale prices for the grain when it was sold on. Farmers and consumers alike assumed that the prices gap could only mean that the *ammassi* administrators, or those who controlled them, were taking a cut way above and beyond allowable administrative, managerial, and operational costs. In 1942, for instance, in the province of Bologna, the *ammasso* agency for potatoes was buying from peasants at 75 lire for 100 kg (220.5 lb), and then selling them for sale to consumers at 160 lire.

Whether the excessive margins were corrupt or not, we can imagine how both producers and consumers were likely to react to such insensitive pricing. The farmer, feeling that he was not being paid a fair and good price for his produce, and that his profits were going into the pockets of others in the food supply chain, withheld his supplies from the *ammassi* or consigned less than he was obliged to, and started selling his produce on the open market. Small peasant farmers who often produced little above subsistence anyway, defaulted on *ammassi* consignments in order to protect their own families' consumption, when the government decided to reduce the amounts of produce the farmer was allowed to retain for family use. With the producer not making his fair profit and the consumer paying inflated official prices, the incentive for both to bypass the *ammassi* system and conduct their selling and buying on open and unofficial markets was irresistible. The effective boycott of the *ammassi* by some farmers was one aspect of the corroding of the Fascist regime's apparatus of control and of its basis of popular support during the war. Farmers, another of Fascism's natural social constituencies, were simply disassociating themselves as individuals from the regime's organs for regulating the war economy in the name, anyway, of the greater national good.

A ready-made apparatus of control and surveillance was the Fascist Party, which during the war resumed the role it had in the years of the Great Depression in the 1930s, setting and policing prices of both rationed and unrationed goods. In the autumn of 1942, Mussolini also mobilized the Party to carry out the totalitarian requisitioning of grain to the *ammassi*. This was done in much the same manner and spirit as Stalin's sending of the Communist Party into the Russian countryside in the late 1920s, to break peasant resistance and obstructionism, and make sure that the cities were fed. The comparisons end here. The Fascist Party's intervention in price regulation was ultimately as futile and ineffective as before, and for the same reasons. Food supply and prices very rapidly moved away from any official attempt to regulate them and became, effectively, beyond regulation. Indeed, official intervention often only accelerated the spin into a self-sustaining spiral with its own inbuilt momentum, leading towards ever-higher prices.

Giuseppe Landi, national leader of the confederation of industrial workers' syndicates and a member of the Central Prices Committee, was forced to admit to his own provincial heads in the debriefing on the industrial workers' strikes of March 1943, that there were three levels of prices in operation. One level was totally unreal or 'virtual', the officially set prices which remained on paper, never to be implemented and never even a guide to actual prices. On another level were what he called 'tolerated' prices, above official prices, of course, but usually left well alone by Party and State authorities, because at least they prevented goods being 'exported' to other parts of the country in pursuit of higher returns. On the final level were black market prices, with huge mark-ups. In practice, the only 'real' contribution of the first level was to strengthen the hold of the third level. Official prices were customarily dismissed by producers and retailers as being too low. As a result, goods disappeared from the official market and reappeared on the black market. Every official attempt to set a price simply created an alternative clandestine market, selling at much higher prices.

The Fascist Party pulled on to itself the full weight of unpopularity as a result of its heavy-handed and counterproductive involvement in a situation it had no hope of controlling, only exacerbating. It found itself devouring its own, taking repressive and punitive action for the infraction of prices and *ammassi* regulations against the farmers and shopkeepers who were the Party's membership spine in many rural communes and small towns. The Party acted partly out of frustration at its inability to control the food situation, and partly to be seen to be doing something as the consumer's protector. Local Fascist leaders became increasingly aggressive and extremist in their treatment of pillars of the community, now labelled boycotters, saboteurs, and defeatists. The Fascist Party was no longer behaving as a national coalition, but as an isolated and embittered faction trying to impose its will on a recalcitrant people, attacking the enemies within. In the few months before Mussolini's first fall in July 1943, the Fascist Party was already shedding its consensual character and on the way to becoming the antagonistic and intransigent minority formation which propped up the Fascist Republic from late 1943.

The development of an unofficial, illegal market was the inevitable outcome of the Fascist regime's official policies on food requisitioning and rationing, and on price-setting. There were plenty of *pezzi grossi* (big shots) who speculated successfully on the black market, including the large wholesalers with enough suitably equipped storage space to accumulate and hang on to goods, as prices rose. The Fascist Party tried to demonstrate that it was capable of taking down its own corrupt leaders who were profiting personally from their official positions in the food regulation bureaucracy. Nobody could be much closer to the government's attempts to monitor and control the supply and price of food than Giorgio Molfino, a Party hack who after long service in the provincial and national Party hierarchy, was made head of one of the regime's most important corporative bodies, the confederation of shopkeepers and tradesmen. Mussolini tended to blame its members for all the country's wartime food shortages, and Molfino's disgrace made a big splash in the spring of 1942. He was expelled from the Party, removed as a member of the Fascist parliament, the Fascist Chamber of Fasces and Corporations, and condemned to *confino* (internal exile), normally reserved for anti-Fascist political opponents of the regime.

Molfino was the peak of a vast iceberg. Pursuing his consumer's vendetta against the nation's shopkeepers, Mussolini tried to humiliate the leaders of the syndical and corporative organizations of Lombardy, Italy's most commercial region, by revealing to them in April 1942 that 100,000 of the 700,000 tradesmen making a living in the region had been charged with offences against food supply regulations. But the regime's pursuit of the nation's shopkeepers and retailers missed the point entirely. The black market expanded as a result of the relentless search of consumers for food, and the opportunities for gain this presented to even the most marginal of rural producers. The market consisted of thousands of small-scale, multiple transactions between town and country, as people roamed into the countryside to find and buy food, and peasant women travelled to the towns and cities to sell their small surpluses of agricultural produce. It was not a big step, either morally or practically, for people to buy a little more than they actually needed and to sell on. In the northern sub-Alpine and Alpine province of Brescia, well placed for servicing the plains of Lombardy and Milan, you could, in July 1942, buy illegal eggs at 2.20 lire each and sell them in the big city at 3.50 lire each. If the authorities, whether Party or State, were too incompetent, corrupt, or impotent to provide what people needed, then the people learned and adapted to provide for themselves, becoming a nation of unlicensed traders, or smugglers and speculators.

The black market became popular and, therefore, irrepressible. It involved too many people for the police to detect and repress. It provided people with the essentials of life, whatever the cost. It benefited not just a small number of shady businessmen, but, as an informer's report stated, 'an enormous mass of people (janitors, workers, delivery men, clerks, etc.) who through high prices paid by the most well-off manage to gain sufficient profit to allow them to get what they need'.[43] One wonders whether the really poor, lacking the means to buy, let alone speculate, would have seen things in quite the same way as a kind of impromptu system of social justice. But a lot of money was being redistributed during and as a result of the war. A sort of social reversal was occurring, with new divisions being created according to whether people were disadvantaged or empowered by the opportunities of the black market.

The scale of the phenomenon at least helps to explain why the public authorities were often disinclined to interfere with the process and to tolerate a system of food supply and distribution which actually seemed to work. In the northern province of Mantua, a prosperous livestock and dairy farming area, farmers met their *ammassi* quotas in full. As a result, the authorities turned a blind eye to the farmers' direct selling of excess production to the public at what was, to all intents and purposes, an official illegal market. The local Fascist Party was certainly relaxed about inadvertently achieving that social truce which it was meant to bring into being by completely different means. Mantua's back-scratching alliance of farmers, consumers, and local State and Party authorities, was an extreme illustration, perhaps the most extreme, of just how impossible it was to do without the black market.

The broad popular consent and support enjoyed by Mussolini and the Fascist regime at the point of the declaration of war in June 1940, was undermined by the failure of Fascism's leaders and agencies to provide the essential needs of the population at war: security and food. The Fascist regime lost credibility among its own people as a result of its apparently chronic and systemic inability to protect Italians from Allied bombing, and to secure enough food on a regular basis for them to live and work on. The outcome was that people ceased to believe in what the regime told them Italy was fighting for, and against, and started looking out for themselves, since the Fascist state was demonstrably unable to defend individual or collective interests. It would have been serious for any kind of government to delegitimize itself, to destroy its right to govern, in this way. But it was especially serious for a Fascist regime which had predicated its existence and continuation on the waging of a successful war.

# 3

# Fascist Italy at War, 1940–1943:
# Collapse of the Home Front

M EASURED in terms of the physical, psychological, and political damage
they inflicted, the Allied bombings of Italy during the Second World
War must count as one of the most successful bombing campaigns ever. It
would be pushing things too far to say that Allied bombing was responsible for
the downfall of Mussolini in July 1943. But the bombings, together with the
food situation, certainly caused a widespread loss of confidence in Mussolini
and the Fascist regime and turned many Italians against the war.

This raises some interesting comparisons, because there was a feeling
among some Allied and Axis political and military leaders that the bombing
of civilian targets was counterproductive, that it stiffened rather than weakened civilian resolve. There was certainly plenty of evidence from contemporary police reports and popular memories of the demoralizing impact of
Allied bombing raids on Germany from 1943, which were generally heavier, more extensive, and more damaging in their effects than those experienced in Italy. A post-war survey of wartime morale in Germany showed
that 91 per cent of the people interviewed felt that bombing was the worst
experience they had to bear during the war. But there was also some
evidence to suggest that the Nazi authorities did more to help and com-
pensate the civilian victims of Allied bombings, and to convey and demonstrate some sense of an equality in suffering and sacrifice. This was
beyond the Fascist authorities in Italy, and it was probably the demonstration of almost complete impotence to either prevent the bombings or
alleviate their effects, which served to demoralize people and sapped their
belief in the Fascist regime.

Some major cities, such as Florence and Venice, were never bombed at
all, and Rome was only bombed once, during Italy's Fascist war. The raids

were concentrated on the southern and Sicilian port cities servicing the Axis military campaigns in North Africa, and on the so-called industrial triangle in the north-west of Genoa, Milan, and Turin. There were lulls or periods of less intensive and regular bombing. The south and Sicily took the biggest hits in the second half of 1941 and in the spring and summer of 1943, immediately preceding and during the Allied invasion of Sicily. The worst raids on the northern cities took place in the autumn of 1942 and they were the heaviest in all senses. Allied bombers used a heavier calibre of bomb and flew in larger formations. It has been estimated that in the twenty-minute raid on Genoa during the night of 22–3 October 1942, they dropped about the same quantity and weight of bombs which had been deposited on Naples throughout 1941.

Allied bombing raids on the northern industrial areas in November and December 1942 led to an estimated 20 per cent loss of production in war industries which were already operating below capacity because of shortages of energy and raw materials. The loss came, obviously enough, from physical damage to factories. But bombings also caused constant interruptions to factory shifts, with workers evacuated because of the bombing struggling to commute between work and temporary places to stay outside the city, and having to go to shelters when raids occurred. Mussolini admitted in early 1943 that with bombing and supply problems, Turin's factories were only working at about half their capacity.

It was the social problems created or exacerbated by the bombings which so shook popular morale. All kinds of inversion of normality were occurring. The war was no longer being fought beyond the country's borders; the war was at home. Bombings took place mainly at night, which became day, with cities illuminated by bombers' flares and fires burning. People were awakened and kept awake when they should have been sleeping. They were, as a result, exhausted by day, especially when bomb damage disrupted and prolonged travel and, in destroying shops or forcing their abandonment, expanded still further the time and energy needed to search for food. People's free time, and rest time, evaporated.

Above all, the bombings caused mass evacuations of the cities, something which Mussolini had, in a characteristically superficial way, ruled out at the start of the war, because the country was not 'big' enough to accommodate the outflow of people. But what should not and could not happen, actually did. The first evacuations had occurred after the first early, isolated, and largely symbolic, but still damaging, Allied bombing raids in the summer of 1940. Rich families took to their second homes in the mountains and on the lakes, starting their usual summer villa holidays a little earlier than normal and staying on rather longer than normal, installing fireplaces and heating where necessary.

The flight of the wealthy from the cities continued throughout the war and was a constant source of social resentment and division among the residents of the large northern cities. Those with money could evacuate properly, by car, truck, or cart rather than on foot or bicycle, and they had somewhere to go. Workers continued to pay rents on their damaged or threatened city tene- ments and also had to find and pay for alternative accommodation in the outskirts, where the city met the countryside. In Turin, industrial workers faced up to twelve hours a day away from their first or second 'homes', travelling backwards and forwards on disrupted and overcrowded suburban transport to work shifts in factories which were under constant threat of bombardment. Some workers, their savings and employers' evacuation and resettlement loans exhausted, returned to live and sleep in the cities. They did it also to reoccupy residences which, otherwise left empty, might be used to give shelter to bombed-out families. The poorest were too poor to leave and had never left, sleeping under bridges and other improvised shelter.

Evacuations were happening spontaneously, under the impact of the bombing raids. They became official, but no less haphazard, once Mussolini had irresponsibly called for the cities to evacuate in his disastrous speech to the Italian people on 2 December 1942. Mussolini's words were taken literally in a rushed and panicky free-for-all. The atmosphere of panic and improvisation created by Mussolini's evacuation call practically invited and encouraged people to behave selfishly and to be at their worst, fighting each other for access to transport and accommodation. In Genoa, perhaps 300,000 people left the city temporarily between October and December 1942. In Turin, by the time of Mussolini's first fall in July 1943, about 340,000 people, nearly half the population, had evacuated the city, and around 100,000 of these were attempting to commute to and from the city for work on a daily basis.

Evacuations brought the city to the countryside, and made the city depen- dent on and subordinate to the countryside, another inversion of the norm. It was strange for everybody. But not all these unexpected and unwanted social and cultural collisions turned out badly. People adapted to the social reversals involved in townspeople being put up by country folk. The commuting breadwinner was hardly ever out of danger and discomfort.

But he and his family were usually better-fed as paying guests in rural homes, and often were and felt safer. Countryside board and lodging could be paid for, and social tensions eased, by bartering urban skills, like reading to and with the semi-literate children of the host peasant family.

On other occasions, evacuations simply put additional strain on rural society and its resources. In our unnamed Appennine village, the pressures of evacuation on top of a deteriorating food situation, generated the first public collective protest in the area for twenty years, in March 1943, when local women gathered outside the communal offices to demand food. There were about one hundred evacuees in the village, which might not appear many, but was quite a significant additional burden for a relatively poor agricultural community of about two thousand people. It was the commune's responsibility to feed and house the evacuees, and the local authorities found themselves grappling with the consequences of a chain of misfortunes and incompetence. There were extra mouths to feed at a time of dwindling food supplies. The fodder quota for the local cattle was inadequate anyway. But the supplies promised for January 1943 only arrived in April and they were half of what was due. The malnourished cows were producing less milk when more was needed. This small-scale drama, where evacuation and food supply problems combined to spark popular protest, was repeated on a far grander scale at about the same time in the industrial cities of the north.

The most significant effects of the bombing raids were political and psychological. The king and queen probably wished that they had not visited the bombed-out areas of Genoa in November 1942, because they were apparently whistled at by the crowds. It might have been somewhat reassuring for them to know that the target of the crowd's anger was not so much the monarchy as Mussolini. The hearsay reported in a letter of a woman to her husband working in Germany, was that the Genoese were shouting that it was not them that they wanted, but 'that other baldie [*testa pelata*]'. She added viciously that 'people are saying that the Duce has cancer; let's hope that it's true'.[1] Practically all the informers' and police reports at the time of the autumn 1942 bombing campaign were saying similar things, that people were connecting the horrors of their own experiences of the raids to those they held responsible for them, and it was not the Americans.

The psychological effects of the bombing were no less devastating. A resident of Catania, in Sicily, after the heavy raids on the south of late 1941, wrote, 'you no longer live with any certainty about tomorrow because the alarms are going every evening and night. We are still feeling the shock of what the English bombers did some nights ago. The air raid alert went on for six and a half hours.'[2] Someone who went through the bombings in Naples felt more nihilistically desperate: 'nothing existed any more, neither time nor anything'. 'There was no tomorrow,' said another, only bombings which 'sapped your energy and your will'.[3] Delayed and lasting shock, the sense of there being no future: these were traumatized people, enervated and depressed by what they were experiencing. Consider the stress in the syntax of this letter, written in April 1943, by a person describing an air raid in Porto Empedocle, near Agrigento, in Sicily, probably one of the grimmest and grimiest ports in Italy, whatever the state of the shelters: 'and there was no alarm—it's always like this—it's torture—here, everyone has run off to the countryside or sleeps in the shelters—it's a terrible life in the shelters, it's filthy-full of lice—of mange—of illness—a disgrace'.[4] This newspaper report in the Turin national daily *La Stampa*, might not have appeared if it had been composed before 25 July 1943. But its account of a visit in early August to a school where bombed-out residents were staying, made no attempt to disguise the traumatized state of the people encountered there, who had 'that almost indifferent expression of somebody who has been very severely tested'. The reporter observed 'a group of women, with their hands resting inert on their laps, looking at a housepainter whitewashing the wall, with a distant air, as if it was a very far-off thing'.[5]

British and American psychologists had apparently predicted the psychological damage which would be inflicted on people subjected to air attacks, and their predictions informed the general inter-war belief in the dreadful efficacy of the bomber. Some Italian psychologists studied the behaviour of soldiers and civilians under bombardment in North Africa in 1941, though the 'withdrawal into mutism'[6] clearly evident among bombed-out Italian civilians, here, was also identified by British doctors analysing the reaction of Londoners to the first air raids on the city.

The industrial workers' strikes of March 1943 were not the first strikes in wartime Axis and Axis-occupied Europe. But they were the first significant mass collective protest in Fascist Italy for twenty years, all the more important because they happened in the first ever fascist state. Such strikes would have been serious in any of the countries at war and would probably have been regarded in the same way by all the governments of belligerent countries. However, they seemed to strike at the heart of fascism, which was premised on the permanent suppression of socialist revolution and of working-class agitation and organization. The strikes appeared to show that the Fascist regime was weakening and losing its grip.

The immediate point at issue was the workers' demand that the special payments envisaged for workers and their families who had been bombed out of their homes, should be extended to benefit all industrial workers. This was hardly an insignificant issue in itself. But it was a kind of lightning conductor for a set of related social and economic grievances arising out of wartime conditions in the northern industrial cities and towns. About six million industrial workers employed in the essential war industries were effectively conscripted and under military discipline for the duration of the war. A tighter and more repressive work discipline went with the requirement to work longer shifts and to work more intensively. This situation was exacerbated by a skilled labour shortage partly caused by the transfer of industrial workers to employment in German factories. Bombings, evacuations, food shortages, ever-higher food prices, reduced rations, including the supplement for heavy industrial work, made life barely tolerable and sustainable for industrial workers.

The strikes began in some Turin factories in early March, spread to other towns in Piedmont in mid-March, and to Milan, Lombardy, some places in Emilia, and to Vercelli, in eastern Piedmont, in late March and early April. Overall, perhaps 100,000 workers were involved. The workers' agitation was canny and deliberately confined to small-scale action, which tested the limits of what was permissible in a totalitarian system while trying to avoid provoking the authorities into even greater repression. It characteristically took the form of the *sciopero bianco* (sit-down strike), with workers stopping work for an hour or so. It was the kind of disruption which made its point, without bringing the factory to a permanent standstill or losing the workers too much in wages. Like most strikes, they spread by momentum, engaging the solidarity of workers across factories. The release of the workers arrested after the initial stoppages became a new demand sparking action among workers in other plants.

The strikes also spread because Communist Party activists prepared for, were involved in, and, to a degree, organized the agitation. It was these PCI organizers who made explicit and public the connections between hunger and intolerable working and living conditions, and the war. These connections would have been evident to any and every industrial worker. But they transformed a grievance over pay into a mass anti-war and anti-regime protest. A factory wall poster in Milan pointedly inverted a well-known militarist

Fascist slogan: 'Believe: what? Obey: who? Fight: why? We're hungry and we want peace.'[7] Another poster similarly linked an economic demand and anti-war feelings: 'Against the twelve-hour day and this damned war!'[8]

Hitler was literally beside himself at the news of the strikes, well aware of their significance for the standing of fascism in Germany and Europe, as well as in Italy. He could not understand why the striking workers were not shot on the spot. Similar noises were heard in smoke-filled rooms in Rome and down the telephone lines linking the capital to the northern cities. Tullio Cianetti was the Minister of Corporations, whose decision on special payments had sparked the initial protests, the man who blubbed at the Grand Council vote against Mussolini a few months later. Now, he urged the Fascist Party boss in Turin, Franco Ferretti, to show a 'hard fist'. Ferretti replied laconically, 'then we'll have to shoot them'.[9] Mussolini demonstrated plenty of bravado after the event. He sacked the Fascist Party chief, Aldo Vidussoni, for the Party's alleged indecisiveness during the strike, and criticized the police for their lack of bite: 'When Italian workers assassinate their fellow Italians who are fighting as soldiers, I would have them shot.'[10]

It was a case of Mussolini, once again, passing the buck. In industrial relations terms, the strikes were quite brilliantly managed by the police, the Fascist Party and unions, and the employers, after the initial panic and uncertainty. It is quite probable that Mussolini himself directed the whole operation. The strategy was anything but exclusively hard line, and that was why it worked. A measured repressiveness and the immediate concession of what the workers wanted—higher wages and payments—defused, contained, and exhausted the agitation. There were a few hundred arrests, including now exposed PCI organizers, which decapitated the movement. Arrested workers were not shot or court-martialled. Some were conscripted for military service, losing their status as exempted essential workers, while others were deported to work in Germany. The police successfully confined the protests to the factories, not allowing them to spread outside and become popular demonstrations in the piazza, which was the intention of at least some PCI organizers.

Not all of them thought that this was a good idea, since it would, once again, expose them to detection and arrest and risk the unravelling of clandestine networks and contacts. Their survival would enable the PCI to continue its anti-Fascist activity in the future. This was the classic dilemma of all later wartime resistance to enemy occupation. The strikes and their resolution were, in essence, a kind of synchronized exercise in self-limitation on the part of the workers and their PCI organizers, and of the authorities and the employers. Each side stopped short of counterproductively provoking the other. The workers did what they could to avoid the full weight of Fascist repressiveness crashing down on themselves and the re-forming Communist Party organization. The police were relatively restrained in their punitive action against the workers, not wanting to create proletarian martyrs and do the work of the anti-Fascists for them. In Genoa, the dual strategy was so successful that it prevented the strikes spreading to the city, altogether, when the conditions for workers there were objectively as intolerable as they were in Turin and Milan.

Significant though they were as a measure of the extent of popular disaffection with the war and the Fascist regime, the strikes of March 1943 had little direct connection to the first fall of Mussolini in July 1943. The indirect connections were, on the other hand, extremely important. The strikes made the internal crisis of the Fascist regime palpable and practically demanded that the crisis be confronted and resolved. They also ensured, ironically (and perhaps tragically), that the resolution of the wartime crisis of Fascism would take the form that it did, an establishment monarchist conspiracy excluding popular involvement. The strikes, ultimately, provide us with another explanation of why anti-Fascist popular forces played no active role in the overthrow of Mussolini. The strikes might have encouraged anti-Fascists, even made them believe, for a moment, in the possibility of undermining the Fascist regime by organized popular protest. But the regime's effectively calculated blend of coercion and concession both removed the anti-Fascist activists from the scene and, for a while anyway, removed the reasons for popular agitation. The regime's response to the strikes had taken all the impetus out of anti-Fascist efforts to turn the war and its effects against Mussolini and Fascism.

For the conservative establishment forces in Italian life, the strikes raised the spectre of class war and social revolution, which it was Fascism's job to suppress and keep suppressed. The strikes destroyed the credibility of Fascism as an anti-socialist force and, therefore, the reason why fellow-travelling conservatives had backed the Fascist regime for over twenty years. Since Fascism was demonstrably failing in its mission as the defence of class interests, it had to be ditched, and in a way which continued to protect those interests. This can be demonstrated in the thoughts and actions of two of the employers who were protagonists of the March 1943 strikes. Vittorio Valletta was the managing director of FIAT, one of Turin's and Italy's major companies, which had profited hugely as a vehicle and arms manufacturer from the regime's autarkic and war economy. Sensing the trouble brewing in the factories, he had fore-warned the authorities, and as an employer, readily met the striking workers' economic demands. His conclusion from the strikes was that employers had to disassociate themselves from the Fascist regime and exert all the pressure they could to get Italy out of the war. Before, during, and after the strikes, he played all sides to the dispute, talking to the police, the Fascist Party, and his workers, and contacting the representatives of anti-Fascist groups and parties, notably the Action Party and the Socialist and Communist parties.

Agostino Rocca was the man in charge of the Ansaldo enterprises in Genoa. Ansaldo was a conglomerate which had made its fortune on First World War arms contracts, been salvaged by the Fascist government in the 1920s, and was another major beneficiary of the Fascist regime's war spend-ing. Like Valletta, he approached all and sundry, anti-Fascists, Fascist Party and union leaders, workers, in a successful attempt to head off strike action in Genoa. His contacts with both Fascists and anti-Fascists, and with his workers, indicated that his primary concern, now, was to save the business. To do that, he was prepared to deal with the Fascists and those who might well succeed the Fascists. The ambiguous playing of all sides, to protect the firm and employment, characterized the behaviour of employers at this point in the crisis of Fascism and through to the end of the war in 1945, doing deals with German occupiers, Italian Fascists and resisters, and invading Allies alike. This was why nobody could really decide or determine whether a man like Valletta had been a Fascist, an anti-Fascist, a collaborator, or a resister in the period from 1943 to 1945, when he had, probably, been all of these, while remaining, certainly and above all, a FIAT man.

Mussolini had the worst propaganda war of all the wartime leaders, when as a fascist dictator, propaganda was what he was meant to be good at. It was obviously difficult to propagandize defeat, and to handle the rapid erosion of the gap between the propaganda aspiration and the lived reality of the war for most Italians. A propaganda of victory and easy gains lost all credibility when it so evidently did not match the actuality of defeat and hardship. But other wartime leaders managed to inspire, reassure, and reinvigorate their people with the right words, even at moments of defeat. This was beyond Mussolini.

One problem was his remoteness and inaccessibility. He made only four public speeches during the war. This reticence in itself created a cycle of disappointed expectations in the country. The fact that he was not saying much to his people generated all kinds of popular rumours about how the war was really going, how ill Mussolini actually was, and ultimately, of course, whether he still had the confidence and gumption to govern the country. The failure to speak became, of itself, a cause of declining popular confidence in the person of the Duce. It was as if Mussolini had nothing to say or, worse, that there was nothing he could say. When Mussolini singularly failed to visit any of the bombed cities and hence demonstrate some solidarity with his people, it could only be taken as a sign that he had given up, that he did not care, and that he was afraid of exposing himself to popular hostility. When the dictator lost belief in himself, then his charismatic authority was bound to fade in the country.

How much that dictatorial charisma dimmed during the war can be gauged from the content of, and popular reactions to, probably the worst ever speech delivered by a wartime leader, that made by Mussolini on 2 December 1942. The only mitigating factor was that Mussolini had been seriously ill and off work with his gastritis and ulcer problems. But that, of course, was the point of the speech. This was his first public speech in eighteen months. It was meant to demonstrate that he was back on his feet and in full command of the situation.

Even reading the speech now over sixty years after the event, I am at a loss where to start with its awfulness. There were quite spectacular own goals. In his speech, Mussolini might have not found it surprising that Soviet troops were so courageous and effective. But his audience would have, after being led by the regime's propaganda to despise the Russians as a backward and barbarous people. The impression could only be that Mussolini had got things wrong and underestimated the enemy. And what to make of Mussolini's assertion that the Italian soldier was a match for anyone, if properly armed and led? The only possible response was to ask who was actually responsible for ensuring that Italian troops were adequately equipped and officered? Why, that must be Mussolini, minister of the armed forces for most of the previous twenty years.

It got worse. This was a speech which actually *caused* demoralization and division among the Italians listening. Mussolini made some gratuitous and rather obscure comments about the inhuman treatment being meted out by the Allies to Italian POWs, presumably intended to arouse that visceral hatred of the enemy which Mussolini regarded as so crucial to winning the war. 'So, it's not true that my Arnaldo isn't suffering,' wrote one woman, echoing the thoughts of all those hundreds of thousands of families who had sons, husbands, fathers, brothers in POW camps spread across the globe, from Texas to India. Mussolini's claim that millions of lire had been spent on air raid shelters should have been derided by all those listeners who had spent a night in the real, ramshackle thing—and it was.

Most calamitously of all, this was the speech in which Mussolini chose to endorse the mass evacuation of bombed Italian cities. He even had the gall to blame the Italians for a situation which was clearly not all of their making. He said that they had ignored his constant urgings to evacuate earlier in the war, making him the leader who was more heard than followed. It was not actually true. Mussolini had long argued against the feasibility of mass evacuations. Now, Mussolini said, 'you mustn't wait for the clock to strike twelve',[11] immediately transferring to the evacuees the responsibility for the chaos caused by his evacuation call. It was too much for the letter writer who had already been distressed by Mussolini's news that her POW son was being maltreated. 'Evacuate,' she wrote in the same letter, 'How? Where?' The double blows of Mussolini's speech induced in this woman nothing but 'terror, my God, what terror . . . As from yesterday, I feel really upset, disheartened, finished.'[12] She was not the only one. Another woman wrote to her mother from Milan, 'today . . . the Duce's speech has demoralized me completely . . . I went home and was unable to eat anything'.[13]

When the leader's speech to the nation put the Italians off their food, then his time was almost certainly up. The police and informers' reports of the time were unanimous in registering how badly the speech had gone down. Everywhere, and everyone, they reported, was actually contesting what Mussolini said, and commenting ironically and critically on the various faux pas of the speech. The dictator was no longer believed. The Duce, who 'was always right', was now almost always wrong. The response to the speech marked the most momentous shift in popular perceptions of Mussolini which occurred as a result of the impact of his war on their lives. The Italian people had lost faith in Mussolini, as well as his subordinates, and that loss was irrecoverable. In Milan, after the 2 December 1942 speech, people referred to Mussolini as 'a dead man talking'.[14]

Mussolini's charisma as Duce was not the only thing forfeited by his conduct of the war. Italians stopped being patriotic, or better perhaps, they no longer associated themselves with a Fascist war and a Fascist nation. In the Grand Council meeting of 25 July 1943, the Fascist dissidents highlighted a break between Fascism and the nation and, in effect, urged that Mussolini, even Fascism, be ditched, the better to save the nation. A summarizing political police report from Rome just before the Grand Council meeting, said that the

Italian people had reached the same conclusion: it was now time for Mussolini to go, in the country's interest. The war was lost. But this also meant that the war would soon be over; the disappointment of defeat carried a sense of expectation of peace. The desire to put an end to the war was greater than the humiliation of losing it. Defeat was to be welcomed, if it meant an end to the war. The *carabinieri* in Enna, Sicily, in October 1942, anticipated what would become a general shift in the public mood, and put it down to the impact of the bombings, reporting that 'the continued bombings of the large and small towns of the island, without sufficient opposition from our side ... has lowered the morale of the people to a point that they pray for the end of the war as a holy liberation'.[15] The police chief of Turin summarized in December 1942 the overwhelming message reaching him and his superiors from informers' reports and censored letters. This was that 'not only do many people no longer believe in victory, they also hope for a quick end to the conflict, whatever the outcome is, and are not even concerned about the consequences'.[16] One woman grappled with the defeatism which came from war-weariness in this way, in a letter written in May 1943: 'patriotism doesn't come into this. I can be a good Italian, but all the same feel tired out.'[17]

Perhaps Italy had become something less than a country of patriotic defeatists by early 1943. There was the sense that in the course of fighting a Fascist war, many Italians had ceased to have an awareness of there being a national community. The impact of the Fascist war between 1940 and 1943 was deeply divisive and disorientating, as was evident in how people responded to and were differentially affected by food shortages, the black market, bombings, and evacuations. Italian society had not stood the test of war. It had disintegrated into so many private and individual worlds bent on surviving as best they could in a difficult and alien, hostile wider world. The privatization of the war meant Italians did not, and could not, extend their hands to help and support others, let alone show any sympathy for other people's predicaments when their own were so dire. They began to resent people who did not appear to be as badly off as they were. They actually wished on others the suffering they were going through, which was a rough and ready kind of egalitarianism.

What follows is an extract from a loving letter to his wife, written by a young army officer stationed in Trento, near Italy's north-eastern frontier, in November 1942. He advised her to learn what he was learning to do, and to teach her mother to do the same, which was, 'not to look 10 cm beyond what is your business'. 'If the world goes to blazes,' he continued, 'let it go: the important thing is to know that I love you, that we love our parents and our children and that in this love we find the strength and the incentive to make any sacrifice for making us happy.'[18] From a man who was serving his country in the armed forces, these were simultaneously warming and chilling sentiments. The retreat or regression to patriotism of the private represented a scouring out of a public patriotism; the void of the nation was, for the moment, anyway, being filled by self and family.

The collapse of the public into the private also offers another explanation for the lack of popular involvement in the first fall of Mussolini. There was clearly a convergence of views from mid- to late 1942 among Fascist and non-Fascist elites, and among most of the Italian people, that Mussolini should go. But the police reports from mid-1942 spoke of the popular mood as being one of tiredness, resignation, apathy, inertia, disassociation, not rebelliousness and rebellion. The war was provoking popular discontent, anger, and resentment, but also a feeling of impotence. A demoralized people did not act. They waited on events; they wanted things to change but were unable to make things change. The war was draining the Italian people of the will and energy and—dare one say it—public spirit, to do anything more than secure their own survival. The removal of Mussolini was left to those who eventually found the will to act in July 1943; the popular exuberance and celebration came after the event.

# 4

# The Forty-Five Days,
# July to September 1943

T HE international consequences of Mussolini's dismissal by the king on
25 July 1943 were significant but contained. The Italian ramifications
of Mussolini's fall were less immediately significant, but ultimately uncontainable. There has been so much controversy over the responsibility for
and significance of the events from Mussolini's removal in July 1943 to the
signing and declaration of the armistice between Italy and the Allies in
September 1943, that it becomes extremely difficult for the historian to clear
a path through the retrospective mutual recriminations and mud-slinging of
the protagonists. The only place to start is with the announcement to the
nation by the 72-year-old Marshal Pietro Badoglio, called out of military
retirement by the king to head the new government after the dismissal and
arrest of Mussolini on 25 July 1943.

Badoglio was a deeply compromised figure, though he probably did not
appear so to those who appointed him. A very political military man, Badoglio
had successfully ducked and weaved with the Fascist dictatorship for two
decades, garnering position, honours, and riches from the regime. He had
managed to assume the credit for Fascism's military successes, including the
extremely brutal pacification of the Italian North African colony of Libya in
the late 1920s and the conquest of Ethiopia, in East Africa, in 1935–6. He had
then evaded responsibility for its military disasters, including the botched
invasion of Greece in late 1940. He resigned his position as head of the
supreme military command, nominally the most important military post
under Mussolini, in the wake of that disastrous campaign. Because he was
regarded as the scapegoat for what happened in Greece, he left with his
reputation, amazingly, largely intact. Approached by the king before 25 July

to be Mussolini's successor, he had two and a half years of apparently clean hands to recommend him as a credible replacement of the dictator.

What Badoglio announced to the nation was that the war would continue, which, once the declaration had sunk in, dampened the popular celebrations which followed the news of Mussolini's dismissal. The days after 25 July saw the defacing, dismantling, and toppling of some of the public marks and signs of the Fascist regime, the now-familiar symbolical cleansing which usually characterizes the transition from one political regime to another. As elsewhere, such popular anger directed against the outward manifestations of a discredited regime was also a sign of the people's sense of impotence. People could only take symbolic revenge on a regime which had already fallen; it was activism and opposition after the event. The impact of Italy's disastrous war on popular morale had destroyed the credibility of Mussolini and the Fascist regime. Quite understandably and predictably, the Italian people expected the end of Mussolini to mean the end of the war, too. It meant the same for the king and the military, also. But they had decided not to take Grandi's advice and achieve it in the risky and compressed timescale of an immediate and simultaneous changing of sides and declaration of war on Nazi Germany.

The war continued because the king and his new government did not want to provoke or provide a pretext for a German-inspired Fascist counter-coup and the German military occupation of Italy. It was the constant fear of German reaction which underpinned and, one has to say, undermined the Badoglio government's action (and inaction) during the so-called Forty-Five Days between July and September 1943. Some of the government's irresponsible behaviour only becomes remotely intelligible if you bear in mind that the concern throughout was to withdraw from the war at minimum cost. It wanted to leave the war with the monarchy and state institutions intact, without fighting the Germans—preferably without having to fight anybody—and in a way which would avoid mainland Italy becoming occupied territory and a war zone. One could say that such aims were desirable, even high-minded and in the national interest. But one could not say in the circumstances that they were in any way realistic. It was this lack of realism, and a consequent overestimation of the country's capacity to function as an international free agent, which ultimately makes the charge of irresponsibility stick.

A sign of the government's lack of perspective was its refusal, or inability, to assess realistically the intentions and actions of Nazi Germany. From the start, Hitler regarded the removal of Mussolini as a betrayal of the Axis alliance, and expected and planned for the eventual Italian exit from the alliance. The Germans substantially increased their military presence in Italy between July and September. Rather than exclusively concentrating its forces in the south for the defence of its ally, Germany also stationed its troops alongside Italian forces in the centre and north, to facilitate their disarmament when the Italian changing of sides occurred. The Germans, in other words, always intended to occupy Italy and always intended to defend their own frontiers not on the Alps, but in Italy itself. The Alps were not the preferred defensive line for the Germans. Occupying Italy would allow them to set up a Fascist government behind their lines, continue to exploit the economic resources of northern Italy, hold on to the Balkans, and keep some of Germany itself out of the range of Allied bombing. There was never any danger of Italy provoking Nazi Germany into action; it was taking action, anyway. The Italian government's dilatory approach to armistice talks with the Allies was presumably meant as a ruse to reassure the Germans of its continuing loyalty to the Axis alliance. The attempt at deception served to bring about the conditions which made a painless exit from the war even more unlikely than it was at the start.

There is no need to imagine how the Germans responded to Italian hopes, probably held up to mid-August 1943, of leaving the war with Hitler's consent. This had been the fanciful thinking of some military figures and diplomats, including Ambrosio and Bastianini, both before and after the Feltre meeting between Hitler and Mussolini on 19 July. The idea was that Italy would negotiate a separate peace with the Allies and a peaceful withdrawal from the Axis alliance with Germany, which would leave Italy at peace, neutral, and with no foreign armies fighting each other on Italian territory. For their part, the Allies were equally uninterested in allowing Italy an easy withdrawal from the war. The idea of a negotiated peace contradicted the declared goal of unconditional surrender. An Italy occupied by the Germans was preferable to a neutral Italy, since the occupation would overextend German manpower and resources, and weaken its capacity to fight on both the eastern and planned western fronts.

Interestingly, this aspiration to international neutrality was reflected in the internal political neutrality of the Badoglio government. The king's new government immediately abolished the organs of the Fascist state, the Fascist Party, the Grand Council, the Special Tribunal, the corporations, the Chamber of Fasces and Corporations. But it went no further in a consciously anti-Fascist direction. It promised elections after the end of the war, and banned all party-political activity for the duration of the conflict. One would hardly have expected anything different in a country still at war, when even democratic states suspended normal politics for such a national emergency.

There was a relaxation of the ban on party activity, allowing some space to organize for reforming anti-Fascist groups. But again, the government's release of anti-Fascist political prisoners was a reluctant drawn-out process and discriminated against Anarchist and Communist prisoners. Certainly, anti-Fascists were kept out of the government. There was no inclination to bring back those whom the king referred to as the 'ghosts' of Italy's pre-Fascist past. Indeed, the royal government was so repressive of popular agitation against the war that it behaved as if it was back in 1922 facing a socialist revolution and determined, this time, not to allow the spread of popular unrest which had necessitated the recourse to Fascism in the first place. The royal government's reluctance to open itself out to popular anti-Fascist forces was a very serious self-limitation. It was entirely consistent with the government's concern to protect against political instability and social change a conservative, monarchical social and political order. Under no circumstances would such a government ever call on the people to help it prevent or expel German occupation of the country.

Goebbels expected the king, after Mussolini's dismissal, to establish a regime like Franco's in Spain. He was close; but Badoglio's government was more like Marshal Pétain's Vichy regime in France. It was conservative, authoritarian, certainly not democratic, but not fascist either. It was a system which the king thought the Germans might be prepared to deal with, as they had done with Pétain in France from 1940. But in its partial disassociation from Mussolini's Fascist regime, it might also be enough to reassure the democracies.

Some tentative diplomatic feelers to the Allies after 25 July produced so negative a response as to make it clear that the Allies were only prepared to talk about an armistice, an end to military hostilities. The Germans were as clearly unwilling to consent to Italian withdrawal from the war and would, in fact, oppose it; so began the protracted pantomime of the Badoglio government's armistice negotiations.

An army general, Giuseppe Castellano, a trusted subordinate of Ambrosio, the head of the general staff of the armed forces, was sent by the government to Madrid and Lisbon to meet Allied representatives and discuss an armistice. Castellano had no official credentials and was not authorized to negotiate on behalf of the government. This caution was presumably designed to keep the trip as secret as possible and to allow Badoglio to disown the mission if it was uncovered or produced uncongenial results. He went there and back by train, which at least was quicker than going on foot, leaving Rome on 12 August 1943 and returning to the city on 27 August 1943. The army general staff was so ignorant or suspicious of the Castellano mission that it confusingly sent one of its men on a similar expedition to contact the Allies while Castellano was still in transit. Ambrosio persisted right up to the declaration of the armistice in keeping his own armed forces very much in the dark about the government's intentions, again presumably to maintain secrecy and avoid any leak provoking the Germans into action.

Castellano's 'present' to the Allied contacts in Madrid and Lisbon and to the Allied military command in Algiers, North Africa, was to reveal something of German troop deployments in Italy. Off his own bat and without Badoglio's prior approval, he also intimated that Italy might well accept unconditional surrender if it was allowed to redeem itself by fighting the Germans alongside the Allies. What Castellano was mandated to outline was Italy's negotiating position on an armistice. This was that there should be Allied landings on mainland Italy *before* an armistice, that these landings should be significant enough to be militarily successful, and that they should take place in central Italy, well north of Rome, to ensure that the Germans withdrew their forces to the Alpine frontiers. The famous British historian of modern Italy, Denis Mack-Smith argues, controversially, that these conditions were those of a country with ideas well above its station, and of a country which was going to wait and see who actually won the war.[1] The first assertion is accurate, the second is less convincing. The Badoglio government had definitely decided to work towards an armistice with the Allies. The conditions were its preferred minimal costs option: the Germans would be expelled from Italy by Allied military strength, with little or no military input required from Italy.

The Allied commanders were insistent that an armistice would have to be agreed before any landings on mainland Italy took place, in order to facilitate those landings by removing Italian military resistance to them, at least. The Allied military command's immovable stance on this reflected the lower priority being given to an Italian, as opposed to a mainland French, invasion. The Allied landings in Italy needed all the help they could get to be successful.

Castellano, during his follow-up meetings with Allied commanders in Sicily at the end of August 1943, was told by his government to bring up the Darlan model. Admiral Jean-François Darlan was the Vichyite commander in French North Africa who had negotiated the end of French opposition to the Allied 'Torch' landings of late 1942. The analogy, or possible analogy, with Darlan was entirely misplaced and, once again, demonstrated the lack of a grasp on reality of the royal government and its inflation of Italy's current international position. Vichy France was collaborating with the Germans, but was not in the Axis and not at war with the Allies. Badoglio's Italy was still in the Axis and still fighting the Allies as an enemy state.

The Allies could not oblige on the timing of the armistice, nor could they promise a landing north of Rome, beyond the logistical range of the Allied forces. But they were so keen to broker an armistice that they promised military help to Italy in order to defend Rome against the Germans, in the shape of a special airborne mission of US forces.

When Castellano met the Allied representatives in Sicily at the end of August 1943, he was instructed by the government to insist on the original conditions broached with the Allies at Lisbon. He still did not have the government's authority to sign an armistice. Practically imprisoned on the island by the Allies, who threatened and cajoled the Italian government at a distance, he was eventually enabled to sign the armistice on 3 September 1943. Given the way in which the Italian government had conducted itself, the Allied military command was hardly going to give a precise date for mainland landings. Despite all the protestations to the contrary after the event, the Italian government definitely knew within a few days of it actually happening on 8 September 1943, that Allied landings at Salerno, south of Naples, were imminent and would coincide with the official declaration of the armistice.

The rational and sensible thing to do, once the armistice was signed, was for the government to prepare militarily for the armistice and for the defence of Rome. In fact, consistent to the end, it did hardly anything. The army high command had already drawn up military directives on how to carry out anti-German military action. From 2 to 6 September, these directives were sent to its commands in Italy. Ambrosio drafted military directives for the army commands under his control as chief of staff of the armed forces in the Balkans and the Aegean islands, but chose not to send them. The directives that were dispatched were certainly more proactive than Badoglio's instructions to the army on 8 September. But they provided insufficiently clear guidance, judging by the very varied ways in which they were interpreted and implemented on the ground on and after 8 September, and by the calls made for clarification by local commanders to the army ministry and supreme command in Rome, on the declaration of the armistice. The calls were unanswered or inadequately answered, because most of the people equipped to deal with them were abandoning their desks in Rome to join the king's flight from the city on 9 September.

The Allies had indicated their willingness to help the Italians defend Rome, to make up for the fact that the landings would be some way to the south of the capital. General Maxwell Taylor, of the US army, made a risky flight to Rome on the night of 7–8 September, to confirm that the Americans were coming and to make arrangements for a landing of an airborne division on airfields around Rome. The top military figures in Rome pretended not to be interested in the US offer of military help. Ambrosio, incredibly, took a train to Turin, in north-west Italy, on 6 September and went walkabout for two days, deliberately missing Taylor's arrival in Rome. General Giacomo Carboni, the nominal commander of the Italian motorized corps charged with defending Rome, told Taylor that the Italian forces would not be strong enough nor ready enough to protect the landing of the US airborne troops and for the immediate defence of Rome. An incredulous Taylor then met Badoglio himself in the middle of the night and, in his pyjamas, Badoglio fired off a telegram to General Dwight D. Eisenhower, the Allied forces' commander-in-chief in the Mediterranean. The message ludicrously requested a delay to the declaration of the armistice, which amounted to a rejection of the armistice: it was, apparently, 'no longer possible', wired Badoglio, 'to accept an immediate armistice'.[2] Eisenhower angrily rejected the request; Taylor understandably called off the operation to help defend Rome.

Later, the king and his advisers were contemplating a rejection of Eisenhower's rejection, until an officer present had to remind them that the government had actually signed the armistice on 3 September. To repudiate it now would mean Italy alienating both the Germans and the Allies. There was no need to anticipate such a consequence. The mutual alienation of both ally-turned-enemy and enemy-turned-ally, was, indeed, the unhappy product of Forty-Five Days of royal government. Successfully offending both sides is perhaps one definition of neutrality!

Behind the passivity and prevarication of the government and the military at this crucial stage of the armistice process lay the concerns which shaped policy from the beginning. There is some evidence to suggest that the message to Taylor about Italian unreadiness to defend Rome was prompted by a determination of at least some army commanders to do what they could to prepare the defence of the city in the time gained by the postponement of the armistice declaration. But this does not seem to have been what prompted the inaction of Ambrosio and Badoglio. They, and the king, were still dreaming the impossible dream, that since the Italian army was deemed to be insufficiently strong to fight and defeat the Germans, the job had to be done by Allied military strength alone. And anyway, they continued to think, if Italian forces did fight the Germans, this would simply provoke the German occupation of Rome and central and northern Italy, and the German capture of the king and the Badoglio government.

Worse was to follow, if that were possible. Faced by the imminent declaration of the armistice, the king and Badoglio decided to abandon Rome and head by car convoy with a large group of senior military staff to the Adriatic port of Pescara, on the opposite eastern seaboard of Italy. From there, they would be shipped to Brindisi, a southern port in Allied hands. Ambrosio quite deliberately destabilized any possible effective military defence of Rome in order to protect the king's departure. He ordered Carboni's motorized troops out of Rome to nearby Tivoli, which also meant the army high command, having just moved to Rome, now had to move out again, totally disorganizing any military resistance to a German attack on the city. It was a very clear demonstration of where, for Ambrosio, the national interest lay. The country's capital city and, indeed, most of central and northern Italy, were sacrificed to save the king's skin. Or as Ambrosio would have put it, parts of the national territory were temporarily sacrificed to German occupation in order to save a man and an institution which embodied the nation as a whole.

On the evening of 8 September, Badoglio's instructions to the military were that *any* attack, whatever the source, was to be resisted. The Italian supreme military command's orders to the armed forces were, 'in no case are you to take the initiative in hostilities against German troops'.[3] The orders were perhaps not so much unclear as wrong. They explicitly ruled out any Italian armed forces' *initiative* against the Germans, any *attack* on the Germans. How the instructions were applied is a story for later. The one dubious merit of the orders was simply that they were consistent with the 'busy doing nothing' approach of the royal government throughout the Forty-Five Days: on no account were Italians to fight Germans and thereby offer any provocation for a German takeover of Italy. In a tragic chain of events which should have been foreseen and guarded against, the king's government had brought about the very situation it wanted to avoid.

# 5

# The Armistice, September 1943

O N the evening of 8 September 1943, Marshal Badoglio, the head of the government, announced the armistice in a radio broadcast to the Italian people and armed forces:

> The Italian government, acknowledging the impossibility of continuing the unequal struggle against the overwhelming power of our opponents, and with the aim of sparing the nation further and more serious harm, has requested an armistice from General Eisenhower, commander-in-chief of the Anglo-American allied forces. This request has been met. Consequently, all hostilities against Anglo-American forces by Italian forces, everywhere, must stop. Italian forces, however, will resist any eventual attacks coming from any other source.[1]

Italian armies were not only located in mainland Italy itself. They were dispersed over the areas they occupied in France, Yugoslavia, mainland Greece, and the Greek islands. For most army commands, wherever they were, this was the first and only directive about the armistice they received. The air force and navy commanders were apparently forewarned of the declaration of the armistice by the armed forces' supreme command. This went some way to explaining why these forces actually managed to change sides, if not intact, then with some kind of residual fighting capacity. Most vessels of the Italian navy sailed out of Italian and Italian-held ports, beating off attempts to stop them, and gathered, as planned, at the British Mediterranean island of Malta or at other Allied-controlled ports. Some of the remains of Italy's air force made it to airfields in those parts of southern Italy conquered by Allied forces and placed under the administration of the king, who with members of his government and military command, had fled there from Rome on the declaration of the armistice. Some aircraft were already located in the conquered areas of the south.

From Malta and from southern Italy, what remained of the Italian navy and air force were eventually allowed by the Allied command and the royal government to help Italian troops who were continuing to fight the Germans in various parts of occupied Yugoslavia, mainland Greece, and the Greek islands, in the expectation or hope of Allied landings and support. Allied and Italian military support was too little and too late to affect the outcome of this fighting.

For those who could actually take it in, Badoglio's deliberately muted declaration of the armistice only contained a specific order to stop fighting the Allies. It did not order Italian forces to fight the Germans, only to respond to attacks from whoever they came, meaning, of course, the Germans, and including, as it transpired, Yugoslav, Albanian, and Greek partisans resisting Axis occupation of the Balkans.

This cautious message kept to the letter, if not the spirit, of the armistice agreement signed with the Allies on 3 September. In this document, there was certainly no explicit mention of the Italians actively helping the Allies against Germany. The commitment was to cooperate with the Allies and resist the Germans. The Allies promised support for any Italian forces resisting the Germans, a promise the Allies felt that they were already keeping by planning the aborted expedition to help in the defence of Rome. But in agreeing to the armistice on 3 September, the king's government knew from the joint Churchill and Roosevelt Quebec declaration communicated to them during the negotiations, that the armistice conditions on Italy would be eased in light of the extent of the Italian government's and people's support of the Allied war on Germany, for however much longer the war lasted. This Anglo-American concession on the principle of unconditional surrender at least gave Italy the opportunity to 'fight its way home', which was what Grandi, back in July 1943, had regarded as the only way Italy could possibly leave the Axis.

But, as we have already seen, this was an opportunity the king and Badoglio were determined not to take. They wanted to leave the war without fighting the Germans. This strategy, if that was the word for it, was reflected in the careful wording of the armistice announcement, and, indeed, in the orders and guidance to the armed forces which were given—and not given—by the military command in the period between the signing of the armistice on 3 September and the king's flight from Rome early in the morning of 9 September. The Italian military command had drawn up directives after the signing of the armistice, which, while repeating the mantra that the Italians were to fight the Germans only if attacked by them, at least envisaged active measures to prepare for such attacks. These directives, 'Memorandum OP 44', were sent to army commands by Badoglio and Ambrosio, head of the supreme command. But despite desperate appeals from some senior officers on the general staff, they refused during the night of 8–9 September to give the order for these directives to be activated. OP 44 remained unopened in sealed envelopes on the desks of army headquarters across occupied Europe, awaiting the order to slice the envelope open which never came.

In the orders which were actually given, the message was basically the same. An order sent to Italian commanders in the Balkans and Aegean stated that if there was no German attack on them, then Italian forces should not make common cause with local partisans ('rebels') nor with Allied troops if they attempted landings. This instruction all but contravened the armistice clause on cooperation with the Allies. Nevertheless, the Italian commander in Greece, General Vecchiarelli, passed this order on to his local commanders, uncoded so that all and sundry would know, after the declaration of the armistice on 8 September. Again, in the very early morning of 9 September, a few hours before the king's flight from Rome, the army ministry clarified something which had obviously been bothering army commands everywhere. German requests to move its troops around in Italian-occupied zones were not to be regarded as hostile acts, and Italian commanders could, if they wished, inform local German commands of their own troop movements and intentions. This instruction practically invited German forces to occupy Italian-held territory and take steps to neutralize Italian forces, something they were already doing and intended to do on the declaration of the Italian armistice.

Finally, there were specific instructions to Italian commands on the central Mediterranean islands of Sardinia and occupied Corsica, which were prepared but not sent at the time of the declaration of the armistice. These were, anyway, effectively countermanded by Ambrosio's response to a query from the Italian military commander on Sardinia early on 9 September. The prepared order was dispatched on 12 September from the supreme command's new location of Brindisi, in south-eastern Italy, when it was too late to make any difference to what was happening on the ground. It envisaged the Italian expulsion of German forces from the two islands, and explicitly ruled out German forces being allowed to transfer from Sardinia to Corsica and thence, of course, to the mainland. Ambrosio, however, on the verge of leaving Rome and still fearful of capture by German forces surrounding the city, told the Sardinian commander that he could allow German forces there to leave the island 'peacefully'. This, again, was tantamount to contravening the terms of the armistice, and once again, confirmed the drift of the other instructions coming out of Rome before the lights went out in the War Ministry. It was, and is, all very well to point to the lack of proper guidance to the army before and during 8–9 September. But if that advice had been more generally forthcoming, then it would have been, 'do all you can to avoid fighting the Germans'.

The behaviour of Badoglio's government during the Forty-Five Days from the overthrow of Mussolini on 25 July to the declaration of the armistice on 8 September; and the military command's orders between the signing of the armistice on 3 September and the flight from Rome on 9 September, including those actually delivered and those which, deliberately, were not, were, ultimately, all one. The king and Badoglio would not contemplate ordering an attack on the Germans, because in their view any such order, or even the whiff of an intention to give one, would provoke German attacks on Italian armed forces and on the Italian population, and bring about the German occupation of Italy. More immediately, such an order would also provoke the Germans into attempting to capture the king and his government.

The king's official declaration of war on Nazi Germany came only on 13 September. But the itinerant military command had, from Brindisi, on 11 September, told its commanders in the field to treat the Germans as enemies. By this time, the king's person was safe behind Allied lines in southern Italy, and it was clear the Allied forces would have to bear the brunt of fighting the Germans and forcing them out of Italy. A declaration of war on Germany made at the same time as the armistice declaration, might, but only might, have induced the Germans to think twice about summarily executing Italian officers and men who had fought them after the armistice, treating them as irregulars rather than combatants with the rights of prisoners of war. But even after the official Italian declaration of war on Nazi Germany, the Germans continued to kill captured Italian soldiers.

Badoglio's announcement of the armistice on 8 September appeared to pro-voke among the Italian people that same mix of enthusiasm and consternation which had greeted the news of Mussolini's fall in July. A mother in the Adriatic port city of Pola, now Pula, on the tip of the Istrian peninsula—a mainly Slav-populated territory annexed to Italy in 1920—reported how the armistice 'arrived as a surprise for everybody, both in Pola and throughout the peninsula and even further afield, where our troops were left without any orders or officers for much of the time'. On the evening of 8 September, the word on the streets in Pola was that 'the war is over',[2] a personal relief to this woman, who had been packing her son's bags for his call-up on 15 September. In fact, the war was only just beginning for the 'Italian' towns and cities dotted along the Yugoslav Adriatic coastline. The woman's son, saved from call-up by the armistice, was enrolled in the army of Mussolini's Italian Social Republic in spring 1944. In Fiume, now Rijeka, further up the Istrian peninsula, a resident recalled that most people were 'disorientated' by Badoglio's broadcast, and 'each one of us had the real feeling that something dreadful and inevitable was about to happen'.[3] It duly did.

Such responses were not confined to Italians who felt particularly vulnerable as Italians because of the places where they lived. A young student at Florence University, back home in Formia, a coastal town just north of Naples and of Salerno, where armistice day Allied landings had occurred, remembered the anxiety caused by what she saw as the ambiguity of Badoglio's statement. 'But what will happen to us, now?', she cried in tears, her panic a kind of counterpoint to the other sounds coming from the street of 'jubilant shouting'.[4] Inland, the same question was being asked in the market square of Isernia, in Campobasso province, where people had gathered once the ringing of the church bells had announced the armistice. While babies and children 'celebrated, the adults put anguished questions to each other: "the armistice has only been signed by the Italians; how will the Allies react? What is going to happen?" '[5] It takes a while to realize that the 'Allies' referred to in this woman's account were the Germans. The answer to these popular anxieties came two days later, on 10 September. The town, an important regional communications fork and soon to become a war zone as the Germans withdrew to the defensive Gustav Line for the winter, was subject to a nasty aerial bombing raid by Italy's ex-enemies and new allies.

The responses to Badoglio's armistice announcement among the senior commanders, officers, and men of Italy's armies resulted in the almost total disintegration of the country's military forces. This was a national disaster, the effects of which reverberated through the remaining years of the war and into post-war recrimination and memory. It was experienced at the time as a national disaster, and from whatever perspective it was experienced, it was remembered as such.

If the general outcome of the armistice declaration was the disbanding of the Italian armies, it is difficult to generalize on how this came about. Italy's armies disintegrated in a variety of ways. Looking back on these events, this was almost bound to be the case. The officers and troops of Italy's widely dispersed armies were forced to make decisions and choices on their own account, in an institutional vacuum without any of the usual reference points which might have guided or offered a direction to how people behaved. For a couple of days after the declaration of the armistice on 8 September, there was no government in Italy, or at least no functioning government. The king, his head of government, and senior military commanders were incommunicado and in transit to their new location in the Allied-controlled south of the country. Telephone calls to ministerial and military offices in Rome were either unanswered, or answered by officials and officers too junior, too ignorant of what was happening, and too frightened and wary to offer any useful or convincing information and advice on how to proceed.

Soldiers listening to Badoglio's broadcast, which was all that most of them would have had to go on, interpreted the armistice as meaning that the war was, finally, over for them. Badoglio was telling them to stop fighting the Allies; that, at least, was clear. He was also not telling them to fight the Germans. If they were not fighting the Allies, and not fighting the Germans, then their war was over and they could expect to return home.

This was a natural and justifiable reaction in the circumstances. The armistice was not so much the cause as the occasion for the break-up of the Italian army. The *tutti a casa* (everybody home) phenomenon after 8 September was the army voting with its feet on the Fascist wars of 1940–3. These wars had demoralized Italian troops, tired them out, kept them from their homes for unjustifiably long periods, forced them into the uncongenial occupation of territories whose peoples rejected them, distanced them from their officers for whom they had little natural respect. After the fall of Mussolini in July—for them as for the bulk of the population, the natural end to the war—they must have been stupefied by Badoglio's decision to continue fighting a war which had lost its initiator and its point.

That the disintegration of the Italian army was rooted in a widespread war-weariness among the troops, seems clear from what happened to the Italian defence of Sicily against Allied invasion in July 1943. Here were the first signs of the dissolution of the country's military forces, anticipating what was to happen more generally after 8 September. Italian military resistance to the invasion, especially among coastal defence units, was flaccid and brief. The police chief of Catania, a major city on Sicily's eastern coast, reported on 20 July, ten days after the invasion started, that there were 'long files of disbanded and hungry Italian soldiers turning up in the Mount Etna area', spreading panic and terror and putting local people in fear of a 'dangerous brigandage'.[6] The policeman had more than enough public order and welfare problems to handle in the city itself, with 30,000 people effectively displaced by incessant day and night Allied aerial and naval bombardment. He probably exaggerated the potential for banditry of fleeing Italian troops, in a report which was passed directly to Mussolini by his superiors. But the picture he portrayed was of an army in the process of self-dissolution.

Eyewitness accounts told the same story. A young woman whose family farm near Ragusa was in the immediate hinterland of the south-eastern coast of the island where Allied forces had landed, recorded an almost Shakespearian encounter with a small group of three frightened and embarrassed Italian soldiers creeping through the fields in the dark 'for fear of being discovered'. Assuming that her account captured at least the gist of their dialogue, it was a meeting and a conversation which was both comic and tragic in its depiction of an army disintegrating and on the run, and almost philosophical in the way the soldiers had already rationalized and justified to themselves the fact that they had given up. The young woman confronted the men,

'Have you run away?'
'Yes, signorina, . . . we are only fugitives, not deserters . . . Here, in Italy, we make war, lacking what we need to defend ourselves . . . and just to have ourselves slaughtered like sleeping dogs.'
'Where are you heading?'
'On whatever road lies ahead of us . . . and which gets us away from that damned hell-hole . . . that mouse trap . . .'

Clearly, these cowed and bedraggled men were not yet at the bandit stage of desperation. The young woman gave them a drink of water, some bread and jam, and off they went. But the shared sense of shame and humiliation remained with her; she observed that when the 'liberating' Allied troops passed through, later, they were received by the locals with 'frightened and bewildered looks . . . at the mercy of a dismay which we could not overcome'.[7]

The invasion of Sicily in July 1943 anticipated the armistice of 8 September in another significant way. According to the Catania chief of police, the German troops were behaving as if they were in occupation of an enemy city, forcibly commandeering cars and trucks for their eventual withdrawal and threatening a scorched earth policy in retreat. The police chief would not have made this up. His own car, along with the prefect's, had been taken at gunpoint by German soldiers, who had fired on him and his police bodyguard as they drove off. The German forces behaved in the same way towards Italian soldiers and civilians in southern Italy during their aggressive retreat of the autumn of 1943 to their first major defensive line, the Gustav Line, stretching across Italy from the coast between Naples and Rome to the Adriatic coast just south of Pescara. Their vindictiveness was now reinforced by their sense of having been betrayed by Italy and Italians on 8 September.

There was clearly a breakdown of normal army discipline and of the hierarchy of command after the declaration of the armistice. Many officers were as bemused as their men by the turn of events and, effectively, decided not to face up to their responsibilities to their men, slipping away themselves without telling them or leaving them with any orders or guidance. In parts of occupied Yugoslavia, some local commanders hared off to the nearest airfield for a flight back to southern Italy, leaving their men behind them. The sense that they had been abandoned and let down by their officers featured strongly in the memories of the aftermath of 8 September. There was sometimes a feeling that they expected no better from their officers. A soldier at Cuneo, in Piedmont, sarcastically asked his commanding officer after the armistice announcement, 'but basically, colonel, sir, what do we have to do, now?'[8] The sarcasm of the soldier's rhetorical question could not disguise his underlying anxiety, nor his lack of expectation of a decent answer and of some leadership from his officer. Elsewhere, there were cases reported of incensed soldiers, full of frustration and rage, smashing up and then, with local people, looting their own barracks and army stores.

In many army garrisons and barracks, authority fragmented, and a kind of democracy prevailed. Some commanders took the mood of their men and before the Germans could intervene, allowed them to leave and disperse to their homes as best they could in a kind of spontaneous disbandment. This, at least, was one step further than simply abandoning their men without saying anything. But abandonment was what it amounted to, ultimately. A man remembered that his brother, who eventually made it home to Macerata, in south central Italy, from service in the Balkans, told him that his commander's words to his unit after the armistice declaration were, 'save yourselves if you can; we no longer have any orders; it's unconditional surrender—look out for the Germans'.[9] Some middle-rank and junior officers, usually closer to their men and how they felt, disputed decisions taken on their force's behalf by senior officers, and hived off on their own, acting unilaterally and taking initiatives which were not authorized by their commanders. In a few notorious cases, the men killed their commanding officers because they ordered them to do something which they did not want to do.

This parcelling out of military authority inevitably stalemated the army units' capacity to act effectively as one fighting force. It also neutralized unilateral initiatives, one group's action or will to act being stymied by the inaction of another group, with sometimes tragicomic outcomes. An officer commanding twenty-five men in an artillery barracks in Alessandria, in north-western Italy, and intending to resist any German attack, sent his corporal to get grenades and ammunition from the depot. The soldier was told by the officer in charge of the stores that he would release nothing without the appropriate chit: 'he does not want any trouble'.[10] The unit was subsequently disarmed by German soldiers. The officer and his men had decided to fight the Germans, which was their response to the vacuum created by the armistice declaration. But they were prevented from doing so by the bureaucratic obstinacy of the quartermaster, who stuck to the normal rules in an abnormal situation, which was his response to the disorder and crisis enveloping him.

Unlike their Italian counterparts, German forces had been prepared for an eventual Italian armistice, and on its announcement put into effect plans to neutralize and disarm the armies of their former ally. Between the fall of Mussolini in July and the declaration of the armistice in September, German reinforcements had moved into Italy itself and Italian-occupied France and the Balkans, positioning themselves near or alongside Italian forces in key strategic areas. Soon after the declaration of the armistice, often on the same evening of 8 September, German units approached Italian commands and confronted them with a choice, or an ultimatum. Italian forces could either cooperate with and join the Germans, continuing to fight the Axis war, or they could lay down their weapons and disarm. Those who chose not to surrender their arms, or not to communicate a decision at all within a short deadline, would be attacked by the Germans and forcibly disarmed. In some places in the occupied Balkans, local German commanders also offered repatriation after disarmament as an inducement to surrender. These promises of repatriation were not normally kept and were probably never seriously made. There were cases in mainland Italy, however, of Italian troops who surrendered their weapons being allowed to leave their barracks and go home, joining those who were disbanding spontaneously.

The fact that German forces had a plan and the will to implement it, and were confronted by Italian troops who had no plan and now had to make a choice, more than compensated for the Germans' numerical inferiority. In the north-eastern city of Padua, home to a large Italian garrison, the entry of a very small advance force of about twenty German troops on 10 September was sufficient to provoke the immediate, panicky dispersal of Italian soldiers, not waiting for but anticipating the German ultimatum. The city just seemed to freeze, or shut down, in the presence of this tiny German force. 'No authority . . . raised its voice,'[11] civilian or military, as Italian soldiers moved out of their barracks, ditching their uniforms and weapons, and clogged up the city's trams and buses in a desperate attempt to leave. By the time the Germans reached the barracks, around one thousand Italian troops were still inside. They were disarmed, taken to the railway station, loaded onto cattle wagons, and dispatched by train to internment camps in Germany and Poland.

Capture, disarmament, and internment was what happened to around 650,000 Italian soldiers in mainland Italy and in Italian-occupied territories. A recent estimate was of over 850,000 men captured and disarmed by the Germans after the armistice, over half of them taken in the Balkans and the Greek islands, the rest in France and Italy. The figures are approximate because the Italian military authorities have never worked out the full extent of the internment operation. The Germans captured whole units in their barracks and garrisons, men passively waiting for something to happen, either because their officers had kept them together to await developments, or by force of inertia, where their officers had deserted them and left them to their own devices. This inactive waiting on events was perhaps the clearest sign of the Italian army just giving up. Many of them had decided not to move, even when there was an opportunity to do so in whatever gap there was, hours, a day, between the declaration of the armistice and the arrival of German troops.

The hundreds of thousands of men who were captured and interned became another 'Italy', in forced exile along with the other hundreds of thousands who were prisoners of war of the Allies. Overall, perhaps 1,300,000 Italians were imprisoned by enemy powers in the course of the war. About 50,000 were in the USSR, taken prisoner during the campaigns on the Axis' Eastern front. Another 40,000 or so were held in French-run camps in North Africa, captured during the last of the fighting in Tunisia in spring 1943. Around 50,000 of the 125,000 captured by American forces, were in camps in the USA, where their labour was needed. About 400,000 had been captured by British forces and were dispersed all over the British Empire, in East and South Africa, Egypt and the Middle East, India, Australia, as well as in Britain itself. Finally, there were the largest group of all, imprisoned in Germany after 8 September 1943 and, again, a vital source of labour for the war economy of their captors.

These men were isolated and separated from events in Italy, some of them for years at a stretch. One artilleryman, called up in 1940, was taken prisoner by the British at the battle of Sidi El Barrani, in North Africa, in January 1941. Initially imprisoned in Egypt, he was transferred to a POW camp in South Africa and thence to one in England, surviving over six days at sea in a lifeboat after his transport ship was torpedoed during the voyage. After being in four separate camps in England, he was eventually repatriated to Italy in April 1946, and had been away from home as a POW for over five years. Admitted to a Pesarò mental hospital in early 1947, his doctors understandably ascribed his depression and eventual schizophrenia to his experience of war and prolonged imprisonment.

Italian POWs were generally reasonably treated in British and American camps, but often maltreated in Soviet, French, and German camps, where they were made to suffer for Italy's invasion and occupation of the USSR and France and for the betrayal of Nazi Germany. They were usually bored by the routine sameness of daily life in the camps and the low levels of subsistence and stimulation on offer. But they were still, in their apathy, inertia, and isolation, required to make a choice about which of the Italies they belonged to, after 8 September 1943.

In the British and American POW camps, the choice was either to cooperate, or not, with their captor-allies. The king's government, once set up in southern Italy, urged Italian POWs to cooperate, and cooperation meant recognizing at a distance that the royal government was the legitimate government of the country and giving their loyalty to that government. Taking this choice made some concrete difference to their lives, and to their status. They officially remained POWs, but could wear the flash on their uniforms which indicated Italy's position now as co-belligerent with the Allies in the war against Nazi Germany. They could expect better jobs, better working conditions, and a better life; they moved relatively freely in their host societies, poised between semi- and full freedom. Some even went back to Italy.

If one chose not to cooperate, then life got no better, but also got no worse; the Americans still expected prisoners to work. In some camps, the non-cooperative POWs were segregated from their fellows, to avoid tension and conflict between them, presumably, but were not otherwise treated very differently. The segregation probably reinforced the initial choice not to cooperate, now a matter which defined and so cohered this sub-group of POWs, and exacerbated their apartness from a world changing around them. A soldier could have made the choice not to cooperate as a Fascist, and become an even more committed Fascist by the point in 1946 and 1947 when he was released and repatriated to a post-war anti-Fascist Italy. Of the 50,000 Italian POWs in American camps, about three-quarters of the officers and of the men opted for cooperation, and numbers increased as the Allies advanced through Italy and the end of the war drew nearer.

At Hereford camp in Texas, Gaetano Tumiati, one of around 900 non-cooperative POWs kept there, clearly could not and did not want to understand what was happening in Italy. Learning of the fall of Rome to the Allies in June 1944, he remarked, 'Why so much joy? How can people be so welcoming to the victors? . . . Just a year ago, the Allies were our enemies, and I would never have imagined that they could be received in this way. What on earth is happening in Italy?'[12] For Tumiati and his fellow 'refuse-niks', the Italian people were behaving dishonourably, while they, of course, were acting honourably, refusing to abandon the German ally with whom Italy entered the war and refusing to be bought into supporting the Allies by the offer of a better life as a POW. For some of these men, Tumiati included, the nation whose honour they were defending was the Fascist nation and the war they wanted to fight was the Axis war. But by no means all of them were Fascists; many became socialists and communists after the war. Their refusal to cooperate presumably, then, sprang from some sense of group identity as POWs and of personal honour and self-respect, the feeling that accepting favours from your captors was a humiliating form of submission to them.

A similar test of national loyalties was required of the Italian military prisoners in Germany. Here, the personal and material inducements or pressures were greater than in British and American camps. If an internee opted to declare his loyalty to Mussolini's Italian Social Republic (Repubblica Sociale Italiana, RSI), the Fascist mini-state set up under German auspices in German-occupied northern and central Italy in late 1943, then he could expect to leave the camps and find 'normal' work outside. Some declaring for Mussolini were enrolled into newly formed Italian SS units or into the reforming army of the RSI, being trained by the Germans for eventual service back in Italy. But this did not seem to be obligatory.

Unlike their men, the 30,000 or so interned officers were not initially required to work in or from the camps. About a third of them were induced to choose the Social Republic, with explicit guarantees that the condition of their repatriation would not be enlistment in the Republican armed forces. If a soldier refused to recognize the Fascist Republic, then he remained a forced labourer, often dispersed to smaller sub-camps nearer the place of employment, where work discipline was harsh and rations so low that he usually went hungry. The Germans were only really interested in the internees as workers. In July 1944, Fritz Sauckel, the Nazi leader responsible for wartime labour recruitment from the occupied territories, obtained Hitler's agreement to convert the internees into civilian workers, which would have made them the responsibility of the German firms to which they were allocated. This conversion to civilian status was initially meant to be agreed to by the internee, who was to sign a work contract with the employer. But, in a further act of resistance which also reflected their resentment at bad treatment in Germany, most internees refused to agree to work contracts. After a couple of months, the Germans were recategorizing them as civilian workers without their consent, to pre-empt their refusal. The change of status might or might not have made a difference to the way they were treated. Generally, refusal to back the RSI also meant the perpetuation of the prisoners' uncertain and vulnerable status—neither POWs nor internees by any international convention—which justified, if justification was needed, their continued maltreatment by their German captors.

Nine of every ten soldiers, as opposed to officers, chose prison and forced labour rather than recognize the legitimacy of the Fascist Republic as the nation's government. It was undoubtedly both humiliating and embarrassing for the RSI to have its legitimacy rejected by so many men, and to be forced to acquiesce in the continued detention of Italians by its German ally. The categorization of the prisoners as Italian military internees (*internati militari italiani*, IMI) was, in effect, an attempt to dignify their imprisonment and so cover up the Fascist Republic's humiliation by these men.

A similar mix of personal, group, and national honour must have motivated this mass refusal. As with the non-cooperators in the Texan camp, it would have appeared undignified and lacking in personal integrity to accept the bribe of a better life offered by their captors. But much more was involved. Men who had been engaged in fighting a Fascist war were now explicitly rejecting the chance to rejoin that war and the claim of a revived Fascism on their national loyalties. In the 1980s, when memories of internment were recorded and anthologized, internment was remembered as anti-Fascist resistance. On this occasion, there is no need to express the usual reservations about the retrospectively rationalizing nature of memories. These military prisoners had explicitly rejected Fascism, and suffered for it.

What is really interesting about the choice faced by men imprisoned by opposing powers which were invading and occupying their country, was that it involved making a judgement on the armistice of 8 September. Similar concepts of personal and national honour inspired, or partly inspired, very different choices. For some of the men refusing to cooperate in the Hereford camp, the armistice had not only meant an end to the war with the enemy, the Allies, but a dishonourable changing of sides and repudiation of the country's alliance with Nazi Germany. The armed forces' commander-in-chief was the king, and he was now ensconced in the south under Allied protection and had made his Italy an ally of the Allies. For men like Tumiati, the king's betrayal of the German ally on 8 September released them from any sense of loyalty and obligation to the king and the Italy he embodied, and enabled them to renew their commitment to the Fascist nation, still faithful to the original German alliance.

Among the military prisoners in Germany, the career and reserve army officers, at least, would have continued to recognize the king as their commander-in-chief and as head of state. Their loyalty to the state and nation as embodied in the king would have overridden their loyalty to Mussolini as head of a past and present Fascist government. As for the men who refused to rally to the RSI from their camps, it seemed unlikely that they did so out of any lingering loyalty to the king and his 'Kingdom of the South'. The king and the military establishment had betrayed them by taking the country into a Fascist war, which they now explicitly rejected, and had continued fighting that Fascist war even after the fall of Mussolini. Both sets of men not cooperating saw the king and his government as betraying the country on 8 September, and did not accept that the monarchy any longer represented their idea of what constituted the nation and national values. A shadow civil war was being contested in the Allied and German prison camps over a country which was and remained physically distant. It was fought for real in a divided and occupied Italy after 8 September 1943.

As the Italian armies broke up after 8 September, most soldiers either disbanded and tried to get home or were captured by the Germans and transported by rail to prison camps in Germany. On the edges of what had become armies of stragglers and prisoners, were officers and men who decided to resist disarmament and fight the Germans, and those who decided to join the Germans. There was relatively little fighting between Italians and Germans on the Italian mainland. Plans had been made for the defence of Rome, and the city was defended, for a while. But the will and capacity to fight were undermined by the diversion of armoured vehicle units to protect the king's flight from the city early in the morning of 9 September, and by the senior commanders' reluctance to engage the German forces moving in on the city.

Their unwillingness was justified at the time and afterwards as the only way of avoiding German reprisals and destruction of the city. The garrison commander's decision to negotiate a ceasefire and surrender on the afternoon of 10 September was at least consistent with the supreme command's general stance on the armistice, to avoid fighting the Germans if at all possible and certainly to avoid any popular uprising. General Giacomo Carboni, head of the motorized units charged with defending Rome, had kept his promise to provide a cross-party 'Anti-Fascist Front' with some weapons for the defence of the city. But most of these were easily located and confiscated by the police from the garages where they had been deposited. There was some combined civilian and army resistance in the west of the city. The memories of Emilio Lussu, a lifetime anti-Fascist who attempted to organize resistance, revealed both the will to fight and the hopeless, desultory way in which the fighting fizzled out. On his rounds, he found 'from behind trees and from house corners, civilians and disbanded soldiers, only one of whom had a rifle, spilling out towards Porta San Paolo'.[13]

Elsewhere, there was resistance to disarmament among some units in Milan and in the surrounding region at Como and Varese, in some parts of Tuscany and on the north-eastern border areas of Alto Adige and Venezia Giulia. The fighting was sporadic and usually did not last long. In Carrara, a marble-mining town inland from the Tuscan coast, resistance went on for two days after the armistice. It was conducted by an ad hoc force of a few platoons of the Alpine regiment stationed there, locally resident soldiers on leave and some local anti-Fascists, who took to the mountains to fight before dissolving after encounters with pursuing German troops. The only successful act of military resistance on mainland Italy seemed to occur in the major south-eastern port city of Bari. Here, General Nicola Bellomo's forces prevented the Germans from disabling the port and held the port area until Allied Canadian troops moved across from the toe of Italy to its heel after crossing from Sicily.

The only places where it could be said that a proper military changing of sides took place after the declaration of the armistice, were the central Mediterranean islands of Sardinia and Corsica, the French island occupied by Italian forces since November 1940. On these islands, the Italian armed forces' numerical superiority over the Germans was so marked that the real issue was whether, and how, German forces would be evacuated to mainland Italy. The local Italian commander in Corsica, General Giovanni Magli, was dining with his German counterpart when the news of the armistice came. Courtesy towards a dinner guest, reflecting the reasonable relations existing between the two commands, at least indicated a peaceful German departure from the island. But, of course, Magli was not informed by anybody that the supreme command had authorized the passage of German troops from Sardinia to southern Corsica, and thence to the mainland.

Incapable of conducting a peaceful withdrawal and not trusting their ex-ally to guarantee one, German forces attacked and seized Sardinian ports to enable their evacuation to Corsica, where the real trouble occurred. The German forces in Corsica joined up with their compatriots from Sardinia and attacked Bastia, Corsica's main city and port of embarkation for mainland Italy. The armistice terms, even Badoglio's radio broadcast, required an Italian military response to any German attack. Under siege from combined Italian military and French partisan forces, the Germans managed to leave for the mainland by 4 October 1943.

This three-way involvement of Italians, Germans, and local partisans in the working-out of the armistice in Corsica, characterized what happened on Italy's north-eastern border and in the Axis-occupied Balkans, but with far less honourable and congenial outcomes. The experiences of a bar and its owner in Gemona del Friuli, about 30 km north of Udine and close to Italy's present border with Slovenia, offer a snapshot of frontier life in wartime. The changing clientele of the bar, commandeered as a military headquarters by everybody who passed through, marked the changing occupation of the area: German soldiers from the fall of Mussolini in July 1943 to just after the armistice in September; then a stream of fugitive Italian soldiers asking for civilian clothes to replace their uniforms, who then 'fled in the direction of Mount Glemina which was near my house';[14] a Croat command; and the Germans again in autumn 1943. To complete the cycle, the bar was taken over by partisans of a communist 'Garibaldi' formation in 1944–5, and then destroyed by an earthquake in 1976.

The presence of Slav soldiers after the September 1943 armistice was an interesting development. In these border areas, in the new territories acquired by Italy after the First World War, and in wartime occupied areas of Yugoslavia further down the Dalmatian coast, the hiatus of authority and control existing immediately after the armistice declaration was an opportunity for Slavs to reclaim territory, both collaborating Slavs and those resisting Axis forces. After the armistice, there was a three-way claim on the city of Fiume (now Rijeka), a mainly Italian populated enclave in territory annexed in 1920: the Germans, Slav partisans, and the fascist statelet of Croatia, set up under Axis auspices after the German invasion and defeat of Yugoslavia in 1941. The Italian garrison commander tried to keep his troops in their barracks, though he could not prevent many spontaneous defections, so that he could surrender them to the incoming Germans. They arrived from Trieste, the Italian border city to the north-west, on 14 September, bombarding positions occupied by Slav partisans in the mainly Croat eastern suburbs of the city.

The coming of the Germans was of some immediate relief to a now very vulnerable Italian population, since it pre-empted an Italian military surrender to the Slavs, of whatever persuasion. The fairly orderly disarming of the garrison could not prevent the city becoming clogged up in the week following the armistice by disbanded Italian soldiers from the interior trying to reach Trieste. One of several compatible eyewitness accounts of Italian residents reported the 'continual passing through of troops' at Fiume, 'an afflux which day by day became more confused and disorderly: the superior officers all seemed to have disappeared, and most units no longer have vehicles; soldiers crossed the bridge . . . tired out, exhausted, covered with dust as if they had walked for long distances on foot. Many of them arrived without their weapons,'[15] which had been stripped from them by local Croats to the east of the city. In this way, the disbandment of the Italian armies in Yugoslavia directly fed the partisan guerrilla warfare which had made the Italian occupation of Yugoslav territory untenable from the start. Local partisan bands and German forces preyed on the disintegrating Italian armies for their weapons, equipment, and vehicles. The competition for Italian military resources complicated, hindered, and in some cases prevented the attempts of Italian soldiers to repatriate themselves from the occupied territories in the Balkans.

In Montenegro, Italian troops disbanded, abandoning their equipment and weapons to the partisans—some of them joined the partisans. In inland Istria, north of Pola, the Italian commander at Pisino (now Pazin) surrendered weapons and the town to Slav partisans and headed for Pola, only to find that the Italian ships had already left for Malta, bottling up Italian troops at the tip of the Istrian peninsula for capture by the Germans. Some of the deals with local Slav partisans worked successfully. On 9 September, near Spalato (now Split), where Croat fascists, and nationalist and communist partisans were jockeying for position, an agreement was brokered with Tito's communist partisans, with the blessing of their British liaison officer. Tito's men provided safe passage for the repatriation of Italian troops who did not want to join the partisans. These first evacuees would not necessarily have been too happy about being landed at Pescara, in German-occupied Italy. Later, Italian troops in this area fought off German attempts to disarm them, with partisan support, and on this occasion were evacuated by Italian ships to Bari, in Allied-occupied Italy.

In Argirocastro (now Gjirokastër), in southern Albania, a 6,000-strong Italian garrison refused the German demand to disarm and began a long march to the coast. Some of them were successfully disembarked by Italian vessels from Santi Quaranta (now Sarandë), before the German capture of the nearby island of Corfu made further use of the port impossible. The force was partly pursued and partly protected by rival nationalist and anti-fascist partisan bands. A deal with the latter enabled the Italians and partisans to fight off an attempted German landing at the port. The garrison commander decided to keep to the protection for weapons deal and handed over his troops' weaponry to the partisans, a premature decision with catastrophic consequences. Some of his officers opposed the handover, arguing that the commander had forfeited the only resource and leverage which the force possessed. Proceeding unarmed up the coast to another port, groups of officers and men flaked off, making for the interior to shelter with the local population as best they could, or joining the Albanian partisans. The remainder of the garrison was captured and killed by the Germans. Its commander was beheaded and his head paraded around impaled on a bayonet.

A similar tragedy unfolded in the Italian-occupied Greek Ionian island of Cefalonia. The local commander, General Antonio Gandin, rejected the orders coming from the Italian command for Greece. These were to surrender to the Germans and to await what the Germans were promising for Italian forces in Greece, which was repatriation. The Italians were numerically far superior to German forces on the island, though admittedly less well equipped. But their resistance was ultimately undermined by divisions within the Italian forces, and by the effects of the temporary vacuum of military authority in Italy itself. Unable to make any contact with the army command in Rome, now en route to Pescara and Brindisi, the garrison commander had to make his own decisions, or allow them to be made for him by his officers and men.

His own inclination, and that of his superior officers, was not to fight an ex-ally, and to temporize and arrive at a deal with the Germans. The will to fight the Germans was strong, however, among his junior officers and the rank-and-file troops. Three officers attempting to organize a surrender of their division to the Germans were shot by their own men. An extraordinary vote allowed by Gandin confirmed that the majority wanted to fight the Germans, rather than be disarmed by them. This democratic decision was one which Gandin could not countermand. He now knew that fighting between Germans and Italians was taking place on other Greek islands, and that the supreme command, from the safety of Brindisi, was expecting Italian forces to fight and promising support from mainland Italian and Allied forces.

Eight days of fighting ensued until the Italian surrender on 22 September. About 1,200 Italian troops were killed in action. Beside himself with anger at Italian treachery, Hitler ordered the local German commanders to kill those who had resisted. About 4,800 captured troops were shot, most of them gunned down where they surrendered. About 340 officers, including Gandin, were systematically executed in batches by their German captors. Some 2,000 soldiers were sent off for internment, and many died in the water when the vessels taking them away hit mines. Of the 11,000 troops there, perhaps 1,000 Italian soldiers escaped German capture, and many of them ended up joining Greek partisan formations on the island. Cefalonia was the most significant and emblematic single incident of Italian military resistance to the Germans. Overall, it has been estimated that about 25,000 Italian officers and men were killed in fighting and round-ups after the armistice.

Where there was resistance to German disarmament on mainland Greece and on the Greek islands, the Cefalonian experience of the disintegration of Italian forces was replicated. Most men were killed during and after the actual fighting, or interned, by the Germans. A small number evaded capture and took to the mountains, enlisting with local partisans or simply seeking shelter and refuge. Where help was not forthcoming from the local people, hunger and tiredness forced these fugitives out into the open, inviting capture and internment.

In Thessalonika, on the mainland, the civil war between Greek nationalist and communist partisans, effectively over who and what should come after the expulsion of the German occupier, worked to neutralize the military use of Italian forces. The commander of the Pinerolo division, General Adolfo Infante, like so many local commanders in Italian-occupied Greece, refused to accept Vecchiarelli's instruction to surrender to the Germans. He genuinely seemed ready to undertake the operation of changing sides after the armistice, which was more or less completed by Italian commanders on Sardinia and Corsica. Changing sides in Thessalonika, where there were many partisans but few German troops, meant joining forces with the Greek resistance against the Germans. This he agreed to do, on 11 September, after contact with partisan leaders and Allied agents working with the Greek resistance. But the division was such a significant military resource, that its use was bound to affect the balance between rival Greek monarchist and communist partisan formations. The communist resistance organization, ELAS, preferred to disarm and intern some of the Italian troops fighting with them, on the suspicion and potential risk of them being poached by the rival nationalist resistance movement, EDES.

What did not happen in Cefalonia, though it did occur elsewhere in Italian-occupied areas, was the defection of some Italian forces to the Germans after the declaration of the armistice. It would not have been seen as a defection by those who joined the Germans, but rather as the honourable standing at the side of one's ally, and in Italian Yugoslavia, the honourable defence of the Italian national interest. These concerns seemed to determine the actions of General Zannini, the commander of Italian forces in Udine and Gorizia which had been fighting Slav partisans in this frontier area since late 1942. He ignored calls coming from some of his divisional commanders to attack the Germans, and from local anti-Fascists offering their support for resistance to German occupation. To him, the communist Slav partisans and anti-Fascists were one and the same, the social and the national enemy combined. The deal he negotiated with the Germans was that German occupation of the region would not be resisted, Italian troops would keep their own arms in order to police the area, and some Italian units would continue the anti-partisan war in Gorizia alongside the Germans. Faced with the choice of fighting the Germans and fighting the partisans, he chose the latter, for class and national reasons.

Similar reasoning was deployed by a young NCO on leave in the Italian enclave of Zara on the Adriatic coast of Yugoslavia, which enabled him to welcome the German takeover of the city a few days after the armistice. 'I had fought with them on the North Africa front,' he remembered, 'and I did not like the idea of turning against an ally like someone changing partners during a dance; the Germans, anyhow, were a defence against a potential Slav occupation after the dissolution of the Italian army, which had occurred in an incredible fashion under our very eyes.'[16] Another veteran of the North Africa campaign also found that his nationalism was compatible with loyalty to the German alliance in this part of the world. Having witnessed the 'slavo-communists' entering his own locality in Istria on armoured vehicles of the now dissolved Italian army, he could see that the worst was avoided with the later arrival of German troops, who ended the partisans' takeover and pursued them into the countryside. Once he and his companions had enlisted in the armed forces of the RSI 'in order to defend our own homes, our own people', he could claim that 'a bit of Italy . . . had taken up arms again'.[17]

Perhaps significantly, the young man on leave in Zara was a university medical student who had actually volunteered for service in North Africa. It seemed to be the case that the military units who went over to the Germans after the armistice were either those with a particular *esprit* and a commitment to the Fascist war, like volunteers, or those who might be expected to have and retain a stronger than usual personal and ideological attachment to Fascism and the Axis. We have already come across the parachutists, those unused assault troops of 1942–3, most of whom ended up fighting as infantrymen in North Africa. In Sardinia, most of the Nembo parachutist division opted for the Axis and for evacuation with their German comrades, and killed one of their commanding officers who attempted to persuade them of their duty of loyalty to the king and his choice of changing sides. In Calabria, in the south of Italy, a captain led over to the Germans part of his battalion of men in the parachutists regiment there, 'for the honour of Italy', as he put it.[18] Joining the Germans in retreat, his men participated in the killing of Italian civilians at Rionero in Vulture, an action for which the officer was tried after the war.

It is difficult to perceive any of the parachutists' motives behind the behaviour of the anti-aircraft defence personnel who, oddly, stayed at their batteries and were taken over by the Germans when they occupied the north-eastern border areas and the Italian-occupied Balkans in September 1943. It might have been something to do with the relatively quiet and uneventful war so far for these units in the Balkans, untouched by Allied bombing raids until late 1943 and early 1944. One man, an officer's adjutant serving in Zara's anti-aircraft battery, spoke of his idyllic situation on the 'splendid Bersaglio peninsula, surrounded by the sea', 'a kind of military villa resort holiday' where anti-aircraft attack exercises were a 'pastime'.[19] All this was to change from the armistice, as Zara was flattened by Allied bombing attacks in 1943–4. But for these men, there was little demoralization and disaffection with a Fascist war, which made them want to leave at all costs. If not a group with a particular combatant élan, they were a group with a special status and function and were nominally under the civilian administrative control of the prefect, the top state official in the area. At least in Zara, the prefect gave clear orders for the men at the batteries to stay where they were, 'to await military developments'.[20]

Some Fascist Militia units attached to regular army divisions in the Balkans also chose to continue fighting with the Germans after the armistice. This happened, for instance, in inland Dalmatia, where Yugoslav nationalist Cetnik and Titoist communist partisan bands were fighting each other as much as the Axis occupiers, a similar situation to that existing in Albania and Greece. The Venezia division was effectively commandeered by Tito's partisans, not the dominant partisan force in the area, on the advice of British intelligence officers operating with the Yugoslav resistance. But the division's Militia forces rejected the Allies' advice and the partisans' pressure, and joined the Germans. On the Dodecanese island of Rhodes, governed by the Italians since the Italo-Turkish war of 1911–12, around 2,000 of about 37,000 Italian troops preferred fighting with the Germans to internment. On the island of Samos, the presence of about 1,500 Militiamen in the garrison, who made clear their continuing attachment to the Axis war, was enough to induce the garrison commander's surrender to the Germans without him testing the will to fight of the rest of his forces.

Deciding what to do after the declaration of the armistice on 8 September would not have been easy for Italian soldiers, especially when many of their officers abdicated their responsibility to lead them. Where a soldier was and what he was doing at the moment of the armistice announcement, clearly mattered, if only because such circumstances could open up or, alternatively, limit his options. Nuto Revelli was the young Alpini officer whose post-war accounts based on personal testimonies have done so much to reveal the wartime experiences of the men who fought on the Russian front. By his own account, his own response to the armistice was 'instinctive, immediate. As soon as the Germans entered Cuneo [his native town, just south of Turin], I ran home. I recovered my three automatic weapons and slipped them into my military rucksack. Then I went off to my first partisan base.'[21] Revelli may have described his reaction as instinctive, but it was hardly an uncalculated one. He had a history of disaffection with the Fascist war and with Fascism's ally, the Germans, as a result of his experiences in the USSR and, especially, of the dreadful retreat from the Don early in 1943. His decision to resist the German occupation of his country after the armistice was evidently driven by the anger and resentment he felt towards the Germans and an awareness of what German occupation would entail.

We know that his decision was not an isolated one. Italian forces in Gorizia, on Italy's north-eastern frontier, were reinforced during 1943 by repatriated Alpini being regrouped after the Russian campaign. Like Revelli, some officers and men hid their arms to escape German confiscation and took to the hills to form partisan units of their own. The 'autonomous'—that is, non-political—Osoppo Friuli partisan formations which operated in Venezia Giulia, were started up by fugitive ex-soldiers and included officers and men from Alpini regiments serving in the frontier areas before the armistice.

These men would have been engaged in fighting against Slav partisans in 1943, as would Italian forces stationed throughout annexed or newly occupied parts of Yugoslavia. It would hardly have been the natural choice for them to join the Slav partisan bands who had been the enemy in a particularly nasty anti-partisan war. A frontier guard recalled how he and his companions had left their base for Fiume and been approached by local Titoist partisans to join them. But 'nobody went with them ... everybody wanted to get home'.[22] One has to assume that the desire to leave the war and return home was the paramount consideration for most Italian soldiers. It was then a matter of whether there was a real chance and expectation of realizing this preference. In this case, the soldier clearly expected, as well as hoped, that he and his comrades would be picked up by Italian ships from Fiume and repatriated.

When that option disappeared, as it did very quickly for many thousands of troops spontaneously disbanding for home, their choices narrowed. The soldiers starting the trek home had not surrendered to the Germans and were treated as fugitives by them, to be pursued, captured, and interned. One choice was to remain a fugitive and hope to last out the war, in whatever circumstances you could. A wartime resident of Pola remembered one of the soldiers she sheltered in her home following the armistice because he decided to stay on in the area for months afterwards, moving into a vacated house in the city until he was bombed out early in 1944. Then, 'good peasant lad that he was',[23] he moved in with the local farmer's family who owned the orchard where he worked. Things became too uncomfortable when the Germans started calling up men for military or labour service. It was at this point, in spring 1944, that he left, taking a boat to Ancona on Italy's Adriatic coast, and from there making, presumably, for his home in a Fascist new town in the reclaimed marshland near Rome.

Some fugitives became official, like those ex-soldiers who were disarmed in Thessalonika and then put up on local farms for the remainder of the war, their board and lodging paid for by the British government through British agents attached to the Greek resistance. These fugitives, far from home, found reasonably safe and comfortable refuge among local communities. For others, it was a matter of lying low and living off the land. A military engineer, evacuating his wife and newly born baby daughter from a heavily bombed Zara in November 1943, holed up in an abandoned and ruined house in the countryside. There, 'in the depths of a thicket', they came across 'a military tent covered with leafy branches',[24] and inside, an Italian soldier, a peasant conscript from S. Donà di Piave, near the Venice lagoon. He told them that he had managed to escape capture by the Germans when they took away all his companions from the barracks.

The engineer was involved in his own tortuous journey home. Refusing to present himself to the Germans in Sebenico (now Sibinek) after the armistice in September 1943, he finally returned home to the Emilian town of Modena in central Italy, at Easter time, 1944. He and his family passed through several hands, the Germans, a Slav peasant family billeting nationalist Cetnik partisans, the Germans again, and finally the Italian police at Zara, where his wife's family connections secured papers for himself, his family, and their Venetian straggler to take a ship to Venice. His testimony revealed the bare bones of a personal 'everybody home' story which illustrated the extraordinary mobility of wartime. It also inadvertently exposed the often highly circumstantial choices faced by Italian soldiers after 8 September. Our engineer had hitched a lift with a vehicle in an armed German convoy travelling from the interior to Zara on the coast. The driver was an Italian 'in German uniform' who 'said that he had preferred driving a lorry' for the Germans to a German 'concentration camp'.[25]

There is plenty of evidence to suggest that some Italian officers and men in the occupied Balkans actually wanted to join local partisans in the struggle against the Germans after the 8 September armistice, and eventually were able to exercise that choice as the forces to which they belonged disintegrated under pressure from Germans and partisans alike. But in the circumstantial, not to say incidental, wartime way of things, disbanded soldier fugitives were as likely to have joined local partisan formations in the Balkans because they could not find a way home out of the bottlenecks in Adriatic ports, because of chance encounters with partisans while on the run, and because joining them provided company, shelter, and food for desperate men who, as fugitives from the Germans, lacked all of these essentials for life and survival. Similar events and motivations would also have characterized the 'everybody home' phenomenon on mainland Italy.

The break-up of the Italian army in September 1943 was something experienced and felt as a national disaster by the Italian people. For some, the armistice meant a very direct sense of personal loss and family separation. A woman remembered as a girl joining the general initial popular enthusiasm at the news of the armistice, near Gaeta, a port on the Mediterranean coast between Rome and Naples. Her uninhibited childish jubilation was chastened by the sight of a group of grieving women who were the wives of marines. 'They were not happy,' she recalled; 'they were crying. They looked out towards Gaeta where on the ships leaving the port were their husbands. Turning to us, they shouted, "Sing . . . sing while you can . . . The worst is yet to come . . . now the war really starts." '[26] This sounds almost too melodramatic to be true. But the women were right. The war was not over for their husbands, and nor was it for the area where they had been stationed. Gaeta was very close to the Gustav Line, the first major defensive line straddling the country from one coast to another to which the Germans withdrew in September and October 1943. The whole area became a war zone, occupied and defended by German troops with little regard for civilian sensibilities or safety, and bombarded by Germans and Allies alike.

Other people literally walked into the war they wanted to avoid or leave. A professional soldier recalled his good fortune in making it home after the armistice. But 'it was worse',[27] because home was inland from Gaeta, in the mountains at Cassino, where the retreating Germans commandeered their houses. As the military front stabilized there in October 1943, local people were forced to take refuge from both German and Allied fire in the wooded countryside nearby, forming a flotsam community with disbanded fugitive soldiers and refugees fleeing the bombing and fighting in Naples and its hinterland.

It is, perhaps, too easily assumed that Italian soldiers and civilians who were near the frontlines at the time of the armistice, were generally safer, and that troops who came from the south and were serving in the south found it easier to reach home. This was certainly the impression given by the writer Norman Lewis, an Allied intelligence officer landing with the US Fifth Army at Paestum, near Salerno. His diary entry for 11 September 1943 recorded that although the Italian soldiers he observed, 'who had walked away from the war . . . on their way to their homes in the South', were in terrible shape, with blood sometimes oozing through the cracked leather of their boots, 'they were, nevertheless, in tremendous spirits, and we listened to the trail of their laughter and song all through the day'.[28] But it is salutary to remember, also, that German troops retreating through southern Italy in September and October 1943 killed over 1,500 people in a violently brief occupation. Most of the victims were civilians resisting the Germans' retreat and their forcible ejection of them from their homes, as in Cassino, or people killed in reprisal for such resistance, or military stragglers.

The army's disintegration happened in the people's midst, and invited, even required, them to show compassion and solidarity towards young men who no longer wanted to be in uniform. It must be said that sympathy was not always forthcoming. The same young university student at home in Formia, near Gaeta, who remembered feeling disorientated by the armistice announcement, also felt bewildered and humiliated by the procession of scruffy disbanding soldiers passing through the streets of her town a few days later. Her father asked one of them where they were going and received the disdainful and defensive reply, 'we're going home. The war is over. How come you don't know?' He compared this end to the war with his own, in 1918. 'We were proud, confident, looking good. And all these men, they are our sons.'[29]

A military chaplain attached to a disbanding infantry regiment on the front line in the southern province of Catanzaro noted the soldiers' sense of humiliation at defeat and having to change sides, which was heightened by the way the local population turned out to welcome the Allied troops and, realizing that they were Italians, 'shouted insults' at them as they passed through.[30] A similar sense of shame and humiliation was shared by a schoolteacher observing the aftermath of the armistice in Merano, an important garrison town near Bolzano, on Italy's Alpine border with Austria, though with considerably greater sympathy for the abandoned and rudderless Italian soldiers she talked to in the streets of the town, the morning after 8 September. She found a group of soldiers, 'silent and disorientated, each one carrying his own little cardboard suitcase', who said that their 'officers had left them free to go. They added with astonishment that they had received no orders.' Further on, in the garden of the garrison command headquarters, she tried to comfort a sergeant 'with his arms wrapped around his knees, shaking his head and repeating in a loud voice the obsessive refrain, "what a humiliation! What a humiliation!"' Most of these men would be picked up as fugitives and returned to the garrison as prisoners.

Merano was in the Alto Adige, or the South Tyrol, a largely German-speaking area which became part of Italy at the end of the First World War. After the armistice, the whole region was effectively annexed to Nazi Germany and placed under a Nazi Party gauleiter. A local Tyrolese police force was rapidly improvised under German auspices, and our schoolteacher witness saw a teenage recruit to this militia shoving through the street to the barracks with a rifle 'which was bigger than him', an Italian officer, 'his uniform tattered and filthy with dried mud, stripped of his belt and pistol', rendered defenceless by the callowness of his captor, who was 'young enough to have been his own son'.[31]

Everywhere, disbanding soldiers needed help if they were to get home. Above all, they wanted civilian clothes to replace the uniform they no longer wanted to wear and which identified them as military fugitives. They stopped people in the streets, knocked on people's doors, asking for clothing, a meal, temporary shelter. The initial spontaneous response, where it came, sometimes developed into a more coordinated enterprise involving groups and networks of people, a mark not only of collective compassion but also of latent organizational skills being put to work. An elderly working-class woman in Turin turned her house into a reception and transit area for disbanding soldiers. She canvassed help with food and clothing from her neighbours and the local nuns, disposed of the weapons, and accompanied the soldiers to the railway station, deflecting suspicion and avoiding detection by treating them as if they were her relatives. Such efforts were among the first examples of popular resistance to German occupation, even more so, in the case of the anti-Fascist woman in Bologna who collected together civilian clothes for disbanding troops which she offered in exchange for their weapons. Her house became not a resting place for fugitive soldiers, but an armoury of their weapons, for use in the armed resistance against German occupation.

People noticed new faces among the porters and orderlies at the local hospital, who were now wearing different uniforms. A victim of an Allied bombing raid on Isernia, in Campobasso province, on 10 September, was treated at the town's hospital where she saw arriving a group of disbanding soldiers, 'tired and in a bad way, in clothes which were half civilian, half military.

They stayed at the hospital to receive help, and to give it.'[32] Women gathered outside barracks to offer food and water, and words, to the young soldiers now imprisoned inside and awaiting transfer to internment in Germany.

Two young women guiltily remembered how on the streets of Zara, one late afternoon soon after the armistice, they had been unable or unwilling to offer help with a place to stay and hide out for a while, to two young soldiers who had approached them, their greyish-green army uniforms peeking out from under their ill-fitting civilian clothes at the neck, wrists, and feet. The two women then later anxiously scoured the faces of the bedraggled captured Italian soldiers being escorted through the city, for a sight of the men they had spoken to, but 'they weren't there'.[33]

It was almost impossible for ordinary Italians not to observe and not to become caught up in the disintegration of Italian armies after 8 September. A woman left Portomaggiore, near Ferrara, in the Po valley between Bologna and Venice, for a tortuous family trip of her own, travelling by train to collect her children who were staying at her mother-in-law's place in the province of Brescia, in Lombardy. On the way out, at Ferrara station, one of her many changes, she noted that it was full of German soldiers loading captured Italian troops onto cattle wagons for transportation to Germany. On her way back, she could not avoid becoming personally involved. In her train compartment, there was an Italian soldier dressed in civilian clothes who 'for fear of being captured by the Germans, begged me to allow him to hold my baby so as to make himself less conspicuous'.[34]

These were typical wartime stories, typical in their incidental, even accidental, nature. The war came unavoidably but unpredictably to people going about their own business, who were forced to make choices, rapid choices, which they would have wanted to avoid, choices which had conse-quences and affected the lives of others and put themselves and others at risk. The woman in the train had arrived in Brescia after curfew and had been forced to solicit a German soldiers' escort to her mother-in-law's house in the city. Now her compassionate, concrete help to a fugitive made her complicit in the soldier's flight and as liable as he was to detection and punishment by the Germans who had earlier protected her and allowed her to be reunited with her children. One wonders whether there was time for any of these calculations of risk to have influenced the women's decision whether to help or not.

Finally, of course, the break-up of the Italian army after the armistice impinged on the lives and outlooks of Italians, because, in their tens of thousands, they came back home, to villages, towns, and cities across Italy. A child during the war, Silvio Trambaiolo remembered the odd hiatus of a couple of months between the ringing of the church bells on 8 September to celebrate the armistice and the end of the war and the arrival of the new authorities, young Fascist policemen and militia in the uniform of Mussolini's Italian Social Republic, and occupying German troops. He was brought up in a small village of peasants and agricultural labourers, Piacenza d'Adige, on the Po valley flats between Padua and Rovigo, in north-eastern Italy. The village's rural out-of-the-way insignificance was probably why the Germans used it to billet and rest soldiers in transit to and from the fighting front as it moved ever closer in 1944–5. But in the autumn of 1943, 'no one seemed to have a clear idea of what was happening. Apparently the war had not ceased, yet servicemen from the village, dressed in civilian clothes, were returning in throngs . . . fleeing from wherever they had happened to be at the time of the armistice.'[35]

The return of the village's young men was both a blessing and an encumbrance. Hiding in cellars and out in hay barns, their presence, and the knowledge of their presence, drew the village to the attention of the Italian and German authorities. These were able-bodied men, after all, who should have been called up to the armed forces of the RSI, representing one of the Italies of the 1943–5 period, or to labour service for the Germans, whether locally or in Germany. Avoiding or rejecting these claims on their labour and loyalties would take some of these young men, fugitives in their own village, into the ranks of the anti-Fascist and anti-German resistance.

The armistice of 8 September has become a mythical event. Its meaning and significance have been endlessly speculated on since the end of the war, and become the object of contentious public and political debate. Over the past decade or so, there has been a feverish and unbalanced debate in Italy about the existence and nature of the Italian nation and Italian national identity. This is the outcome of, and one of the responses to, sometimes related political and social developments. There occurred in the 1990s the apparent collapse of the institutional and political alignments characterizing the Italian parliamentary republic since the late 1940s. A cause and a symptom of political realignment were the emergence and presence in government of the Northern League, a secessionist movement which has questioned whether the south has a place at all in the Italian national state. Recent influxes of economic migrants and asylum seekers from the Balkans and Africa have, as in other European countries, reopened debates about racism, colonial pasts, and the kind of national society which Italians have now and might want in the future.

In the overheated debate about national identity and national consciousness, the armistice of 8 September 1943 has for some commentators, journalists, and historians, been seen as the start of the 'death' of the nation, the start of the dissolution of a sense of nationhood which has apparently blighted post-war Italy. From this viewpoint, what disintegrated after the armistice was the army, arguably Italy's most important national institution, the guarantor of national independence and internal order, and since it was a conscript force in which the nation's male citizens had to serve, the most evident expression of national unity and strength. The giving in and going home of most of Italy's soldiers after the armistice, denoted for some a deeply seated failure of nation-formation and a weak to non-existent sense of nationhood among Italians. This is really an old debate taking a new form. Ever since the late and imperfectly realized political and territorial unification of Italy in 1870, people have agonized over whether a country so internally divided by class and local and regional identities did, and could, constitute a nation. Fascism's aggressive nationalism and imperialism, and its attempt to mould a new nation through totalitarian organization, was one attempt to resolve Italy's national problem.

It may now be time to see the armistice in its proper historical proportions, without forgetting that the disproportionate use and interpretation of it by different groups has already become part of Italy's history and the way Italy remembers its own past. The most evident and immediate consequence of the armistice, or rather of the way in which the armistice was managed and handled by Italy's military and royal establishment, was that the capital city, Rome, was inadequately defended and allowed to fall into German hands. Nobody at the time anticipated that it would take another nine months of warfare for the Allied forces to liberate Rome from German occupation. But the failure to hold on to Rome in September 1943 prolonged the war and the German occupation of central and northern Italy.

The armistice also conditioned how the Germans occupied Italy, which mirrored how the Germans treated those Italian soldiers who fought them after the armistice. To the Germans, the armistice and changing of sides of 8 September were a second betrayal. The first betrayal was Italy's decision not to remain in the Triple Alliance with Germany and Austria-Hungary and to enter the First World War on the Entente side against Germany and the

Austrian empire in May 1915. The armistice confirmed for the Germans the existence of a defective Italian mentality which became evident in what they saw as Italy's derisory and half-hearted contribution to the Axis war effort between 1940 and 1943. Italians were seen and stereotypically as a congenitally untrustworthy and deceitful people, and were to be treated and occupied as such. The Germans very rapidly transformed Italy from being a useless ally to being an occupied enemy country, a change accelerated by the transfer to the Italian war of German military units who had already demonstrated how to handle 'inferior' peoples in occupied eastern Europe and western Russia.

The harsh nature of German military occupation of Italy, in part determined by the armistice betrayal, had important short-term and long-term effects. It helped to undermine from the start the credibility among Italians of Mussolini's Italian Social Republic, installed in German-occupied Italy from the autumn of 1943. As with Marshal Pétain's government in occupied France, Mussolini's Fascist Republic could have tried to justify its existence as a collaborating regime on its capacity, by merely existing, to prevent the worse, and to mitigate the most punitive aspects of a Nazi German occupation. After the armistice, the Germans treated occupied Italy as if it was occupied Poland; they annexed territory, ruthlessly exploited the labour and economic resources of the country, and defended Germany in Italy with no regard for the lives and livelihoods of Italian civilians.

The longer-term effect of a harsh German occupation, predicated on a perception of Italian betrayal, was historiographical, or to do with how the war would be remembered in Italy in the post-war period. This takes up an important point already made in the Introduction. The disintegration of Italy's armies following the armistice had involved German troops disarming and killing Italian officers and men in the occupied territories, and forcibly interning in prison camps in Germany and Poland over 600,000 Italian soldiers. This was enough to make people forget that these same Italian officers and men had conducted their own forcible occupation of other people's territory between 1940 and 1943. From being the victimizers, Italian soldiers were now the victims of German oppression. The status of victimhood could then understandably enough be conferred on all those Italians who were forced to endure the full rigours of the Nazi German occupation of part of their country. Their wartime suffering and misfortune were caused by the occupier. This was how, and why, in so many retrospective personal testimonies of experiences during the war, people reminisced as if the war really started for them in 1943, not 1940.

In a very evident and literal sense, Italy ceased to exist as a national state between 1943 and 1945. The country was divided and occupied by invading foreign powers; the Germans effectively annexed the borderlands of north-eastern Italy. More importantly, perhaps, three different versions of Italy came to exist within the country. Each of these competing Italies was a child of the armistice. There was a calculation behind the royal coup against Mussolini and the Fascist regime in July 1943. It was that the king, and behind him, Italy's conservative military and political establishment, could achieve a soft landing from Fascism and the Fascist war, and manage the transition from Fascism to post-Fascism in a way which would both ended the war and protected the position of these conservative forces who had been Fascism's fellow-travellers.

To an extent, it would be fair to say that the operation was botched. The monarchy's and the military's credibility as the forces representing the nation and the national interest was undermined as a result of the Badoglio government's decision to continue the Fascist war while conducting ludicrously protracted negotiations with ludicrously inflated expectations for an end to the war with the Allies. That credibility was all but destroyed by the national humiliation of the 8 September armistice. But not all was lost. The king and the military had secured something from the armistice. The armistice itself was Allied recognition of the king's government, the signatory of the agreement, as the legitimate government of Italy. The Allies would want to keep this government in existence, because having signed the armistice, it was the Italy which could be made to comply with the terms and obligations of the armistice agreement on the occupation of the country.

As the Allies moved slowly north, they released liberated areas of the south to administration by the king's government, which allowed and justified the partial recuperation of the state's military and civil apparatus in the south. This, alone, is probably sufficient explanation for the continuation in office of a largely unpurged and unreconstructed civil service, the state machine which had serviced Fascism, into the post-war Italian Republic. A military force of sorts was reformed, after the total collapse of the armistice, and, now that Italy was a co-belligerent, participated in the Allied military campaign against the Germans in Italy. A civil service, or part of it, returned to their desks. There was some justification for the view that the king had maintained the continuity of the state in the south. It was hardly coincidental that a majority of people in the south, which was the king's Italy between 1943 and 1945, voted to retain the monarchy in the 1946 referendum.

It was, of course, the case that the Allies insisted on the king broadening out his government to include other national anti-Fascist and anti-German forces which Badoglio had attempted to exclude from political life during the Forty-Five Days. The fact that there was a referendum at all on the monarchy was the clearest indication that the king had not been able to guarantee a politically and socially conservative outcome to the fall of Mussolini. But this was the political price paid for the botched operation of the armistice. What had been gained in late 1943 was the opportunity, at least, for the king to remain in the political game, and the continued existence of a monarchical Italy which could attempt to influence, even determine, what happened in the country after the war. Given the extent of the king's complicity in twenty years of Fascism, still being in the picture was probably more than the monarchy deserved to extract from the disaster of the armistice.

The impetus behind the emergence of the two other Italies of 1943 to 1945 also came from the armistice. That minority of soldiers who went over to the Germans after 8 September, and that minority of Italians, Fascist or otherwise, who rallied to Mussolini's Social Republic in northern Italy in late 1943, felt or were made to feel that they were restoring national honour by sticking with their German ally and rejecting the betrayal of the nation by the king and Badoglio. That Mussolini's client Fascist regime in the north was Social and a Republic denoted a repudiation of the king and a conservative fellow-travelling establishment, which, in the wishful thinking of the RSI's apologists, had compromised the Fascism of 1922 to 1943. Much of the RSI's propaganda was directed at contesting the legitimacy of a king who had betrayed the country in September 1943.

The armistice was also a liberation and a stimulus for political anti-Fascism in Italy. The collapse of the Italian army after 8 September fed directly into anti-Fascist and anti-German armed resistance. Soldiers trying and failing to get home after the armistice declaration took refuge in the hills and mountains of the country, sometimes forming their own apolitically national partisan bands, sometimes becoming or joining political anti-Fascist formations. The anti-Fascist political movements and parties denied an effective voice by Badoglio's government during the Forty-Five Days, could now organize and resist without restraint.

The sense of relief and release among anti-Fascists was apparent immediately after the armistice. On 11 September, the broadsheet of the Action Party, a liberal-socialist anti-Fascist resistance movement, made a rallying cry to its readers, characteristically placing Italy's national struggle in a European-wide context: 'we do not have to write on walls, at night, in a secret and under-hand way, "Long Live the Heroic Danes!" We too are now like them, like the French, the Belgians, the Dutch, like the Yugoslavs and the Greeks, like the Czechs and the Poles.'[36] The day after the armistice, it was Rome's anti-Fascist front organization, including socialists, communists, and actionists, which attempted to mobilize popular resistance against the German seizure of the city. These anti-Fascist groups were the first to take to the armed struggle against a revived Fascism and German occupation. A broad alliance of anti-Fascist movements formed the Committee of National Liberation for Northern Italy (Comitato di Liberazione Nazionale per Alta Italia, CLNAI) in January 1944 to run the activities of the armed resistance and to act as an underground government in German-occupied northern Italy. Representatives of these movements were then incorporated into the king's government in June 1944, after the Allied liberation of Rome. Both the Italian Social Republic and the anti-Fascist resistance refused to recognize the legitimacy of the king, and justified their own legitimacy as representing Italy on the basis of his treachery at the armistice, where he had betrayed respectively the German ally and the Italian people.

In this light, it is just tendentious to want to argue that the 8 September armistice meant the end of the Italian nation. Those who do so are really lamenting the passing of a particular version of the nation, the conservative nationalist one. Arguably, not even the Fascist version of the nation, nationalistic, racist, imperialist, totalitarian, had died or been killed off in late 1943. It survived in an attenuated and less than independent form, in the RSI. What the armistice entailed, was, finally, the opening up of the succession to Fascism which should have or might have occurred after the fall of Mussolini in July 1943. The effect of the armistice was to lead to a contest between different ideas of nation and nationhood, in a country which was divided by more than invading and occupying foreign armies. It was not the end of the nation, but a battle for the nation.

# 6

# The Invasion and Occupation of Italy, and the Kingdom of the South, 1943–1945

I N spring 1943, General Sir Bernard Montgomery, commander of the British Eighth Army, gave an order to the head of MI9, the military intelligence service responsible for escaped prisoners of war in Axis-occupied Europe, which in turn was to be communicated secretly to the camps in northern and central Italy which were holding over 85,000 captured Allied servicemen. The instruction was to the effect that in the event of an Italian surrender, Allied POWs should 'keep fit and stay put' and await the arrival of Allied troops.[1] In the actual event of the Italian armistice of 8 September 1943, and in light of what happened afterwards, this was rather stupid advice. But at the time it was made, the order reflected a confidence among Allied military commanders that Italy could be easily and rapidly conquered and occupied. Apparently, their military plans anticipated that after crossing from Sicily to Calabria on the mainland in September 1943, the Allied forces would take the Italian capital city by Christmas 1943 and the rest of the country by the summer of 1944.

In the event, Allied forces spent the Christmas of 1943 stalled at the first of the Germans' major defensive lines, the Gustav Line, straddling south central Italy from the Mediterranean to the Adriatic, which protected Rome and prevented the Allies from relieving the beleaguered Allied bridgehead south of Rome, at Anzio. Rome was not liberated from German occupation until June 1944. During the summer of 1944, Allied forces liberated much of central Italy. But the advance was already slowing down again by the autumn before the Gothic Line, another German fortified defensive line thrown across Italy from near Pisa, on the Tuscan Mediterranean coast, to near

Rimini on the Adriatic coast. There were advances, but no complete breakthrough, in the ensuing battles on the Gothic Line, and Allied forces spent another winter in neutral gear, this time south of Bologna and the Po valley. The rest of central and northern Italy was liberated in the spring of 1945.

There were political, strategic, and military reasons which explain why Italy, in Churchill's phrase, 'the soft underbelly of the Axis', turned out to be a 'tough old gut', in the words of US General Mark Clark, commanding the American Fifth Army in Italy. Churchill, already thinking of the political shape of post-war Europe, was all for pushing hard in the Italian war and getting Allied troops into central and south-eastern Europe to pre-empt Soviet armies advancing from the east. For President Roosevelt, however, and his military commanders, the only 'second front' which would satisfy Stalin and the USSR and win the war against Nazi Germany was the invasion of continental Europe from the west through France. While never losing his enthusiasm for the Italian campaign, Churchill was obliged to recognize that the Allied priority was the planning and implementation of the Normandy landings in France, which took place in June 1944.

Certainly, after the Allied taking of Rome in June 1944, the Italian theatre of war was absolutely secondary to the invasion of France. The main Allied commanders, Eisenhower and Montgomery, had already, in December 1943, left Italy to others and assumed command of the 'Overlord' campaign. Seven divisions of Allied troops were withdrawn from Italy after the taking of Rome, to participate in landings in southern France, and were barely replaced by newly formed Italian army units. The Italian campaign was now even less important than the minor Allied invasion of southern France.

Allied commanders in Italy were slow to recognize and tap the military contribution which a growing Italian armed resistance to German occupation could make to the liberation of central and northern Italy—as slow, in fact, as the laborious military advance up the peninsula from north to south. There is evidence to suggest that during the late summer and autumn of 1944, partisan bands harassed retreating German forces in coordination with Allied advances, until partisan and Allied fronts converged. Allied support to the Italian partisans, in the shape of intelligence agents, special operations forces, and drops of equipment and weapons, only reached and benefited a relatively small proportion of partisan formations. From the autumn of 1944, help to the Italian partisans slowed down and was diverted to internal resistance movements which were then of greater military significance to the Allied war and which seemed to be doing a more effective job in driving out the German occupier, whether in France, Yugoslavia, or Greece.

Field Marshall Sir Harold Alexander, the Allied forces commander in Italy, had foolishly informed the Italian partisans in November 1944 that the exhausted Allies were taking a winter break on the Gothic Line, and advised them to disband and suspend their operations until the renewal of the Allied offensive in the spring. The Germans and the Fascists were aware of the announcement, which practically invited their forces to move against the partisan movement in a concerted way, knowing that it would be the only enemy they would have to fight over the winter. Alexander at least acknowledged his mistake by attempting to restore Allied material support to the Italian armed resistance and shore it up until the offensive could be resumed. But the whole disastrous episode showed how little the Allies thought of the Italian resistance at this point, and how little they thought of the Italian campaign. In 1944–5, the point of the war in Italy became holding down German forces there and so preventing German reinforcement of the main fighting fronts in France and eastern Europe.

The Allied decision not to commit themselves fully to the war in Italy, matched the Germans' decision to make a defensive stand there. Encouraged by the containment of Allied landings at Salerno in September 1943, Hitler decided not to follow Rommel's plan to withdraw German forces to the Alps and, instead, backed the (then) air force commander Kesselring's strategy of fighting over everything in Italy and to defend in depth and delay the Allied advance for as long as possible. The outcome of these corresponding strategic decisions was a kind of military parity in the Italian war. The Allies had almost complete air superiority, but could not always make it count, since bombers and fighters had to operate over mountainous terrain and sometimes could not operate at all, kept on the ground by the exceptionally bad weather which marked the successive autumns and winters of 1943–4 and 1944–5. Even if they had wanted to commit more effort and resources to the war in Italy, the Allies would have found it logistically difficult to do so. As it was, they faced problems in supplying and backing up their forces by sea, since they used southern ports which they had to clear of German mines and scuttled ships and to repair from the effects of their own bombing raids of 1940 to 1943.

A lengthening occupation of the south by the Allies and of the north by the Germans was also both cause and effect of a military stalemate. By the 1944–5 winter, armies of about 600,000 Allied troops nominally confronted German armies of around 500,000 men. But most troops on both sides were behind the front lines in occupied territory, as reinforcement and for control of the territorial hinterland to the actual areas of fighting. In terms of real fighting forces, perhaps 40,000 German troops faced about 70,000 Allied troops. Such a balance of forces was unlikely to produce a rapid, decisive breakthrough. German forces were never routed in battle. They generally withdrew in reasonably good order to planned and prepared defensive lines across the country, elongated 'trenches' from which they could stabilize the fighting front.

The German armies fought a well-organized and tenacious defensive war in Italy, exploiting the mountainous terrain of the Appennines and the lousy weather to slow down the Allied advance. Both sides used their vehicles to get their infantry to the front lines, and then fought on foot. The Allies preceded their infantry offensives with lengthy and sustained bombardment, from the air (where this was possible) and from land. With heavy autumn rains in both 1943 and 1944 churning up mountain tracks into mud and further reducing the pace and momentum of the war, it was little wonder that British officers and men felt that they were reliving the static attritional campaigns of the First World War. A fusilier on the river Volturno, near Capua, north of Naples, in late 1943, was clearly demoralized by 'a steady, drenching rain which in no time produced inches of water in the bottom of the slit trenches'.[2]

The opposing armies were both multinational affairs. The Germans had Italians, Czechs, Russians, Ukrainians, and Cossacks fighting for them. But the Axis forces in Italy were Eurocentric in comparison with the Allied 'United Nations', who were a global village of black and white troops from the British and French empires and from the USA, including a segregated American Negro division. There was a large Polish contingent, some Belgians, Greeks, Danes, Hungarians, Russians, Czechs, Austrians, and, of course, Italians. There were even a Palestinian Jewish force, some Egyptians, and a Brazilian expeditionary force.

The problems encountered in the liaison between and coordination of the multinational Allied forces might well have also slowed down the Allied advance, since the commanders could deploy them to fight alongside each other, but could not really mix them up if circumstances suggested it. A British officer recalled how he was ordered to take the bridge at Pontecello, near Cesena, in Emilia, central Italy, in October 1944. The Polish liaison officer failed to show up, and having started the operation on their own, the British troops eventually 'found the Poles, and, after a feverish and comic conversation in French, confirmed where we were on the map...and where the enemy was'.[3] Such incidents were probably common enough. But it is difficult to say how many more lives were lost, how much less ground was gained, how much more time was wasted, as a result of these linguistic obstacles.

Those most affected by the multinational composition of the Allied forces were likely to have been the Italians, who found themselves being liberated by the rest of the world. They witnessed a passing and sometimes frightening pageant of different peoples in uniform, including Americans, British, New Zealanders, Canadians, South Africans (black and white), Rhodesians, Indian Sikhs, Afghans, Nepalese, and Free French forces largely made up of white French-officered black and arab troops from Senegal, Morocco, and Algeria. It was certainly confusing. Some of the inhabitants of liberated villages in the province of Pesarò-Urbino, in south central Italy, recalled the black troops in their midst as being Senegalese, when these West African soldiers were never on their section of the front line. Some of the people around Cassino remembered the rape and pillage by Moroccan troops after the eventual fall of what remained of the town in May 1944, in particularly blood-curdling and stereotypically racist terms. The Fascist Italian Social Republic certainly tried to extract what advantage it could from the invasion of the country by such a polyglot force. Much of its poster propaganda exploited the racially composite character of the Allied enemy forces, though it was usually the image of the American Negro soldier which was employed to represent the threat to European civilization posed by what was portrayed as a racially hybrid and degenerate invading extra-European army.

The prolonging of the war in Italy, and its grinding nature, had very dramatic repercussions for the Italian people. The war of 1940 to 1943 had touched practically every family in the country, self-evidently because of the conscription to military service of husbands, sons, and brothers. Cities were bombed, and people evacuated them, sometimes permanently, but usually commuting between city and countryside. As the Fascist regime's control of the home front broke down, people's lives and livelihoods were shredded by shortages of food and fuel, rationing, and recourse to the black market.

All these detrimental facets of wartime civilian life continued, as the war continued, between 1943 and 1945. But the situation was worse, because Italy was now itself a battlefield. The war moved from south to north in destructive waves, as the front and the armies passed through both countryside and town.

Peripheral rural areas which had not seen or experienced a war or invasion for centuries, now went through the most terrifying modern war, where civilians, if not exactly combatants, occupied the front line of fighting and were treated as combatants by both armies in the war zones. 'We thought we were right in the wolf's mouth,' recalled a woman in Portomaggiore, near Ferrara, in north-eastern Italy, as the Eighth Army approached in early April 1945.[4]

Between 1943 and 1945, the war arrived in areas of the country which had not been affected physically and materially by the war of 1940 to 1943. Some towns and cities were bombed from the air by the Allies for the first time, and then regularly, for as long as the war lasted for them. Padua, for instance, a city just south-west of Venice, suffered its first Allied air raid on 16 December 1943, and then twelve more, until its liberation from German occupation in March 1945. Nine out of every ten buildings in the city were damaged or destroyed. Padua was a target because it was on a main railway line, had a military garrison there, and as a relatively large urban area was an administrative and services centre for that part of Venetia. In destroying it, the Allies destroyed the infrastructure of German occupation.

But the war also came to Sant'Alberto di Ravenna, a village in the low-lying marshlands around Ravenna in east central Italy, which had absolutely no objective military and strategic importance at all. It was only a target for three Allied bombardments by air and by land artillery in December 1944 and January 1945 because it was in the way of the Allied front. The laborious progress of the fighting and the tenacity of German military resistance involved the war coming not once, but twice, to this provincial backwater. Having retreated from the village in December 1944 when its loss to Canadian troops appeared imminent, the German forces were able to return for another month of occupation because the Allied advance was held up elsewhere. As the Canadians gradually fought their way into the village in mid-January 1945, the evacuating villagers were caught in cross-fire and counter-attacks. Those fleeing included people who had earlier evacuated to the village from the provincial capital, Ravenna.

The slow advance of the military war also meant that many parts of the country experienced two waves of foreign occupation. Just two provinces, Brindisi and Lecce, in the deep south-east of the country, which together constituted what there was of the 'Kingdom of the South' in September 1943, avoided any real kind of German occupation. Italy's two major north Italian cities, Milan and Turin, were occupied continuously by the Germans from the armistice of September 1943 until the liberation of late April 1945. In between, there were two sets of occupation of varying durations. Naples was occupied by the Germans until early October 1943 and then by the Allies until 1946. Rome was occupied by the Germans until June 1944, then by the Allies. Florence was occupied by the Germans from September 1943 to August 1944, thereafter by the Allies. Zara, the ex-Italian enclave on the Yugoslav Adriatic coast, was occupied by the Germans from September 1943 until the end of October 1944, and then by Tito's partisans.

It was certainly the case that the Germans, as opposed to the Allies, were never seen as liberators. But it cannot be assumed that, initially anyway, Allied occupation was more benign than German, or that conditions for the population improved significantly from one occupation to another. This was partly because the conduct of both German and Allied occupying armies was driven by the same logic of invasion and occupation, to control the territory in pursuit of the priority for them of waging the war. In a slow-moving war, the Allies had to administer liberated areas which were still close to the front lines, and as a result, felt that they had to try to control everything.

So the Germans forcibly evacuated the population of Pesarò, a town on the Adriatic coast in September 1944, as the Allied armies approached and the area became an active war zone. After the front line passed, the Allied military administration maintained the evacuation of the coastal port sections of the town and prevented people from returning to their homes, which were requisitioned for use by Allied troops and officials in areas regarded by the Allied commanders as still militarily and strategically sensitive. The continuation of German systems of occupation was one reason, among others, why the leader of Pesarò's provisional local council complained that Allied liberation was turning into Allied occupation, hence alienating popular sympathies.

It was hardly to be expected that Allied occupation would make much initial difference to the wartime conditions in which people lived. The Allied military government in liberated areas inherited a physical and psychological terrain devastated by the effects of war and German occupation. In other words, the war continued, even though the war had moved on. In Umbria and the Marches, regions largely liberated by Allied forces in the course of the summer and early autumn of 1944, the local people continued to provision themselves throughout the following winter by making long, regular hikes on foot by mountain paths in bad weather, carrying sacks of grain on their backs and heads. Much of this self-provisioning was smuggling, of course. The prefect of Pescara province estimated in

April 1945 that over half the provincial population were living off the black market and illegal trading. The army of smugglers were mainly small peasant farmers who, partly because of war damage to their land and the uncleared and still dangerous debris of war, were unable to farm and produce enough for subsistence or the black market. To survive, they had turned to trading in rather than supplying the black market.

The persistence of the black economy was, indeed, the mark of the essential continuity of the war in Italy. Successive governments and successive occupations in both the south and north of the country attempted to regulate the production, supply, and distribution of basic foodstuffs to consumers. Peasants everywhere, whatever the government or occupation regime, went on evading the requirement to supply a good proportion of their crops at officially set prices to public deposits, whatever their guise as Fascist *ammassi* or non-Fascist 'granaries of the people'. They did so because prices were always higher on unofficial markets, which consumers increasingly had to resort to if they were to feed themselves at all.

South central and central Italy between the two main German defensive lines, the Gustav Line and the Gothic Line, was the most fought-over territory of the Italian war from the winter of 1943–4 to the winter of 1944–5. The fighting was heavy, and the Allied advance was often laborious. It took six weeks, in August and September 1944, for the Allied forces to fight their way from Ancona, a port city on the Adriatic, to Pesarò, 40 miles on, partly because of the problem they had to confront all along the eastern coast. They were advancing from the south to the north across rivers which ran to the coast from west to east.

To be a civilian in the actual fighting zone was terrifying. Everybody was vulnerable, especially those who were already so. The psychiatric hospital at Volterra, a Tuscan hill town near Siena, was hit during a bombardment in July 1944, inducing panic among the nursing staff whose charges included over 450 increasingly agitated criminally insane patients. It was usually just as bad to be in the immediate hinterland of the fighting zones, especially on the German side of the war. This was because German forces beat very aggressive retreats and intensified their occupation methods to ensure total territorial control of the areas just behind the front. A peasant farmer, forced by the Germans to leave his home with his family and lodgers, evacuees from Pesarò, described what the soldiers did to the land which had been in his family's possession for over two hundred years, in order to construct and protect an anti-tank ditch

3. The people of Rionero in Vulture, Potenza, in southern Italy, grieve the killing of fifteen hostages by retreating German troops in late September 1943. The sign on the wooden cross says, 'to the martyrs of Nazi-Fascist savagery'.

on Monte Cabbate, near Pesarò: 'the area to the north and south of the ditch was mined with anti-personnel and anti-vehicle explosive ordnances. In these areas, all the vegetation was cut down to make the advancing troops more visible. The houses of the local peasants, scattered along the line of the ditch, were blown up with large amounts of explosive.'[5] The family returned to their land once the fighting had passed through, and some of them were injured by mines awaiting clearance, in November 1944. The massacres of civilians by German troops which occurred should really be seen as part of the military campaign to secure an area totally. This was the aim and effect of the 'march of death' of the German SS armoured division which started and ended with massacres at Sant'Anna di Stazzema in August 1944 and at Marzabotto in October, brutally pacifying the Tuscan and Emilian countryside inland from Pisa on the western extremity of the Gothic Line.

The intensity of the fighting meant that the physical devastation of war was enormous. In the province of Chieti, in Umbria, central Italy, a quarter of the towns and villages, including Ortona, were literally razed to the ground as the front passed through. On liberation in June 1944, there were over 72,000 homeless people in the province. Whole areas were rendered impassable and incommunicable as a result of the physical damage to the roads, railways, and telegraph lines. Normal economic life was disrupted, not only for the period of the fighting, but afterwards as well. Mills and bakeries did not function, because owners and workers were too afraid to risk going to work, electricity supplies were interrupted or cut off altogether, and grain and flour could not

4. A British army photograph showing an evacuee carrying her belongings returning to the ruins of her home town, Ortona, on the Adriatic coast south of Pescara, in late 1943.

be produced or delivered. The planting and harvesting of crops had to be delayed or could not take place at all, again because farmers did not want to work in the open or could not properly farm damaged or mined fields. The Germans, for instance, laid nearly 10,000 mines in the valley between Pesarò on the coast and the Renaissance new town of Urbino inland, which was the province's main area of agricultural production. On liberation, it was initially impossible either to produce or distribute foodstuffs, and, indeed, for the Allied occupation authorities actually to reach some villages badly damaged in the fighting.

Much can and should be made of the differences in the experiences of people living in the north and the south of the country between 1943 and 1945. But much should also be made of the similarity in people's circumstances as the war moved north.

When Allied troops entered Naples early in October 1943, on the back of the famous 'Four Days' of popular risings against German occupation, it was the largest city to be liberated in Axis-controlled Europe. It also became the Italian city which had the longest period of Allied occupation, from October 1943 until January 1946. Much of the surrounding region of Campania was returned to Italian governmental administration fifteen months earlier. This was how Mario Palermo, the Communist Party leader in Naples, saw his city at the point of liberation:

> there was no water, no electric light, no foodstuffs of any kind, no means of public transport. Rubble obstructed the streets. Unburied dead bodies, devastated factories, people without jobs, and tens of thousands, thousands and thousands of disbanded soldiers, bombed-out houses, while the others, the best of them, were requisitioned by the Allies as offices and residences. Fishing was banned. The port half-destroyed, full of vessels of every kind. And in this picture of squalor, desolation, and chaos, thousands and thousands of soldiers from all over the place, Americans, English, Canadians, Brazilians, Indians, Moroccans, Poles, French, Algerians, who wandered through our streets looking for adventure and entertainment. The black market which they encouraged was operating at full steam. Prices increased to giddy heights. Prostitution was spreading.[6]

Much of what happened in Naples under Allied occupation had already occurred on a smaller scale in the naval port of Taranto, on the heel of Italy, taken over by a polyglot Allied force on the day after the armistice, on 9 September 1943, without any German occupation. Both port cities enjoyed a precarious and volatile dependence on an occupying force which became the major, almost the only, source of legal and illegal employment. Taranto was used to repair damaged Italian and Allied shipping, and both ports supplied and reinforced the fighting front and provided rest and recreation for tens of thousands of multinational Allied troops. The long stalemate on the front at Cassino during the 1943–4 winter had the effect of bottling up Allied troops in Naples and extending their stay in the city. The reliance of Naples' social and economic life on Allied occupation was so marked that a visiting Italian official reported to his political masters in the Bonomi-led government in March 1945 that 'what people fear most is the end of the war'.[7]

The new dimension which the presence of Allied troops brought to the cities of the occupied mainland south was an incredible spending power, which fuelled both inflation and the black market economy. Both phenomena existed before the arrival of Allied troops. But inflation rocketed and the black market expanded exponentially after liberation. It was estimated that up to the liberation of Rome in June 1944, nearly 40 per cent of all spending in liberated areas of the south was being done by Allied occupation troops. On the island of Sardinia, where, as we have seen, German troops evacuated quickly for Corsica after the armistice, and where there was no Allied occupation to follow, price levels were under half of what they were in the liberated mainland south.

What combined with Allied purchasing power to send prices to the skies were continued shortages and need in the city's population. In a move which was both laughable and serious at the same time, the Allied administration's insensitive and misfiring contribution to the food needs of the city was the distribution of a ghastly soup powder made of peas, which no Neapolitan could cook or actually wanted to eat. The Allied authorities miscalculated that a largely agricultural southern economy would enable the liberated areas to be self-sufficient in food. But even though the fighting had stopped, producing and marketing foodstuffs which met Italian eating patterns and dietary needs, were inhibited by the lasting wartime damage to land and infrastructure. The Allies were obliged to import food through the port to feed the city. The same wartime transport and communication difficulties which continued to isolate Naples from the rest of the south, also made the newly printed Allied occupa-tion money, the 'am.lira', an exclusively Neapolitan currency. Am.lira notes which were intended to facilitate trade and exchange throughout the liberated south, stayed and circulated in the city, giving another kick to inflation.

So plenty met scarcity in Naples. The Allied troops were supplied in abundance and had a generous surplus to trade in a city which needed to live and provide for itself. The bulging Allied depots at the port, and the large supplies of goods of all descriptions passing through the city, were inviting targets for theft, diversion, corruption, smuggling, and illegal trading. These activities eventually bound together Allied officials and troops and the city's population in complicit self-sustaining networks of low-level criminality.

The writer Norman Lewis was a British intelligence officer in Naples with the impossible job of policing British forces in the city and their multiple daily contacts with the local population. He recorded in his diary for 18 April 1944 a report by the Allied military administration's propaganda and 'culture' branch, the Psychological Warfare Bureau (PWB), that 65 per cent of the Neapolitans' per capita income came from dealing in stolen Allied supplies, and that a third of all imported supplies and equipment found their way on to the black market. Whatever the accuracy of the estimates, they denoted the extent of the phenomenon, which Lewis himself confirmed by being drawn into the system himself. Dispatched to police Benevento, a town about 40 miles inland from Naples, with a bunch of gung-ho and drunken Canadian military policemen, he obtained from a friendly pharmacist in Naples the drugs which his main Italian informant needed but could not obtain on prescription or otherwise in Benevento. The chemist 'had every drug known to modern medicine, and I knew where his abundant supplies came from'.[8]

Since the black market was, effectively, the only market which worked in the city, and was at the heart of the interaction between the Allied occupiers and the occupied population, one might regard it as a humanitarian crime wave, crime with a human face. But here, as elsewhere, the black market had very distorting and dysfunctional economic and social effects.

In repairing and reopening the port, the Allies were soaking up much of the unemployment caused by the wartime collapse of the city's industries. But pay was, relatively, still low, certainly in black market conditions. Lewis wrote that an ordinary British soldier earned more than an Italian foreman in the naval shipyards. Working for the Allies obtained a ration card for a worker and his family. But many people could only survive by getting involved in the black market as well, often stealing and dealing in the goods they came across in their Allied workplaces. The employment agencies set up by the Allied administration to manage the city's workforce were kept busy by a constant turnover in labour. It was unheard of for workers to stay at their jobs for more than a week. Only one in five workers stayed on to the next day, and many simply faded away from the work site after the distribution of the daily meal.

The lethal combination of scarcity in the midst of plenty, of urban poverty with Allied troops flush with money and time on their hands, encouraged the spread of an informal and unprofessional prostitution. Lewis recorded another PWB statistic that 42,000 women in Naples, out of a nubile female population of about 150,000, were regularly or occasionally prostitutes, a figure he regarded as 'incredible',[9] and not because he doubted whether it could be true. In his work in the city, he came across both the lighter and darker sides of the phenomenon. He was responsible for vetting young Italian women who wanted to marry British servicemen, and had to test the credibility of the relationship by checking whether they were prostitutes or not. If they lived in poor and squalid districts and yet had food stocks in clean and well-looked-after apartments, the assumption was that they were living off immoral earnings. He also, by his own accounts, was personally approached several times by young women or their pimping mothers and fathers, offering sex 'for a good square meal once a day'.[10] The fact that these young Neapolitan women were driven to sell their bodies out of personal and family need, in order to obtain what was otherwise unobtainable, made their work essential to family survival and so, presumably, tolerable to their parents and siblings.

But widespread prostitution could threaten the cosy market-driven sociability which was developing between occupying Allied troops and the city's poor. Lewis records being called out to handle an ugly confrontation involving 'mobs of youths' who were attacking and humiliating local girls walking out with Allied soldiers, and beating up their Allied boyfriends. By the time they had armed themselves and reached the scene of the trouble, 'the storm had come and passed . . . All the local black market activities, involving the sale of American cigarettes, articles of military clothing and food, were being carried on with absolute normality . . . a drunken American negro slept in a flower bed. We could go home.'[11]

One wonders whether this heady symbiosis of a city and its occupiers had any lasting effects on Neapolitan and Italian culture and life. The unbalanced, frenetic, and false prosperity of a black market economy lasted long enough. But it was temporary, and bound to be so. The urban poor had shared in the 'good life' for a while, and been exposed to the consumerist civilization of the Western Allies. This was one reason why Italians' memories of Allied occupation tended to concentrate on US soldiers especially, whose spending power and consumption were considerably higher than British troops', even though British officials and soldiers had a bigger role in the Allied occupation and administration of liberated Italy.

Even living for twenty years under Fascism, Italians were well aware of the USA as the epitome of a better material life. The myth of the land of plenty was conveyed to them by the experience of mass emigration to the United States. But the emigrant model of material wealth being secured by hard graft and sacrifice hardly fitted the reality in wartime Naples of an impoverished city population feeding off the spending sprees of young soldiers on leave. The feel of an American consumerist society was passed on rather better in the Hollywood film romances and their home-grown imitators which filled out the cinemas of 1930s Fascist Italy. It figured, indeed, in the Fascist regime's own wartime propaganda, which attempted to elevate a materially poor but ideologically armed Italian people above a materially endowed but spiritually degenerate enemy, 'blood' over 'gold'. It was, of course, the gold which appealed and attracted, and which won the war. One cannot imagine more counterproductive propaganda than this.

It was not really until the so-called economic miracle of the 1950s, when the country's politics were moulded by the cold war division of Europe into Eastern and Western blocs, that Italy adopted, or adapted, US-style consumerism, or at least, put itself in a position to do so. The economic miracle finally built in self-sustained economic growth, belatedly fulfilling the dreams of the American Marshal Aid planners of the late 1940s who filtered US post-war aid to Western Europe, including Italy. Marshal Plan posters declared to southern peasants that 'you, too, can be like us'.[12]

If the Neapolitans learned anything from the experience of Allied occupation, it was dependence. The Allies were the people's new and powerful patrons in straitened wartime circumstances. Naples voted to retain the monarchy in the 1946 referendum, and elected monarchists to the post-war Italian parliament and city council. Their populist, welfarist, clientelistic hold on the city's poor most resembled the parasitic dependence of the wartime occupation period.

Once it was liberated in June 1944, Rome never quite developed the same rapport with the Allied occupying forces as Naples did. After Naples and what lay between Naples and Rome, the Roman cityscape must have appeared really strange to Allied troops, because its status as a so-called Open City under German occupation had protected it from war-inflicted damage. The only ruins were those of ancient Rome. The Lazio region around Rome had, however, been a war zone and was badly damaged in the fighting, which helped to account for the influx of over 200,000 refugees and evacuees into the city after its liberation. The incomers' swelling of the population to about three million was one of the most evident signs that the city was at war, along with a collapsing infrastructure and an estimated 300,000 unemployed. Like Naples, the city initially had only precarious transport links with its sources of food supply. Nevertheless, its liberation temporarily worsened the food situation in Naples, as southern agricultural producers and suppliers chased a better market in the capital. The single railway line to Naples took freight and military traffic, but only in January 1945 did the first passenger train leave from Rome for Naples. The 120-mile journey took twelve hours.

One interesting thing about the Allied occupation of Rome was the way in which, very rapidly, the economic situation worsened to match that in occupied Naples. This, in fact, was a feature of the Allied liberation of the south. Conditions of life in the already liberated areas spread or were carried into the newly liberated areas. The introduction of the occupation currency, the am.lira, and the ever wider ramifications of the black market which accompanied occupation, pushed prices sky-high and involved practically the whole population in the black economy, whether as consumers, wholesalers, or more characteristically, as the small traders who dealt in tiny amounts of foodstuffs and goods, not as a matter of gain but of subsistence.

The unemployed and near-destitute people living in the city's new suburbs or *borgate* had been moved out of their city centre Renaissance slums when these were demolished to clear the space for the Fascist regime's imperialist-minded town planning projects during the 1930s. These were marginalized suburban communities whose 'community spirit' was engendered and sustained by their own very high levels of petty banditry, crime, prostitution, and black marketeering, all activities designed to cause as much trouble as possible for the authorities. During the nine months of German control of the city, the criminal anti-authority activities of the suburban gangs could almost be construed as resistance to Nazi occupation. But in January 1945, the leader of one of the *borgate* gangs, known by his nickname or *nom de guerre*, 'the hunchback of Quarticciolo', was killed in a shoot-out with police, and this time, his criminality was no longer regarded as patriotic.

The acclimatization of the city to what conditions were like in the rest of liberated southern Italy was probably the reason why Rome's substantial middle-class and lower-middle-class white-collar population never took to the Allied occupation. In Naples, the people felt that the Allied occupiers were their new defenders and saviours, the solution to their problems of wartime survival. In Rome, people tended to see the Allies as the cause, or the aggravation, of the city's wartime problems. The fact that the mainly resolutely English-speaking and self-contained Allied military administration was not a big local employer, added to the Romans' resentment.

The Allied officials were not particularly sociable. Sponsored by the PWB, British and American artists, poets, and musicians came to work, perform, and be in the city. Young and hungry Roman intellectuals, and would-be intellectuals, gatecrashed their gatherings, for the food and drink as much as the culture. One of them recalled listening to a reading by the Welsh poet Dylan Thomas, though it was probably more of a slurring than a reading: 'he was completely

5. Meeting of cultures: Scottish soldiers wearing their tartan kilts examine the Coliseum in Rome in June 1944, while a Roman woman examines their dress.

drunk, always'.[13] Most of the city's musical and cultural events during the Allied occupation were organized by the occupiers for the occupiers, British, American, and other Allied troops and officials. It was not exactly the case that interaction with the locals was banned. This happened in Taranto, where eventually Allied troops were barred from entering the city centre. But interaction was not exactly encouraged, and for this reason, among others, Rome never warmed to its occupation.

In the summer of 1944, twenty German divisions were retreating across Umbria, the Marches, and Tuscany towards the Gothic Line. On the eastern edge of the Gothic Line was the coastal town of Pesarò, which was to become, in German plans, a kind of trench. Local communities immediately to the north and south of Pesarò came under intense pressure from German forces. Reinforcements poured into the villages to the north. Local men were press-ganged on threat of death and reprisal to transport equipment and munitions on their oxen and carts, and to work to German orders on preparing trenches, fortifications, and shelters, or sabotaging the area's infrastructure.

Similar German round-ups of local men and their cattle to carry munitions occurred in Mombaraccio, an inland agricultural commune, but at a later stage, when the first fighting hit the area in late August 1944. Preparatory to the fighting and, again, in an attempt to clear a war zone, German troops and Italian police of the Fascist Republic took to the hills to root out the local partisan band, formed in March from Mombaraccio peasants evading the Republic's military call-up. In June, the band had ambushed and killed a few German soldiers, and captured and executed a man who was probably known to them, since he was born in Mombaraccio and had returned from working in Milan to act as a guide and interpreter for German forces in the area.

To the south, the inhabitants of the small town of Marotta, about halfway between Ancona and Pesarò, were chased out of their homes by a company of Russian soldiers in the German army, who billeted themselves in the local Catholic orphanage.

Pesarò itself, with a peacetime population of about 50,000, was a reception area for evacuated people. From late 1942, the town received a huge influx of evacuees from Rome, Naples, and other bombed southern cities, and of the families of military and civilian officials and emigrants repatriated from Italy's now defunct East African empire. They lived without jobs and on welfare in the town's hotels and guesthouses.

The town suffered its first Allied bombing raid in November 1943, inducing a first movement of people from the town to the surrounding countryside. In January 1944, the Germans publicly warned the inhabitants that they could order the total evacuation of the coastal zone to a depth of 10 km (6.2 miles) to take place within two days. The town's public offices and officials were transferred and dispersed to inland communes, while the 'new' provincial capital became Urbino, its own population now increasing by a third to over 30,000. The German warning had itself encouraged a more or less managed, if voluntary, further evacuation of many of Pesarò's population, mainly to communes on the outskirts of the town.

Then, finally, in June 1944, the Germans ordered the complete evacuation of the town and the coastal zone, and this time, it was everybody for themselves. The evacuation order posted on the town and village walls gave no real indication as to where the evacuees should go, and since there was no transport or fuel available, people had to evacuate on their own, 'even on foot'.[14] The prefect's advice was to head south, in other words, towards the Allied lines. But he recognized that this could not be a planned evacuation, because of the previous more or less spontaneous evacuations, which had saturated the province. The evacuation of Pesarò had, then, repercussions throughout the province, which was now being criss-crossed by long columns of homeless people looking for somewhere to stay. Mombaraccio, with a population of about 4,000, had, in fact, been designated by the prefecture as an obligatory evacuation zone for Pesarò after the German warning in January 1944. Its population now reached twice its normal size, with the arrival of a new wave of refugees.

The Germans, again as common practice in areas which were becoming war zones, stripped, plundered, and transferred by rail to the north, the machinery, raw materials, and stocks of Pesarò's two main factories. One of them was Benelli's, a motorcycle manufacturer converted to war production, making bikes for the army and motor parts for the air force. The other was a metallurgical manufacturing plant owned by Montecatini, a huge industrial corporation. The Benelli management had attempted to save and hide what they could before the Germans arrived to dismantle and then mine the factory. But, again characteristically, the Germans kidnapped and held a Benelli brother as hostage, and the location of the caches of equipment had to be revealed.

The Germans had demanded a total evacuation, and it had been total. After the Allies had liberated the town, the military government's census in

October 1944 counted one hundred people still living there. The enforced evacuation, here as elsewhere, was the German attempt to clear and control the area for military operations. In this case, by pushing the town's population inland, they had created what they might well have wanted to avoid in a war zone. The province was now teeming with a hungry, homeless, and moving population, getting in each other's way. Perhaps that was actually the intention, to expel and set on the move a mass of people who would be a kind of human shield, clogging up and complicating the Allied offensive.

The evacuations of the town before the final, definitive one, in June 1944, did, in some cases, meet a planned and organized response in the agricultural communes inland from Pesarò. Some communal administrations requisitioned houses and facilitated temporary rental agreements between evacuees and local residents, or made available public buildings and schools as reception areas for the incomers. But evacuees were a considerable financial and welfare burden for under-resourced local councils, and as the countryside filled up with each successive influx of refugees, evacuating families had to find shelter where they could on peasant farms. They often occupied the stalls and barns emptied by the German requisitioning of livestock and grain.

It is important to realize that evacuation, this unexpected and emergency interaction between town and countryside in the spring and summer of 1944, was something which was largely handled and managed by the women of both peasant and urban families. The men were usually absent, or at least, inactive, lying low and keeping out of sight, to avoid German and Republican round-ups which were intensifying as the Germans prepared to defend the area and, if necessary, retreat from it.

It was hardly surprising that the host peasant women seemed to adapt better to the new situation created by the influx of evacuees. They were, at least, on home ground, and were accustomed to mucking in with other peasant families and their relatives where circumstances required it. Evacuation, like the war generally, was another admittedly extreme emergency of peasant life, to which they had to adapt in order to survive.

For the wives of urban evacuee families, evacuation to the countryside was a distressing and disorientating experience. To the anxieties and difficulties of fleeing from Pesarò were added the problems of adaptation to a different kind of life. Cohabiting in cramped and unsalubrious conditions with unfamiliar people, other evacuees, the host peasant family, was personally and collectively uncomfortable. From their memories of the experience of evacuation, it appeared that they tried, in difficult circumstances, to transplant the separateness and privacy of the urban nuclear family to the farm courtyard. They cleaned up their own space and ate their meals on their own as a family. But it clearly did not always work. One woman recalled distastefully that it was 'a completely public kind of life'.[15]

As the person now responsible for the welfare of her evacuee family, the town wife's one daily pressing priority was to find enough food to feed the family. This was probably not very different from what was required in her previous wartime urban existence. But the context was different. 'You walked and walked if you wanted to eat,' remembered one woman,[16] and you developed your own ersatz food replacements, making bread from potatoes, and coffee and tobacco from anything. Women and their children scrumped, that is stole, fruit and vegetables from farms and fields. 'We lasted a month on pears,' recalled another woman,[17] remembering her life of exile in the countryside in the spring of 1944.

Age seemed to make a difference to how women responded to the experience of evacuation, and this was confirmed by the memories of women who evacuated from other towns in other places in 1943–4. The then girls' and young women's memories of evacuation were full of the innocence of being young and of the lack of awareness of the gravity of their situation, which weighed down the recollections of their parents. But they had a sense of how different things were, living in the countryside during the war. Their friendships were wider and more varied, as a result of families being thrown together by circumstances, and they found company and activity outside the family and, to an extent, beyond family restraints and conventions. They had a good time, in other words; no school (it was the summer, anyway), not washing or changing their clothes much, playing and gossiping in the fields with new friends, holding impromptu dances in the barns.

In the industrial town of Terni, to the north-west of Rome in central Italy, which had over one hundred Allied air raids in the ten months from August 1943 to liberation in June 1944, practically the whole population decamped to the surrounding mountainous countryside. The adults remembered the evacuation as an uncomfortable and undesirable return to nature, sleeping on the ground, eating without utensils, living with the fleas and insects in abandoned, semi-destroyed, and plundered farmsteads. For the children, it was the best of a return to nature, an extended holiday in the countryside. As one then 12-year-old girl recalled, 'every day was like a Sunday, for us'.[18]

The Balkan Adriatic port and naval base of Zara, along with Italy's north-eastern frontier provinces and the rest of Italian-occupied and Italian-held Yugoslavia, were effectively annexed to Nazi Germany after the armistice. In May 1944, the German military ordered the complete evacuation of the city because of heavy Allied bombing raids. As in Pesarò, this was an order which finalized a process of leaving the city which had started in late 1943. Zara was an Italian island in a Slav sea, and the greatest threat to the German occupation, other than Allied bombing, were Tito's Slav partisans. Zara's position as an Italian outpost in German-occupied Yugoslavia gave a definite additional frisson to the relationship between Italian evacuees and the Slav peasant families they roomed with in the countryside of the interior. In Còsino, a small town 8 km (5 miles) from Zara, overlooking the city, an Italian evacuee remembered how their Slav hosts 'slammed their right fists into the palms of their left hands, saying 'neka, neka [that's good, that's good]', as they all watched the city burn below them in the distance.[19] A well-off Italian family evacuating from their villa on the Zara seafront to one room in a house in Diklo, in the Slav hinterland to the city, had a similar experience. They recalled the locals 'witnessing the Allied bombing raids from the terraces of their houses, or standing on roofs, jubilantly applauding the columns of fire, the crashes of bombs, the curtains of dense smoke hanging heavily on the horizon'.[20]

In this case, evacuation had led to an incongruous cohabitation of Italian city dweller and Slav peasant. The fact that the Italian evacuees paid rent for their Slav lodgings undoubtedly helped; it was a deal, an arrangement, in other words. Family connections and previous acquaintance also eased the way. Rather than a place in the stalls of a farm, one Italian family, for instance, stayed in the house of the local Croat elementary schoolteacher, who was known to them because of his marriage to an Italian from Zara.

But, however inherently or potentially tense the cohabitations might have been, it was clear that some kind of mutually supportive complicity between evacuee and temporary landlord developed out of the common wartime situation which they had to find a way of coping with, and surviving. The Zara evacuees were living in rural areas which were nominally occupied and held by the Germans, but where Slav partisan bands were active. One Italian evacuee remembered that in the village where they stayed, the partisans held meetings in farmyards specifically for the re-education of Zara refugees, who were treated to what came across as menacing speeches in barely understood Croat. When the Germans periodically hit the area, looking for partisans, they similarly improvised meetings to warn people off helping the partisans, addressed to all the local inhabitants, Slav residents and Italian evacuees alike. The complicity came, in other words, from neither Slav host nor Italian evacuee doing or saying anything which could compromise the other in the eyes of either the Germans or the partisans, and hence threaten the survival of both. Several Italian evacuees remembered that their peasant families had regular contact with the partisans, even if they were not partisans themselves, and that the peasants made no attempt to hide these contacts. When you think about it, this could only mean that the peasants had confidence in the evacuees, and believed that they would remain silent in the event of a German round-up or raid.

The Pesarò urban housewives had not exactly enjoyed their evacuation to the countryside. But they had, because of wartime circumstances, become the decision makers for their families. Did this last? Did they take this wartime-induced self-confidence and sense of their own worth into post-war life? They certainly employed some of it on their immediate post-liberation or post-war return to Pesarò. Some of them got involved in the local branches of one of the Communist Party's many wartime and post-war capillary organizations, the Union of Italian Women. These functioned in Pesarò as community groups which tackled the still pressing concerns of returning families about food supplies, accommodation, welfare, and the resumption of schooling for their children. In these activities, the men remained in the background as much as they had done during the war. The women organized community fund-raising events and parties, and as one of them recalled with evident pride in her independence of her husband, 'I went dancing, even on my own if he wasn't around, and he didn't say anything about it.'[21]

The experience of evacuation and the involvement of village communities in the violent and brief front-line fighting, probably did not have the same liberating effects on the outlook and behaviour of peasant women as they did for their temporary guests from the city. The parish priest at Montmaggiore al Metauro, in August 1944 one of the villages directly on the front running along the river Metauro, which flowed from the mountains eastwards to the coast at Fano, described the Allied liberation as an exotic week-long procession, 'a dense, uninterrupted passing through of trucks, cars, sidecars, motorcycles, weapons of all kinds, with soldiers from different races and different national-ities, English, Canadian, Australian, Negroes, all in different uniforms, with different looks and behaviour'.[22] He and his fellow Catholic priests found the war deeply disturbing, or rather, deeply ambiguous. The priest of the village of Cerbera rather pathetically wondered aloud to his archbishop in July 1944 how he was to celebrate mass now that his church was full of evacuees and local people made homeless by the Germans' blowing-up of their houses. He was clearly too overtaken by events to realize that the wartime suffering of his parishioners was an opportunity to excite and strengthen their natural religiosity. In the same diocese, at Mondavio, his colleague was organizing prayer meetings and hymn singing in the local shelters.

But for the priests and their bishops, the invasions and occupations of their parishes by foreign troops in the summer of 1944 were a potential threat to religion, morality, and good order. One is naturally sceptical as to whether local people would have necessarily perceived an Allied occupying force dispensing 'lots of money, goods, entertainments, distractions',[23] in quite the same way as the bishop, who was concerned about the undermining of faith and morals in his flock. That is, until one realizes that the priests' reports to the bishop, admittedly written up to a year after the 1944 summer, all unequivocally stated that the presence of Allied troops had not encouraged sexual licence and promiscuity among the local women. The priests were not reticent in expressing their often prurient fears about the behaviour of their women around Allied soldiers, which is good reason to accept their word when they said that their female parishioners kept their distance, and their virtue.

Even the girls and young women who were living in the countryside as evacuees spoke very little about any sexual adventures in their time of relative freedom, and they certainly ruled out, in their memories anyway, dalliances with Allied soldiers. In Marotta, the parties held there by the Allied troops were for, and attended by, the female workers who came from the nearby town, Fano, to clean their vehicles, not the local women. One does get the sense from these testimonies, of priests and women alike, that the soldiers, German or Allied, were all the same, as arrogant and intrusive as the other, another unpleasant visitation which the war had brought on them, and to be coped with by remaining and holding on to what they were.

By the middle of October 1944, after battles on the Gothic Line, Allied forces were within 12 miles of the major central Italian city of Bologna, a transport and communication node for the whole country, which was close enough for them to start artillery bombardments. The Allies expected the city to fall before the winter, and so did the Germans, who from the late summer of 1944, implemented their chaotic but planned aggressive retreat and reinforcement of the new defensive position they intended to retreat to. In a pre-allocated exercise in asset stripping, German military and civilian agencies based in the city moved to plunder and destroy the area's agricultural and industrial economy. Industrial plant and raw materials were seized and moved north, as were grain stocks in the *ammassi* and the region's livestock, some of which was slaughtered, butchered, and stored, the rest herded together in special collection centres in other places. German divisions were paid a bounty for each animal they delivered to the improvised pens. Bologna was becoming a farm-yard, anyway, because the massive influx of reinforcing German troops to the province was driving peasant farmers and their families into the city with their produce and farm animals, a reverse evacuation from countryside to town. In the autumn of 1944, the planned German withdrawal from Bologna resembled a giant cattle drive out of the gates of the city.

Reinforcement German army and Waffen SS units, joined by German police, trawled the front-line areas in the hinterland and mountainous Appennines villages near the city, not only attacking partisan bands, but also rounding up able-bodied men and women for deportation to work in Germany. Over 7,000 people were captured in this attempt to clear the front line of its human resources, and the great majority of them were not partisans or those taken in specifically anti-partisan operations. The German round-ups of August 1944 paralysed the life of the province. Everything closed down, as the population, effectively, went into hiding or left for the city, deterred from their normal activity by the fear of being caught up in the German terror.

The round-ups ended, or were curtailed, in October 1944, partly because they were proving so counterproductive, with local young men joining the partisans in order to escape capture, and partly because the front had stabilized. Bologna's fall, which appeared imminent, was postponed. In Bologna itself, the German air force organized its own swoop on skilled industrial workers, and snatched eighty men to work in aircraft factories in Germany. But the effects of this raid were to stall German war production and administration in the city. Hundreds of blue- and white-collar workers absented themselves from factories and offices. Men were still sought for what was effectively forced labour, but were now mainly deployed on German work projects in northern Italy, including the building of new defensive fortifications in the neighbouring province of Ferrara. If a Bolognese agreed to work closer to home, then at least he received a ration card and some guarantee that he would not be deported to labour camps in Germany.

Since the front outside Bologna stopped at the point it had reached in October 1944, the city existed through the 1944–5 winter until the front moved again in April 1945, as an overcrowded, under-resourced, and underserviced frontier town. The Germans had planned and carried out their usual plunder in an area of imminent retreat, and many of the city's administrative offices had been transferred to the north, by the time it became clear that Bologna would not fall, yet, to the Allies. Refugees and evacuees had poured into the city, and even the famous arcades of the city centre streets were walled up to provide temporary accommodation for refugee families. And the Germans, unexpectedly, were still there, in occupation. Local manufacturing was at a standstill, because of pre-emptive German asset-stripping, and there was not much work or welfare available for a swollen labour force. There was a run on candles, in heavy demand because of the large number of families living in temporary shelter and with no electricity supply. Lacking raw materials, local producers closed down. The official price per candle was 2.10 lire in November 1944, but hardly any were available at this price; the black market price was 22 lire. The city was beleaguered from within by the Germans and from without by the Allies, existing in a precarious, dangerous, and dimly lit limbo. Germans, Fascists, and partisans were penned up together in the besieged city, which was one explanation for the desperate ferocity of the civil war being fought there during the winter of 1944–5. Reprieved by the halt of the Allied advance, Germans and Fascists hunted down partisans unable to leave the city, who responded in kind, attacking anybody in uniform.

But the towns strung along the banks of the river Senio, either side of Faenza in the province of Ravenna, went through an even crueller frontier existence during the winter of 1944–5. The front ran along the river, with Allied forces on one bank and German trenches and lines on the other. Where towns straddled the river, they straddled the front. Cotignola, a town of about 7,000 people to the north-east of Faenza, was first bombarded by Allied artillery on 29 November 1944, and then for the next 145 consecutive days. The town was on the front line for four months. Over 80 per cent of its houses were destroyed and one in ten of the population were killed or wounded. The Germans started evacuating the parts of the town they controlled in late December 1944, blowing up the houses and mining all the landmarks, including the churches. By the time the Allies crossed the river and captured the other bank, early in April 1945, their soldiers had nicknamed Cotignola 'the Cassino of Romagna', after the terrible attritional stalemate on the Gustav Line during the previous winter. As in Cassino, towards the end of the fighting, it was a case of the Allies' continual shelling destroying the ruins created by earlier bombardments.

A local priest and an impromptu council of other citizens attempted to run things, or rather, as the priest's diary put it, to confront 'times of impossible choices and sufferings. I remember the consultations, the perplexities. How were we to behave in round-ups?'[24] One can only empathize with the local family carefully feeding up the other member of the family, their pig, only to have it seized at the point of slaughter by German troops who had obviously been following the fattening process. Three days after stealing it, the German soldiers returned the pig's head to the family. Was this a gesture of humiliation, a trophy confronting the family with the thought of what they had lost, or of sympathy, since something, anyway, could be made of the head?

It was more of the same in the small spa town of Riolo Terme, west of Faenza. Constantly bombarded by artillery exchanges and constantly in a line of fire, the town was effectively cut off for days at a time. It was full of evacuees from neighbouring areas, who were forcibly evacuated, once again, by the Germans from some parts of the town. About 3,000 locals and evacuees were crammed into the town centre districts, forced to live 'a desperately troglodyte existence' in basements, ditches, the pits left in the ruins of bombed-out houses, 'at the mercy of observers in two opposed lines, who scrutinized every movement whatsoever in order to counter it'.[25] 'You lived the life of the catacombs,'[26] recalled one survivor, who knew his history. Five hundred people were killed, 250 were wounded, which was, again, about one in ten of the town's expanded wartime population.

It should be clear from this account of the passing of the military war from north to south after the armistice of September 1943, that with Italy as a battleground, the war affected practically all Italians in some way. The conditions of civilian life got progressively worse and remained poor, even after the fighting had moved on. The destructive reach of the war, whether experienced as bombing raids, evacuation, hunger, and malnutrition, or any combination of these and other damaging impacts of war, reduced life to a matter of bare survival. Those for whom life was never much more than this, anyway, had to find new ways of surviving. The war was a greater shock and challenge to those Italians who used to have a cushion in life, for whom life was not normally a question of subsistence.

The war in Italy was such a different and difficult experience for Italians that it provoked sometimes extraordinary behaviour among them. There was, above all, a very noticeable mobility of people during and as a result of the war. The countryside, especially, was just teeming with people on the move, people who belonged there and people who normally did not, many of whom were the flotsam and fugitives of war. Roaming around the countryside were soldiers of many different nationalities, as well as Italian troops, both those who had disbanded and were still on the run and those who had enlisted, or been enlisted, to fight alongside the Allies or in the armed forces of the Fascist Republic. There were Allied prisoners of war who had escaped from or simply walked out of their camps after the armistice, some of whom were trying to cross to Allied lines to the south or to neutral Switzerland in the north, while others kept moving, or sought refuge, hoping that the advancing front would reach then. There were deported central European and Balkan Jews, Slavs, and Gypsies who had similarly melted into the countryside from their camps in south central Italy after 8 September 1943. There were evacuees and people who came into the countryside on a regular basis to forage for food, smugglers, black market-eers, young men avoiding military conscription and labour service, partisan bands and those who pursued them, and all the other fugitives of war, the men of the German police and of the Fascist Republican police and militias.

The Italian countryside became a crowded and dangerous place, exposing everybody there to incongruous and incidental encounters with people from other worlds. How else, but for the extraordinary mobility caused by war, could one explain the marriages, in 1946, of three local women in the small rural commune of Cartoceto, in Pesarò province, to respectively, an ex-naval officer from Cagliari on the island of Sardinia, an ex-soldier who came from Genoa on the Ligurian Mediterranean coast, and an ex-driver in the Polish army (who could have been Polish or Italian), or the birth of a child in 1945 to the local schoolteacher, the father of whom was a German officer?

It has become fashionable in recent Italian writing on the war to draw attention to the behaviour and conduct of the silent majority of Italians. This is often done for quite tendentious reasons, to demonstrate what, in fact, was always obvious, that those who actively resisted German occupation and those who actively collaborated with it, were small minorities. Resisting or collab-orating were not how most people responded, the argument goes. Most people occupied a grey zone between resistance and collaboration, or rather, beyond resistance and collaboration. They chose to make no choice at all, to do nothing and wait out the end of the war, in a passive and non-committal way.

Such reasoning is double-edged or, at least, can be employed to do different things. It can be used to undermine the myth that the country was practically unanimous in its opposition and resistance to Nazi occupation, and that those who collaborated with the Germans were an isolated, exiguous minority. It can also be used to condemn a nation for its loss of national and collective identity. *Attendismo*, a 'wait and see' policy, negatively understood as 'a plague on all your houses' fence-sitting, was the mark of a people who had forfeited its soul and its ideals, putting the individual struggle for survival above the country's survival.

This division of the Italian people at war into active minorities and an inactive majority is also a superficially appealing one, because a non-involved wait-and-see attitude would appear to be the most likely and appropriate way in which people could hope to survive the war and, with survival being the priority, was bound to be the way out of the war adopted by the great majority of Italians. Such a view bases its credibility on what is taken to have been the actual behaviour of most people in the war between 1943 and 1945. It is, though, a misrepresentation of the reality of wartime life for many people. This was not a war people could stand aside from; the war came at them from all sides and it was impossible to separate themselves from its effects and from the demands and choices it imposed on a daily basis. To survive at all, people had to act, and react, make hard, unpalatable, inconsistent, contradictory choices from day to day, as circumstances demanded. How were people to feed themselves today, and tomorrow, and the next day? How were young and middle-aged men and their families to respond to military call-up, to labour service? How were people to respond to the presence of evacuees from the town, of an escaped Allied serviceman wanting food and shelter, of a partisan band, of a foreign or Italian Jew? How were people to respond to police and army round-ups and sweeps in their area?

One has only to think through the ramifications of, say, hostage-taking, to realize how impossible it was for ordinary people to have or adopt a wait-and-see attitude to the war and its impacts. Both sides—the RSI and the German forces, and the partisan bands—took hostages from among the civilian population. To some extent, they did so for similar reasons, to use them as prisoner exchanges or as a means of counter-reprisal, and to throw the moral responsibility for the mutual violence on to the other side. For the Germans and the RSI police, hostage-taking was also, and primarily, a crude way of controlling and terrorizing the local population, since it made the community as a whole responsible for the lives of its own people, the individual hostages, and for the presence and actions of the partisans in their area. Whatever they felt about it, hostage-taking required the community to make a choice, and the choice was a really difficult one, since how they behaved put lives at risk. This was the point of taking hostages, to involve a wider group of people in the fate of a few individuals, to make the community collectively pay for the activity of a few partisans operating among them.

It is important to realize that these choices were highly charged, intense ones for the people having to make them. Those making demands on them and demanding choices from them, the partisans, the Germans, the Fascists, always polarized the choices and made them a matter of either collaborating or resisting. The RSI required its civil servants and public employees to take an oath of loyalty to the Republic. One response of the anti-Fascist resistance organizations, the National Liberation Committees (Comitati di Liberazione Nazionale, CLNs), was to say that 'whoever swears is a traitor'. Where did that leave the civil servant wanting to keep his job and support his family? The CLNs urged people not to pay taxes to the RSI, and some wanted to punish those who did. People constantly faced tests of their loyalties, tests of which side they were on.

These were hardly situations in which people normally wanted to find themselves, or choices which people normally wanted to make. But the proliferating and corrosive effects of the war required most Italians to make such choices, some or most of the time. People had to find ways of coping and surviving in extraordinarily difficult circumstances. Their conduct and behaviour matched the extraordinariness of the times. Prostitution, petty crime, black-marketeering, resistance to or collaboration with author-ities making unpalatable demands on them, were all popular, majority activ-ities and responses, and can be regarded as part of the Italian people's wartime survival kit.

It can be said with some justification that these difficult choices of war were faced for longer and with greater intensity by people living in the north and centre of the country than people living in the south, simply because the lengthening of the war prolonged the German occupation of the centre and north. The whole argument about the grey zone of an apolitical, apathetic majority materializing between the actively resisting or collaborating minorities, has arisen from a re-evaluation of what it was really like to be in the north and centre, as opposed to the south of the country, where, it is assumed, the concept has no meaning.

It is sometimes forgotten that there was popular opposition to the brief and violent German occupation of the south in September and October 1943, in the regions of Puglia, Campania, Abruzzo, and Molise. There is some evidence that in Naples, at least, such resistance was organized or channelled by reviving anti-Fascist political parties. As in Rome, a National Liberation Front made up of Communist, Socialist, and Action Party members had existed in Naples since the downfall of Mussolini in July 1943. But the Four Days of popular disturbances in Naples between 28 September and 1 October 1943, which could pass as the city's act of self-liberation, were largely a matter of spontaneous combustion. The people were reacting against the cumulative effects of the oppressive and taxing system of German occupation, the requisitioning and plundering of the human and material resources of the city, and the policy of reprisals following any resistance to these measures, something which escalated and maintained the momentum of popular protest. An unorganized, reactive popular response to German occupation, rather than anti-Fascist party-organized opposition, also mainly characterized what resistance there was to the Germans in Lazio, the region around Rome, in late 1943 and early 1944. This kind of resistance to German occupation in the south was not, in fact, at all southern. Although there developed in the centre and north of the country a strong, organized, armed resistance to the Germans, which never really occurred in the south before Allied liberation because of the relative brevity of occupation, most popular resistance there, also, took the same forms as the civil disobedience in the south in 1943–4.

There was apparently little *Fascist* resistance to the Allied occupation of the south, in contrast with the anti-Fascist resistance to German occupation of the north. In the north, resistance to the Germans also meant resistance to the Fascist Republic, the client state installed by the Germans under Mussolini's leadership in late September 1943. The presence of the Fascist Republic gave a civil war—Italians fighting Italians—dimension to resistance in the north. Some local Fascist parties had spontaneously reformed after the armistice and offered their services to the German occupier. But the Germans always realistically envisaged that the Fascist Republic's remit would be in northern Italy. While there were undoubtedly Fascists overtaken, as it were, by the Allied invasion and occupation of the deep south in September and October 1943, organizationally, the Fascist Republic had only the time and the resources to situate itself in those parts of south central Italy which were north of the Gustav Line.

Some eighty or so Fascists were tried in one southern province, Catanzaro, for resistance to Allied occupation between October 1943 and April 1944, when the area eventually passed to the king's government. This hardly constituted a Fascist rising against the invader. But the fact that any Fascists attempted anything at all, pointed to the presence of social and political conditions which enabled a conservative restoration, rather than a democratic reconstruction, to occur in the post-war south. Peasant land agitation, combined with the impromptu and shallow formation of CLNs and anti-Fascist parties, enhanced the southern middle and landowning classes' fear of communism. The perceived threat of social revolution justified the use of the same heavy-handed and repressive handling of peasant grievances by landowners and local authorities which had characterized the Fascist and, indeed, the pre-Fascist periods. That same fear of social upheaval weakened the resolve of the Allied military government to proceed with a serious purge of local police and officials compromised by Fascism. The royal government had no resolve at all, when it came to replacing 'Fascist' state officials. The old ways, and the old personnel, were clearly the best, when it came to repressing social unrest. Southern conservatives were at one with the king's administration in projecting a lurid scenario of a liberated south apparently sliding into communist-inspired social anarchy. The neo-Fascist Italian Social Movement (Movimento Sociale Italiano, MSI), partly based its post-war revival in the south on this resurgent and largely manufactured anti-communism, and the opportunity it provided to rehabilitate Fascists and 'Fascist' officials of the old Fascist regime. In the late 1940s, the MSI was active in developing legal and welfare support groups to protect Fascists and officials from the courts and the purge commissions, as both a surrogate for and future basis of political activity.

As with German occupation of the north, the Allied occupation authorities in the south did have their own client state in the royal government of the Kingdom of the South, to which they progressively passed the administration of liberated territory. While it might have had different characteristics to anti-Fascist and anti-German resistance in the north, there was resistance of a kind in the south to Allied occupation and the king's government.

The armistice of September 1943 was not just a ceasefire agreement between the Badoglio government and the Allies. Italy was to change sides and fight alongside the Allies against Nazi Germany. Badoglio eventually declared war on Germany on 13 October 1943. It was a political as much as a military decision, needed to establish the royal government's credibility with both the Allies and the Italian anti-Fascist political parties. All sides were now united in wanting to drive the Germans out of Italy. Italy could bury the Fascist regime's alliance with Nazi Germany and, indeed, twenty years of Fascism, by fighting its way back to being, and being recognized as, a free and independent country. The declaration of war was also, very importantly, the opportunity for the king and Badoglio to redeem themselves and reaffirm a monarchical leadership of the nation, when the monarchy's standing as a patriotic and national force had been so damaged by the disaster of the armistice. The organized, armed anti-Fascist and anti-Nazi resistance movement in the north came to see itself as the one single expression and symbol of national recovery and national redemption after September 1943. It is important to recognize that there was an opportunity and a chance for this national redemption to come from the newly liberated south. The royal government, it must be said, did not appear to want to grasp the opportunity. Its reticence now was consistent with its behaviour at the time of the armistice, and with its conservative, establishment nature.

At issue was the kind and extent of the military contribution the royal government and the liberated south could make to the Allied campaign in Italy, the degree to which the south could participate in the liberation of the north. The Allies were concerned to limit the Italian military role, partly because they did not wish to see the re-emergence of armed forces which were a badge of national sovereignty and which gave real muscle and independence to the Italian government. A government with its own army could well affect and even predetermine how the Allies would dispose of an occupied Italy. The British commanders, especially, also tended to continue to regard Italy as an ex-enemy power which should be penalized for the Axis alliance and whose armed forces could not really be trusted. These were precisely the reasons why Hitler, on the other side, was reluctant to allow Mussolini a reconstituted army in the north, which would be largely recruited from the 'traitorous' Badoglian army captured and interned by the Germans after the armistice. As Field Marshal Wilhelm Keitel, chief of the Supreme Command of the German armed forces, put it, 'the only Italian army that will not betray us is an army that does not exist'.[27] The Italian military units Hitler grudgingly permitted to be formed, had to be trained and equipped in Germany, and were not usually deployed in the fighting against the Allies.

In the south, the Allies permitted the raising of an Italian force of an anticipated nearly half a million men. They were happy for the great majority of these men to be used either for internal policing and defence of liberated territory, or for servicing and service in Allied armies. But they insisted that only about 60,000 men were to be trained and equipped as separate combat units for use in the Italian campaign.

There were calls from among the anti-Fascist parties in the south, and others, for the creation of a new volunteer army in the south to fight the Germans alongside the Allies. Such a force would mark a definite break with the monarchical and Badoglian army, and would allow the incorporation of career regular army officers who were disgusted by the way the king had allowed the army to disband and disintegrate after the armistice. This view of a new Italian army was unacceptable to the Allies, who felt that such a force would escape its control, and absolute anathema to the Badoglian Italian military command because of its democratic, volunteer character.

By October 1944, there was still a shortfall of about 100,000 men on the Allied target or limit of half a million men. One explanation must be both Allied and royal scepticism about the validity and utility of raising such a force. But after the taking of Rome in June 1944, in a significant realignment encouraged by the Allies, the Italian government was broadened out to include the anti-Fascist parties, headed not by Badoglio but by Ivanoe Bonomi. He was an old politician and former prime minister from Italy's pre-Fascist and anti-Fascist liberal past, who had emerged from the shadows just before Mussolini's dismissal in July 1943 as the possible figurehead of a moderate anti-Fascist succession to Fascism. Probably only an anti-Fascist, non-monarchical government would have taken the decision to proceed with the recruitment of the remaining 100,000 men.

It was a disaster, in some ways comparable to the disaster of 8 September 1943. Essentially reflecting the compromises between the monarchy and political anti-Fascism and between moderate and more radical anti-Fascist forces which lay behind the formation of Bonomi's government, the operation was managed by a still unreconstructed military command in the conventional and traditional fashion. It was a call-up, an obligatory enlistment, conscription, in other words, not a recruitment call for volunteers. The decision to conscript, rather than recruit, was a very significant one. The government, or rather the military command, intended to raise and train a regular army of conscripts, who became soldiers because they had to, not because they wanted to. The contrast could not have been greater with the armed forces of the Resistance in the north, who were volunteers fighting not a conventional, but an irregular guerrilla, war, and who believed that they were fighting a popular anti-Fascist and anti-Nazi war with a definite idealistic and ideological component.

There was something more to the call-up of November and December 1944 than the fact that it was decided on more than a year after the king's declaration of war on Nazi Germany. The call-up papers were addressed to the young men of the south aged between 20 and 30 years old who had been in the army on 8 September 1943, and had disbanded after the armistice. The military command estimated that there were about 200,000 of them, who had made their way home in September 1943. It was not a call-up, but a recall-up.

This was probably enough to guarantee failure. The war had ended for these men over a year earlier, in ignominious circumstances and after three years of useless combat. It seemed to be an act of revenge on men who were blameless, enacted by the men who were actually responsible for the national catastrophe of 8 September 1943, for the war which was now dividing and destroying Italy, and for the Fascist war of 1940 to 1943. The conscripted men refused to show, and in great numbers. Tens of thousands of names were referred to the military courts for not responding to the call-up. The attempt to round up, arrest, and charge the military defaulters was as cack-handed and counterproductive in its effects on the southern population as the German and Fascist pursuit of the draft-dodgers in northern Italy was. In the Lazio region, 14,000 were conscripted, but only 3,700 turned up at the barracks. It was a military strike which became a matter of social and popular protest, and in some places, mass civil disobedience. In Ragusa, in Sicily, where the opposition to the call-up and its social resonances were greatest, there were five days of violent civil disorder, with popular demonstrations, attacks on public buildings, even exchanges of fire, until, eventually, the army regained control. The *tutti a casa* (everybody home) movement of the armistice was reborn as the *non si parte* (nobody leaves) movement, spreading to Sardinia, Puglia, Calabria, Campania, Lazio, Umbria, across the liberated south.

The evident connections between the army's disbandment of September 1943 and the no-show of November and December 1944 would suggest that the mass refusal of military service was the specifically southern reaction to the armistice. It was an indication of how seriously the armistice events had discredited the king and the military as national and nationalizing institutions. In a wider setting, the protests of the *non si parte* campaign were yet another demonstration of southern Italy opposing national central state authority, and refusing incorporation into one Italy, a feature of the wayward and imperfect nation-forming which had occurred since the political and territorial unification of the country in 1870–1.

It seems unlikely that these tens of thousands of young men in the south were refusing to participate in the war against Germany because they were committed Fascists. It might perhaps be nearer the mark to say that they rejected call-up because they were not Italian patriots. Ideas of and hopes of Sicilian autonomy and separatism had some political and popular currency at the time, and the experience of the war so far was hardly conducive to a sense of belonging to Italy. Although the methods of conscription were conventionally military, and so this was not necessarily how the call up would have appeared to those being called up, it was nevertheless the case that the young men of the south had refused to take part in a national, anti-Fascist war to drive the Germans out of Italy. The south was refusing to liberate the north, and as a result, did not fully share in what, elsewhere, was being portrayed and experienced as a war of national liberation and redemption.

Taking part might have helped to make the anti-Fascist liberation struggle popular in the south. Whether the call-up of late 1944 was a missed or botched opportunity can perhaps be gauged from what happened to the four Italian combat groups of about 50,000 men in total, who did, eventually, fight alongside the Allies in the Italian war. Their input was carefully controlled, as the Allies wanted, in a quite deliberate devaluing of their military contribution to the campaign. They fought among other Allied units and under Allied strategic command, between January and April 1945. The 'Cremona' combat group, for instance, was attached to the first Canadian army corps, on the Adriatic sector of the front. It was the one combat group to enrol as volunteers in its ranks, men from the partisan bands of newly liberated Tuscany and Emilia. The ex-partisans gave the force its democratic élan, and to a degree, took the places of the young men from the south who rejected the call-up. It was troops of the Cremona who derisively cat-called and barracked the king's son and their nominal commander-in-chief, Prince Umberto of Savoy, when he visited and inspected the combat groups. This public display of disloyalty and lack of respect towards the monarchy expressed and fused the feelings of the two anti-establishment components of the force, the democratically national ex-partisans of the centre and the north and the post-armistice soldiers of the south, the combination which might have liberated all of Italy.

It is possible to speculate that the south's mass abstention from a national war in late 1944 might have nourished the political phenomenon of the immediate post-war period which both marked and exploited the south's sense of apartness from the rest of the nation. 'Down with everything! Fed up with everything!'[28] expressed the sceptical and aggressively apolitical stance of *l'uomo qualunque* ('the ordinary bloke' or 'the man in the street') movement, which at its peak won a fifth of the vote among the south's lower middle and middle classes, a constituency which later moved on to the Monarchists and the post-war neo-Fascist party, the MSI. If this was the case, then the *non si parte* movement was the nearest Italians got to widespread Fascist resistance in the liberated and Allied-occupied south.

# 7

# The Other Two Italies, and their Three Wars, 1943–1945

D URING a conference in Pesarò held in 1984 on the war along the Gothic Line, an ex-partisan defensively took issue with some specific contributions, but really with the whole tenor of the conference: 'when people ask me how many partisans there were, I never reply with a number, because in reality we were an entire people who had taken to the woods, because everyone contributed in various ways, with the exception of a minority who served the Nazis'.[1] Unfortunately for this protagonist of the armed struggle, and for her restatement of what was the conventional post-war view of the wartime Resistance, others had been playing the numbers game.

Shortly after the war ended, a partisan was defined as someone who had been under arms for at least three months (presumably before the final liberation of the country in April 1945) in an armed formation recognized by the Volunteer Corps for Liberty (Corpo Volontari della Libertà), the army of the Resistance. To be recognized as such, partisans had also to have participated in at least three actions of sabotage and war. This definition helped to produce a figure of around 250,000 partisans on liberation in April 1945. Of course, this was bound to be the point at which the partisan resistance movement was at its fullest extent. Estimates of its dimensions up to liberation do vary somewhat, but are broadly compatible. The first partisan bands were formed in northern and central Italy after the armistice of 8 September 1943. They were mainly made up of fugitive disbanding soldiers escaping German capture and internment and trying to get home, and then ex-soldiers evading military call-up to the RSI's armed forces. The bands' members numbered perhaps around 10,000 by the end of 1943. Everybody seems to be agreed that across the summer and autumn of 1944, there was a big expansion in partisan forces, which grew to about 80,000 in August and over 100,000 by the time Field Marshal Alexander advised the partisans to stand down for the winter. Numbers declined back to August 1944 levels over the winter of 1944–5, before growing rapidly again as the end to German occupation became imminent in spring 1945.

The Fascist Republic and the German occupying forces could call on a greater number of armed Italian men, perhaps around 400,000 at the peak period of the spring to summer of 1944. The number crunching is complicated by the sheer range and variety of the sources of Fascist and German armed manpower. The yield of the November 1943 call-up to the new Republican army was about 51,000: 45,000 conscripts and 6,000 volunteers. An estimated, or claimed, 100,000 were recruited over time to the Republican National Guard (Guardia Nazionale Repubblicana, GNR), the re-formed Fascist Militia, which operated as a political police force. About 20,000 Italians joined the German army, through the Waffen SS, and others joined German police forces operating in occupied central and northern Italy. Private, freelance militias proliferated under the RSI and the German occupation, patronized and more or

6. Italians being trained for service in SS units, October 1944.

less controlled by the Fascist and German authorities, and combined violent criminality with violent anti-partisan operations and policing. The ex-naval units turned anti-partisan force of the Tenth Anti-Submarine Torpedo Boats Squadron (Decima Flottiglia Motoscafi Antisommergibili, or Decima Mas), led by a charismatic nationalist adventurer, Prince Junio Valerio Borghese, recruited about 10,000 young men during the lifetime of the Fascist Republic. The largest and most criminal of the autonomous, freebooting militias were La Muti, operating mainly in Milan and with over 2,000 gang members.

We could also include members of the new Fascist Republican Party (Partito Fascista Repubblicano, PFR), who numbered around 487,000 in March 1944. These men could be taken as armed, but only in the loosest sense. In response to the fall of Rome in June 1944 and the great leap in the strength of the partisan bands, Mussolini had, in July, declared that all PFR members were to regard themselves as being under arms. This was a ruse which Mussolini had employed in late 1921, before coming to power, when all Fascist Party members were made simultaneously members of the armed Fascist squads, a tactic designed to inhibit any government attempt to dissolve the party and its paramilitary formations. In 1944, the context and meaning of the move were very different. It was an attempt both to inflate and galvanize support for a Fascist regime with an increasingly faltering and tenuous hold on the country. The Party militia formed to militarize PFR members, the Black Brigades (Brigate Nere), probably recruited about 30,000, of whom perhaps 12,000 were actually trained and armed.

The figures given here can be and have been put to many uses, historically and politically. The numbers appear to be both small and large, according to the perspective. The population of the regions more or less under the control of the Germans and the RSI was about twenty million. From this viewpoint, the men under arms in the partisan movement and those at the disposal of the RSI were active minorities, with the latter rather larger than the former. The numbers seem to confirm the assumption that Italians in the German-occupied centre and north of the country between 1943 and 1945 were unevenly divided into active, that is fighting, minorities, and an inactive *attendista* majority living in the grey zone between the two extremes of positive commitment to one side or the other. But the figures also indicate that hundreds of thousands of armed men fought each other, Italians against Italians, in a nasty, violent civil conflict, the civil war within the war, which, in fact, lasted beyond the end of the military war itself. Around 45,000 partisans were killed. To this figure should be added the 10,000 ex-soldiers who died fighting in the partisan bands in the Balkans, participating in other people's civil wars and wars of liberation. There are no consensual figures for the number of Fascists killed either in the civil war of October 1943 to April 1945 or in its extension after April. Perhaps between 12,000 and 15,000 were killed in the immediate post-war period, though Fascist and neo-Fascist sources put this death toll many times higher.

For our unreconstructed ex-partisan, an entire people had resisted the Germans, and the idea of there being a civil war in Italy between 1943 and 1945 was out of the question, as it was for much of the post-war historiography of the wartime Resistance. Fascists at the time and post-war made great play of the civil war theme. Post-war neo-Fascism wanted to have it all ways and exploit both the good and the bad connotations of civil war. As post-war political pariahs, written out of history as the agents of the Nazis in wartime Italy, arguing for civil war was a way of saying that Fascists had fought on their own account and for Italy, not for a foreign occupying power. The concern was to deny a monopoly of patriotism to the victorious Resistance and reassert their own nationalism, by pointing to a rough equivalence on the ground between those who had fought for the RSI and those who had fought for the resistance movements, which was then translated into a moral or ideological equivalence. The Fascists of the Salò Republic were not wrong; they had just lost the battle. But civil war was also internecine, fratricidal conflict, a war of factions where not ideals, but territory and power, were at stake. The responsibility for provoking such a grubby and discreditable war of Italians on Italians lay with the Resistance, in this neo-Fascist reading of wartime events.

The validity of the term 'civil war' to describe what went on in central and northern Italy between 1943 and 1945 does not ultimately depend on the questionable uses to which the concept has been put. The anti-Fascist resistance movements embraced the term from the start. The Rome edition of the Communist newspaper *L'Unità*, spoke in October 1943 of 'war against the Nazi aggressor; civil war against the Fascists, their allies; political struggle against reactionary forces'.[2] The Communists placed civil war alongside the other national and class wars, and often tended to dignify the national war above the others. But civil war was absolutely central to the outlook of the inter-war liberal socialist anti-Fascist movement Justice and Liberty (Giustizia e Libertà), which became the wartime Action Party and gave its name to a significant partisan force. The Actionists consistently portrayed the war in Italy in ideological terms, as the decisive battle in a more general European civil war between Fascist and anti-Fascist values and civilizations, the exact mirror image of Mussolini's own projection of the Fascist war in 1940, and of the RSI's self-legitimation from late 1943.

Civil war seems an entirely appropriate way to view the events in central and northern Italy between 1943 and 1945, and even beyond. Italians fought and killed Italians over, ultimately, differing views and versions of the nation. This was why the RSI and the partisan movements both stigmatized the other as traitors, why the RSI attempted to delegitimize the partisans by calling them bandits, outlaws, and rebels, and why the partisans always referred to the enemy as Nazifascists, connecting the Fascists unpatriotically to Nazi German occupation. There were countless incidents and examples of this civil war in action. The intransigent, non-cooperating Fascist prisoner of war in his Texan camp, Gaetano Tumiati, learnt with stupefaction that the Fascist authorities had executed his brother as a partisan, in May 1944. The GNR reported on a family quarrel in Nogarola Rocca, near Verona in north-eastern Italy, in October 1944. They had arrested two brothers, RSI draft-dodgers and anti-Fascists, who were denounced to the Fascist police by their own father, an active PFR member, who had been beaten up by his sons the evening before after a political argument. A similar civil war cycle, or chain, of reprisal and counter-reprisal could be observed in the working-class and doggedly anti-Fascist Oltretorrente district of Parma, in Emilia, in August 1944, when the ambush and killing of two GNR men by a local cell of the urban Patriotic Action Groups (Gruppi di Azione Patriottica, GAP), provoked in response the execution of a draft-dodger held as hostage for just such an eventuality by the Fascist police.

What the numbers cannot tell us was why and how Italians became actively involved in either defending the Fascist Republic, or in the armed resistance to German occupation and the Republic.

The decision to install a Fascist statelet in German-occupied Italy was apparently Hitler's alone. Mussolini himself seemed to be utterly demoralized by his dismissal and arrest by the king in July 1943. He simply went along with the drift of events and decisions which were being determined and made by others, and this included his dramatic release, or capture, by the Germans from his mountain-top hotel-prison in the Appennines of south central Italy in September 1943. He showed little appetite for resurrecting his political career, perhaps partly because he knew that he would be expected to sort out his family problem, who was Ciano, the son-in-law and heir-apparent who had voted for Grandi's motion at the Grand Council meeting of 25 July 1943.

7. The dictator in physical decline: a gaunt and impassive Mussolini at his desk in the offices of the Fascist Republic, 1944.

The top Nazis were contemptuous of Italian performance in the Axis war and of the betrayal of the Axis in September 1943, which for good Nazi racists like Goebbels, signified an ineradicable Italian-ness. They preferred to see Italy treated as a defeated and occupied country, as punishment and revenge for the armistice betrayal and as a more secure basis for the plunder and exploitation of Italy's human and material resources for the German war effort. But Hitler's view of the need to restore Mussolini to nominal power prevailed. His decision was not so much a show of personal loyalty and attachment to Mussolini, as a political demonstration that fascism, internationally, was still a force and could be reinvigorated by the re-emergence of the first fascist in the first fascist nation.

This calculation certainly worked in terms of the revival of Fascism and Fascists in Italy itself. The creation of the Fascist Republic marked the return of Fascists who were more fanatically Fascist than Mussolini himself. The Fascists of the last hour were the Fascists of the first hour, many of them protagonists of the violent squadrist paramilitary Fascism of the early 1920s, and now middle-aged men with paunches, squeezing themselves back into party uniform. Some, of course, had never really been away, like Farinacci, the pro-Nazi and intransigent Fascist irritant of the 1930s, sidelined but never quietened by Mussolini, and Renato Ricci, the boss of one of the most ferocious local squadrist Fascisms in the Tuscan marble-quarrying province of Massa and Carrara, a Minister of Education and of Corporations during the regime, and now back as commander of the reborn Fascist Militia, the GNR. Some were younger middle-aged men who had become more extreme in the late 1930s and during the war, like Pavolini, once Minister of Popular Culture—that is, propaganda—the one Fascist to respond to Mussolini's fall in 1943 with a call for armed resistance, and now head of the re-formed Fascist party, the PFR.

Below them, re-emerging as provincial Fascist Party leaders, prefects, and police chiefs, were men who belonged entirely to the 1920s squadrist generation and were returning from long periods of political exile or disgrace. These were men such as Mario Giampaoli, the rehabilitated PFR leader in Milan, back in the post he occupied in the late 1920s until he fell foul of the prefect, the exposure of a corrupt squadrist-enforced protection racket in the city's fruit and vegetable markets, and the more general desire to be respectable of a Fascism consolidating itself in power; Tullio Tamburini, a violent Fascist Militia leader packed off to Libya until the late 1930s, when he became a prefect, who was now appointed Chief of Police; in Verona, where the founding conference of the PFR took place in November 1943, Nino Furlotti, a local squadrist commander before 1922 who had retired after the disbanding of the paramilitary squads in the mid- and late 1920s, and was now back as the city's chief of police, so hands-on that he commanded Ciano's execution squad in January 1944 and fired the final shots; and Piero Cosmin, a decorated veteran of all Fascism's wars, who had restarted the Verona *fascio* in October 1943 and became prefect of Verona until May 1944, and then of nearby Venice.

In its political programme, racist, corporatist, republican, anti-establishment; in its political outlook, wanting to take revenge on the traitorous Fascists and monarchy responsible for July and September 1943, and, indeed, for the compromises which from their pure, extremist viewpoint, stalled the Fascist regime in the 1930s; and in its methods, violent one-party rule, the RSI exactly mirrored the stance and mentality of these born-again Fascists. These hard men of the past were joined in the PFR and the various Fascist polices and militias of the Republic, by younger men who usually volunteered for such membership

8. Young volunteers enrolling for the Decima Mas in La Spezia, probably in 1944.

and service. So a typical *fascio* was largely composed of men under 25 and over 40 years of age.

Prince Junio Valerio Borghese, the founder and commander of Decima Mas, claimed that what attracted young men to join his militia was the adventurous, swashbuckling, rebellious spirit which pervaded it. Borghese was making a virtue of the lack of conventional military discipline and procedure to be found in the regular army, not a deficiency at all, in fact, but appropriate and functional for a force fighting an irregular, guerrilla war against the partisans. The relaxed, informal discipline generated by comradeship in shared risk and danger, rather than the formal exercise of rank, probably did appeal. It might, of course, have been a way of rationalizing away his Fascism. But the account of his own exploits by one volunteer, Teodoro Francesconi, who served with the Republican army in the northeast borderlands of Italy, depicted a young adventurer rebelling, through his service, against the playing-safe mediocrity of his own middle-class background and upbringing.

Some of these young male recruits were just too young to have fought in Fascism's wars, but old enough to have gone through and been affected

by the militarized activities and outlook of the Fascist regime's youth
organizations. In the militias, the young men who joined could behave as
the Fascists they were educated to be. The same sense of recklessness and
adventure would equally, of course, have been one of the elements inducing
young men to join the partisans, rather than the Fascist forces. We are, after
all, speculating on the attitudes of a committed minority; under one in four
of the 180,000 adult males conscripted to the RSI armed forces in November 1943, actually turned up to enlist.

The PFR struggled to recreate the collateral organizations of the original
single party of the Fascist totalitarian state, in order to realize the civil
mobilization of a society at war. One of these organizations, the Fascist

9. Young women volunteers for the Fascist Republic's Women's Auxiliary Service,
line up in Venice, August 1944.

Women's Auxiliary Service (Servizi Ausiliari Femminili, SAF), set up in April 1944, seemed to be the female equivalent of the Fascist militias, both in spirit and composition. Young women were recruited to replace young men who were meant for military service, in auxiliary work in hospitals, in the offices of military commands and barracks, and in canteens. Wearing a uniform, banned from smoking and using make-up, and trained in the handling of a weapon for use in cases of legitimate defence—though not permitted to carry one, they were the nearest the RSI came to enlisting women soldiers. It was clear from letters and memories that many of these auxiliaries wanted to fight against the partisans, but only a very few managed this. The closest some of them got to any fighting front was taking and running mobile snack bars to the rear of military operations, though this job was for young women who were single, had some German, and could drive.

Many of the young women who joined the auxiliaries had recent Fascist pasts, participating during the late 1930s in the student games (*Littoriali*) of culture and sport, or in the colonial training camps for young women held in the Italian North African colony of Libya, or in the physical education courses of the Fascist teacher training academy at Orvieto. Some came from the lower middle class and had Fascist parents: they were therefore, born and raised in Fascism. The wartime auxiliary service would have seemed a natural, patriotic progression from these activities. Some clearly resented the contradictory mobilization of women for stereotypical passive, caring, and family roles, which was a characteristic of Fascism's female organizations. 'All I do is wash piles of dishes, wash the sheets, cook, tidy up the rooms where people sleep, do all the office work, telephoning all and sundry, deciphering coded messages,' complained a 16-year-old auxiliary to her mother, in March 1945.[3] It was evident she hankered after real action, a chance on what she called 'the front line', and only felt 'right' when she was wearing her uniform. Being the 'little sister' to the 'boys' must have seemed a poor return on her life. Her letter was written from prison, and she was later shot for her participation in the SAF. Another auxiliary, a 20-year-old, recorded the uneasy and reluctant welcome she received from the military commander whose unit she was to service: 'women were more useful at home'. It struck her, as well, that it was 'work more for men than women'. But she made the adjustment, nevertheless, since, as she said, 'I needed to work and then realized that there was no way out'. She was 'proud' of what she did, 'but not at the beginning'.[4] This was quite a revealing testimony, because it indicated that her real incentive for joining was the need to work, and that once in the job, the choice was definitive. There was no going back on it, or escaping the obligations and consequences of the choice to work for a Fascist organization. The choice was determined by the situation and the circumstances. For her, as for many others, it was an existential, not an ideological, choice. But a choice dictated by circumstance could harden into solidarity and loyalty to the organization she worked for and the people she worked with. The young SAF recruit became the 'little sister' of a new or surrogate family of Fascists.

There were plenty of similar instances of what might be called circumstantial collaboration with the RSI and the German occupier. A woman resister in Bologna, Aurora Beccari, recalled that her boyfriend joined the Fascist police in the hope of getting a desk job and a ration card. What was interesting, also, here, was how this woman's rather promiscuous love life during the occupation crossed the boundaries between resistance and collaboration. A later wartime lover, an ex-soldier from Naples, became a paid informer for the Fascist political police, eventually reporting to the German police, in order to stay in Bologna—not to be with her, as it turned out, but to be with another woman with whom he had had children.

It is difficult to discern much popular support for the RSI beyond the embattled core of hard-line young and middle-aged Fascists, whose extremism and fanaticism fitted both the emergency conditions of wartime and their concern to return Fascism to its uncontaminated squadrist and syndicalist origins of the early 1920s. Their compressed public and private lives came to resemble the garrison or ghetto-like existence of fascist collaborationists and their families, such as the Rexists in occupied Belgium, for instance, during the final stages of Nazi control in Western European countries, small communities physically, psychologically, and ideologically turned in on themselves.

After the institutional vacuum of the days following the armistice of 8 September 1943, some people would have been grateful for the RSI's filling of a void, and the return of a kind of order, security, and provision of public services guaranteed by the presence of a government. The fact that the RSI claimed to be and acted as the state, would have eased the transfer of civil servants from Rome northwards to the government ministries relocated in small towns along Lake Garda, between Brescia and Verona. Some people, at least, went on paying their taxes to the RSI, even subscribing to municipal and state loans at a point when the Republic's survival was unlikely, despite calls for a popular tax boycott by both the resistance movement and the other Bonomi government.

There were good reasons why the RSI was unlikely to gain more than the natural or automatic aquiescence of the governed towards their government. It became pretty clear to everyone that the Germans were losing the war in Italy, and were fighting not to win it, but to delay an inevitable Allied victory. The progress of the war and the near-certainty of Allied victory removed the point of the Republic's existence, even as a de facto authority. What could the RSI actually offer and provide for the people of northern Italy in 1944–5? Defeat with honour? RSI police reports on popular opinion and the public mood, constantly bemoaned what they saw as the *attendismo*, the wait-and-see inertia, of the great majority of the people, without ever really quite realizing what it was they were observing. The Fascist police were actually criticizing the people not for *attendismo*, but for not supporting the RSI. They were not supporting the RSI or doing anything to sustain its existence because they knew that the war was being lost and that the RSI was on the losing side. *Attendismo* could denote a conscious neutrality in conduct and behaviour, while the contest was being decided. But it was meaningless to assume or expect such neutrality in 1944–5, when everybody realized that the outcome of the contest was not in doubt.

To this limitation on consent and support for the RSI, which derived from the circumstances of war, was added an important element of self-limitation, which related to how the Republican Fascists responded to the circumstances of war. There was a real sense that the Fascists of the RSI did not actually want the people's support. The Republic was not much more than an exercise in revenge against those deemed to have betrayed Mussolini and Fascism. These 'traitors' were, above all, the false Fascists of the Grand Council, the monarchy, and the military, and more generally, all those vested establishment interests which had compromised and vitiated the revolutionary aims of the Fascist regime; hence, the rebranding of the Fascist state as social and a republic. But Fascism had also been 'betrayed' by the Italian people; the lost war was the 'failure' of the Italians, not Fascism. Mussolini had reached this self-justifying conclusion in the course of 1942, and scolded Fascist Party audiences about the endemic mental and character defects of a people who had wilfully refused to be fascistized. 'The regime controls something like twenty-five million individuals,' he declared in a speech in May 1942; 'well, what are all these people doing? I ask myself, what are they doing?'[5]

We know that hardly any of the armed military and police forces raised by the RSI were actually deployed alongside the Germans to fight the Allies. One explanation for this was German reluctance to use Italian troops whose loyalty and commitment were regarded as suspect. The parachutists fought, fragmented and diluted though they were among German units, on the Anzio bridgehead and in the defence of Rome, from February 1944. Their sense of loyalty and attachment to the Axis alliance was unquestioned, and no wonder. Mario Rizzatti, commander of the parachutist battalion which had defected to the Germans in Sardinia after the armistice, had found a cause which took him beyond the defence of the nation and national honour: 'the people are what they are, morally defeated and rudderless...I have the oath of loyalty to the Führer, and I fight under the tricolour, with the swastika, an Aryan symbol much older, much more sacred and much more serious than the Etruscan Fascist *Littorio*.'[6]

The other explanation was that the Republic's armed forces were raised with the intention, from the start, of fighting a civil war against the partisans and against the Italian people, and were imbued, from the start, with a civil war mentality. The Fascist militias carried out their own anti-partisan operations, as well as the more customary joint expeditions with German police and military. In both unilateral and combined operations, the hunt for partisans involved terrorizing the local people who were held responsible for protecting them or even tolerating and not reporting their presence, which, to their German and Fascist pursuers, amounted to the same thing. Perhaps one in ten of the incidents where civilians were massacred, involved Republican units operating on their own. What was noticeable about these killings was that they were usually discriminating, targeted, and political. The Italian massacres which occurred in German-occupied Italy were normally of hostages taken before and during an expedition, anti-Fascist politicians, the parents and relatives of deserters and draft dodgers, executed as reprisal and punishment for local non-cooperation in the round-up of partisans.

This was the wording of a poster displayed on the walls of Vittorio Veneto, a small town in the mountains north of Venice, right on the old Italo-Yugoslav border, by the commander of a Decima Mas unit policing the area, in response to the killing of one of his men by partisans, in January 1945.

Everybody knows that we consider to be on the same level as the bandits those people who at any time help them in even the smallest way, even if only putting them up, or only keeping quiet about their whereabouts. All this will undoubtedly mean terror and blood, but I have to say that terror and blood are what you yourselves have wished on yourselves. Once the population shows itself to be firmly against the bandits, then we will be able to protect and help it. There will be trouble for anybody who dares to obstruct our work, which is preparing for the real battle against the enemies of the fatherland.[7]

The 'enemies of the fatherland' on the far north-eastern frontier were, of course, the Slavs, and this added real poignancy and ferocity to the Fascist commander's sense that he was conducting a legitimate war on the traitors who were the local Italian population. It was clear that the Decima Mas were determined to get their retaliation in first: the reprisals, which started with the burning down of houses, had already been initiated before the poster went up on the walls of the town. What the poster displayed was the contempt and distrust of the commander for his fellow Italians and his reluctance to consider them Italians at all. He was behaving as the occupier of his own country.

The perpetrators of civilian massacres during round-up operations commonly expressed the feeling on their return to base that they had attacked people who were not really Italian, who were unworthy of being called Italians. The intransigent wording of the poster was not just a matter of local initiative in a particularly tense and volatile frontier situation. It resembled in word and spirit, the official warning on the Republic's proclamation of the call-up to the armed forces in November 1943: 'he who does not turn up will no longer be considered an Italian. First we have to chase away the enemy, then we will have time to fight among ourselves.'[8]

Portraying themselves and behaving as a heroic elite fighting for a nation which did not deserve them, was cause and effect of the Republic's isolation and lack of sympathy among the people it nominally governed. Since the nation did not really exist at the time for these Fascists, and was actually shrinking in territorial size as a result of German annexations and the Allied advance, the nation they invoked was an imagined Italy peopled not by the living Italians around them, but by the dead, the fallen comrades of the Fascist and Axis war. Facing the certainty of defeat, the Republic's Fascists could only offer themselves and the rest what a post-war neo-Fascist book called a 'beautiful death'.[9]

This lugubriously defiant patriotism was expressed in a letter of a trainee pilot, another parachutist, who was off to the fighting front at Anzio early in 1944: 'we will die happy, in the flowering of our 20 years, making a holocaust of our youth . . . to demonstrate to the whole world that the Italians know how to fight and know how to die for their country and for their Faith'.[10] This young man's faith was not Catholicism, but Fascism. Death with honour was a rallying cry for fanatics and diehards. But it was unlikely to mobilize a war-weary and introspective population concerned with survival. A 'beautiful death', however, came at the very end, in April 1945, for one Pavan, the commander of the 'Monterosa' Alpini division of the Republican army, at the hands of a Communist 'Garibaldi' partisan formation liberating the town of Saluzzo, between Cuneo and Turin on the north-western border. Facing his execution squad, the commander shouted out, 'Viva l'Italia grande!' (Long live the great Italy!) But the man who was about to die was not allowed to have the final word. The partisans countered with 'Viva l'Italia libera!' (Long live the free Italy!)[11] This was the essence and meaning of the civil war, in one scene. This was why Italians were killing Italians.

Our understanding of the nature of armed resistance to the Fascist Republic and to German occupation has been illuminated by the recent work of an Italian historian, Claudio Pavone,[12] who gives us the most sophisticated and nuanced sense of what the Resistance was and claimed to be, within an anti-Fascist historiographical tradition. His view that the armed resistance of 1943 to 1945 was, simultaneously, a national war, a civil war, and a class war, has become the new orthodoxy. The explanatory matrix of the 'three wars' in German-occupied Italy can also usefully be applied to the other side of the civil war in northern Italy. This may have been his original intention, since his book gives a lot of attention to Fascist as well as Resistance wartime choices. So for the RSI and its supporters, the Republic was fighting a war of national liberation to throw the Allies out of Italy, a civil war against both anti-Fascism and the monarchy, and a class war against the internal and international forces of capitalist plutocracy. As with the Resistance movement, or sections of it, the RSI gave a European dimension and aura to its internal civil war. The Republic, with its Nazi ally, were fighting to defend European civilization against the extra- and anti-European forces of Russian Bolshevism and Anglo-American capitalism and their Italian lackeys.

The class war aspect of the RSI was rather stretching a point, since the syndicalist-corporatist policies of the Republic, as of the earlier Fascist regime, were meant to induce class collaboration and supersede class conflict. But the Republic stepped up its 'back to the origins' anti-capitalist rhetoric, and its corporative reforms were hailed as rebalancing the forces of production in favour of the workforce and as a way of engaging the industrial working classes. So the third dimension just about holds up, even though Italian workers were unlikely to be inspired by a revamped syndicalism after experiencing twenty years of a Fascist regime built on the permanent denial of workers' rights.

The three wars motif could coexist in any armed resistance movement, and, indeed, in any individual partisan band, but was not necessarily present in all of them. Different facets were often more evident in some bands rather than others, and to some extent, the combination depended on the political affiliations adopted, or not adopted, by partisan bands. From the summer of 1944, the CLNAI started categorizing politically the bands which were nominally coordinated by this inter-party Resistance organ. An estimated 40 per cent of all partisans were in Communist Party-aligned Garibaldi formations; another 25 per cent were estimated to be members of Justice and Liberty bands under Action Party auspices; and the remaining 35 per cent were nominally and variously Socialist, Christian Democrat, and Liberal, or in autonomous, non-political bands.

The autonomous bands were, in a sense, the first bands to form themselves, and all bands might have been considered such if the main anti-Fascist political parties had not made contact in order to politicize them. They were usually made up of ex-soldiers and their officers. Non-political was something of a misnomer, since these bands generally recognized the distant Kingdom of the South and the monarchy as being the legitimate Italy. They were often resented by the political leadership of the other more overtly party-political bands, because they were Badogliani, loyal to the 'traitorous' monarchical and military forces culpable for the armistice. In some cases, these resentments led to tensions within individual bands which often had a mixed composition anyway, and overlaid rather more basic turf wars between partisan bands over control of territory and access to civilian and Allied-supplied resources. At other times, these conflicts were muted or submerged in the dynamics of the common struggle on the ground against the Fascists and the Germans. In general terms, however, the autonomous formations, which remained a significant component of the partisan movement, perceived their function as a primarily—sometimes exclusively—military one, to support the Allied liberation of the country. They did not look much beyond the eventual liberation to the shaping of post-war society, and regarded the liberation as the point and end of their lives as partisans. The war of national liberation was the only war which mattered to them.

The propaganda flyer printed and distributed in the north central region of Romagna after Allied bombing raids in the summer of 1944, combined the three wars simultaneously in the same document. 'Germans, get out of Italy,' it stated; 'get out, the Nazi barbarians and their Fascist servants . . . Why are we being bombed? Because . . . we're working for the enemies of the people. Let's sabotage the production which is going to them. Let's all show together our support for the freedom and independence of our homeland.'[13] The elision and mutual reinforcement of the three wars theme were evident in this product of one of the Communist Party's resistance organizations, its Womens' Defence Groups. The Italian Communist Party, the PCI, developed the most ramified resistance movement in German-occupied Italy and had the most nuanced perspective on the aims and purposes of the Resistance. Although all three elements of the resistance's war were expressed here, the PCI always tended to emphasize the national liberation aspects of the armed struggle. To cold war anti-communists, this stance was, and is, suspicious, and is often written off as a subterfuge to disguise the Party's real revolutionary intentions and its inter-nationalism, in other words, its subordination to the strategy of the Stalinist Soviet Union. It was clearly the PCI's intention to draw as many people as possible into the armed struggle against Fascism and Nazi occupation, and to transform itself into an authentically national political force, capable of mobili-zing all social groups, not just workers, behind a reforming social democracy rather than proletarian revolution. The PCI's stance was entirely consistent with the pre-war Popular Front and wartime National Front strategies followed by all western European Communist parties, which aimed to insert themselves into national political life by concentrating on what united people in a general European battle against fascism.

In this light, the PCI found itself in the rather paradoxical situation of trying to mute or contain the class war aspects of the armed resistance, for the sake of preserving the broad anti-Fascist unity of the CLNs. A Communist militant in the 'republic' of Montefiorino, an area in the mountains of Romagna to the south-west of Bologna, which was temporarily liberated and governed by the partisan bands in 1944, could claim that 'we are living in a real revolutionary climate'. But he and others like him had to be called to order by their divisional Garibaldi commanders. One such rebuke embodied the official party line: 'the communists are not fighting at the moment for the proletarian revolution but for the liberation of the nation' and a 'progressive' democracy.[14] The qualifying 'at the moment' was clearly meant to reconcile the revolutionary partisan to the Party's position, while, of course, providing further ammunition for contemporary and later criticism of the apparent ambiguity of their stance. But the PCI maintained its line to the end. In Lombardy, the Garibaldi divisions were told on the eve of final liberation in April 1945 not to display their red banners or show the clenched fist salute, as they took the public's acclamation for liberation, because it made sense not 'to make gestures and displays which divide'.[15] The very redness of the Garibaldi partisans' insignia, and, indeed, the choice of the name of Italy's great hero of nineteenth-century unification, Giuseppe Garibaldi, for Communist-led bands, were deliberately designed to invoke not social revolutionary, but national revolutionary, aspirations.

The nature of the armed resistance struggle itself imposed its own limitations on the use of the class war theme. On the one hand, it was very natural to give a class edge to acts of resistance. There was no mistaking the crude personal and class envy in the recollections of Annunciata Cesani, who joined the Womens' Defence Group in Osteriola, near Imola, between Bologna and Forlì, which for her, in retrospect anyway, was 'a group of friends rather than a political cell'. It certainly behaved like a female gang. She remembered them beating up the work supervisor at a local firm who was hard on her female labour force, 'a beautiful woman, heavily made up, with white hands and lacquered finger-nails'.[16] A partisan, Giuseppe Balduzzi, spoke of the practicalities of the band's existence when he said that 'we needed money and it's obvious that we went to get it from well-off people, above all, whom we knew were in some way compromised with the Fascist regime'.[17] Being rich and being Fascist was the kind of equation which suited both the pragmatism and idealism of the bands.

In some cases, the class war was the way to engage popular support for the resistance struggle which was indicated by the workers themselves. Vasco Lugli, a GAP commander from Rovereto, in Venetia, remembered his first nervous proselytizing contacts with rice workers in the fields. His attempt to read out a PCI leaflet urging the workers to support the partisans was inter-rupted by a rice worker who demanded to know why they were being paid lower wages than in other rice-growing areas. At least, Lugli was sensible enough to take the hint. Calling on the employer, he told him that 'you must give them what they want. The next time the partisans come by, we'll drop in to see if you've done it. If not, then we'll take action.' The rice worker's interruption sparked a campaign to win hearts and minds in the rice fields: 'then we went to other farms and made the same speech . . . with these actions, our influence . . . grew even more'.[18]

On the other hand, class war was, in many cases, simply inappropriate to the situation both employers and workers found themselves confronting under German occupation. It was undeniably neat for the resistance movement to be able to make political capital of the extensive industrial strikes in German-occupied Italy in February and March 1944. Strikes for better wages and conditions were, after all, an attack on the employers who had backed the Fascist regime and who were now producing for the Germans and the RSI. Such demands were immediately political, since so many of the workers' material grievances could be made the responsibility of the occupiers' and the Republic's punitive social and labour measures, from rationing to deportation. But in calculating the level of risk involved in striking in such a repressive climate, both workers and employers were united, not divided, in their common interest in protecting their factories and employment from the depredations of the Germans and the RSI. Workers who stopped working on German contracts faced deportation to work in Germany; idle plant and machinery were liable to be transferred elsewhere in Italy, or to Germany. The employer might well be able to justify his drawing up of a list of subversive workers for deportation, an act of class war, on the grounds that the sacrifice of the few safeguarded the livelihoods of the many who were allowed to remain and work in Italy. Industrial employers inhabited whatever middle ground there was in occupied society, but not inertly. They had to play both sides simultaneously, if their businesses were to survive the war. They collaborated in meeting German war orders, and they resisted in protecting their labour force from deportation and in funding local partisan bands who, in return, were the security guards on their factory premises.

In the highly ambiguous and compromising circumstances in which such choices had to be made, it was little wonder that the class war was played down by the resistance leadership, and could not be pursued unequivocally by the partisan bands. In the Seriana valley, in Bergamo province, in November 1944, an increasingly maverick and independent-minded partisan leader, Angelo del Bello, was eventually captured and killed on the orders of the Justice and Liberty partisan command, to which del Bello was nominally accountable. His elimination was motivated by undisciplined behaviour, which included his attempt to extort money from a local industrialist who was, in fact, a major patron of the Justice and Liberty organization in the province. He had brokered a deal between partisan commands and electricity supply companies to protect the pylons and generating stations from sabotage, whether by partisans or the Germans.

The most emblematic case of all was the inability of the Turin workers' committees to press home their indictment to the local CLN in November 1944 of the entire management of FIAT, the city's major industrial employer which had profited hugely from the Fascist regime's and the German occupiers' war production contracts. FIAT's managing director, Vittorio Valletta, condemned as a traitor to his country, could prove, with documentation, his resistance credentials and his wartime contacts and deals with the Allies. The fact that employers played a double game, and felt that they had to in order to save their businesses, also shows how difficult it was to purge from their positions of power and influence, men apparently compromised by their complicity and association with Mussolini's regime and the German occupier.

There was barely a trace of the class war in the outlook of some Justice and Liberty partisan formations, where, often, the most congenial combination was of patriotism with anti-Fascism, the national war and the civil war. The association was evident, as was the absence of class concerns, in the final verse of the partisan song composed by Revelli for his Justice and Liberty Alpini division: 'the partisan fights | his battle | Germans and Fascists | out of Italy!'[19] The themes of the song reflected the relatively homogenous social composition of Revelli's band, many of whom were ex-Alpini of peasant, mountain stock whose basic sense of belonging lay with a village community, rather than class. The Action Party, of all the political parties involved with the bands, was the most committed to using the resistance experience to create a new post-war Italy, new in respect both of Fascism and of the liberal Italy which had preceded Fascism and enabled Fascism to flourish. Its political programme of liberal socialism, of reconciling individual liberty and social justice, was very much along the lines of other West European non-communist resistance movements with no previous political history and whose origins lay exclusively in resistance to fascism and German occupation. Its ideology and programme were basically inter-class, rather than class against class, deliberately mirroring what it mythologized as the essentially unifying effect on participants of the struggle against Fascism and German occupation. The Action Party was keen to project the anti-Fascist co-operation of the CLNs into the post-war period, and it was appropriate that one of its men,

Ferruccio Parri, the party's representative on the CLNAI and the resistance's military commander, became prime minister of a short-lived resistance coalition government after the war between June and November 1945.

The partisan bands were both homogeneous and heterogeneous in their make-up, drawing in both local men and women and the flotsam of wartime society, including evacuees, draft-dodgers, the politically and racially persecuted, refugees, even ex-POWS. Some were in the bands as a matter of a definite and coherent anti-Fascist political choice, and their participation was consistent with a previous record and experience of anti-Fascist militancy. Some of the Garibaldi brigades operating in the mountains of inland Liguria between Genoa and Alessandria were typically made up of men from the local villages and evacuees from the big city, Genoa—mainly workers and students who had been active in PCI organizations there. Some of these anti-Fascist militants were present because of the anti-Fascist parties' attempted politicization of the bands. This was pursued actively by the Action Party, and the PCI, which had decided from the autumn of 1943 that Party members should join the bands, and from early 1944 that Party cells should be formed within them.

For the younger men and women who made such politically motivated choices in joining the resistance movements, family and community background and upbringing were important influences on their choices. Such influences predisposed or made likely a choice for resistance which, nevertheless, could have been catalysed by a particular wartime incident or circumstances. The personal profiles provided by some of the women partisans in Bologna bear out this sense of there being a transmission of values from one anti-Fascist generation to another, of some people being born into anti-Fascism, as others had been born into Fascism. Odette Righi's uncle was an Anarchist, sent to *confino* (internal exile) under the Fascist regime. Her father had refused to take out Fascist Party membership and been beaten up by local Fascists. Tolmina Guazzaloca's brother had been arrested for anti-Fascist activities in 1930. Gina Negrini, who joined a Garibaldi brigade, had seen her friend and workmate killed by Fascist Militiamen while scavenging ('looting') for what she could find in the ruins of a bombed-out train. Most of these Bolognese women came from Il Pratello, a rough working-class and lumpenproletarian neighbourhood of the city with a tradition of petty criminality and rebelliousness, both features accentuated by the wartime influx of fugitives, refugees, and other marginalized individuals and families. One gets the same sense of political conviction being translated into active resistance by a particular event, in the memories of another young woman, this time from Venetia, who became a courier for the partisans in 1943, a conspicuously early point in the German occupation. 'I joined the Resistance', she said, 'without really knowing why at the beginning... we instinctively did what had to be done, without anyone forcing us... Anyway, they wounded [my brother] and then that evening they killed him. And from the moment that they killed my brother, I officially joined the Resistance.'[20]

It was the occupation itself which really created the bands. In the spring and summer of 1944, the various Nazi agencies responsible for labour recruitment in the occupied territories, engaged in a massive round-up of able-bodied men in Italy, either to deport them to work in Germany or to put them to work on German war projects in Italy, through the Todt organiza-tion, a Nazi military construction agency. In the German-annexed parts of north-eastern Italy, this compulsory labour service was enforced by the German agencies and authorities themselves. In the rest of occupied Italy, the RSI was delegated to meet its quota of forced labour, while the German agencies, including those from the armed forces combing out skilled labour from Italian factories, duplicated and competed with the RSI and each other. In annexed north-eastern Italy, all adult men and women were conscripted for war service in October 1944, mainly for work in Italy with the Todt organization. But so few responded to the call-up that in Fiume the German police took to raiding the city's shelters during and immediately after Allied bombings. It was hardly a coincidence, then, that partisan bands developed so rapidly in the middle of 1944, as thousands of young men took to the hills and mountains to escape labour deportation sweeps. These men joined the partisans in order to survive and remain in Italy. But their choice still contained a fine calculation of risk, since sanctions were applied against the families of those evading the labour round-ups, including the cutting of pension and social welfare payments, and hostage-taking.

One can hardly say that these choices to join the armed resistance were politically or ideologically driven, though they clearly had a political con-sequence and became a political choice, since people were choosing to reject occupation. But they did reflect something rather more fundamental than press-ganging by circumstances, and this, I think, held also for those who resisted German occupation without necessarily joining an organized, armed resistance group. The young woman who recalled her experience as a courier for the resistance movement in Pesarò province, definitely ruled

10. Members of the armed resistance communist Garibaldi Eighteenth brigade posing for a photograph in the mountains around Cuneo, north-west Italy, *c.* spring 1945.

11. Two brothers, captured members of a partisan band operating around Alba, north-west Italy, being led to execution, *c.* 1944.

12. A German army propaganda photograph shows Italian young women enjoying themselves with German soldiers at a fairground in northern Italy, c.1944.

out any political motivation for joining. 'It was a natural instinct,' she said; 'I can't explain it myself.'[21] The testimony of a man who was a teenager in 1944 attempted to articulate the same reactive principle behind his resistance in the Tuscan province of Arezzo, which did not, in the end, involve him joining a band. His story rings true, because he records the doubts, hesitations, and uncertainties which marked the process of his eventual decision to act, in part created by the conflicting demands on his will of his mother, who constantly implored him not to get into trouble, and of his role model, the young bearded partisan Carlo Grazzi, himself just 20 years old, who was publicly shot in June 1944 after capture for a partisan attack on German troops. 'I remember that I felt inside myself a feeling of rebellion which I could not suppress, an impulse to react that never left me,' he wrote, recalling emotions he claimed to have some time before the actual moment of resistance, the throwing of Molotov cocktails, which Grazzi had taught him to make, at an unguarded German truck. The 'rage inside me', he went on, 'made me feel an intense, uncontrollable desire to act on instinct'.[22]

These words express what was most elemental behind popular resistance to German occupation. The instinct was to do with the person's survival, or sense of himself or herself, as a human being, understood not simply in terms of material existence but in terms of the self-worth of the individual, secured by reacting against tyranny. It appears glib to say that resistance to German occupation was an assertion of the human spirit against a system designed to suppress or control it, a kind of instinctive anti-fascism, but it does seem to capture what these young people felt they were doing it for.

The key to the survival and activity of the partisan bands was the relationship of the bands with the local community inhabiting the area of their operations. Most bands were nomadic and lived off the land, though some were composed of part-time partisans, men who might periodically return to their homes and work. No band could survive unless the local people, grudgingly or not, provided them with food, shelter, and protection. From a village's viewpoint, the presence of a partisan band was a huge risk and threat to their survival, since it brought down on that community the full weight of RSI and German repression. Popular memories of the period of armed resistance often held the partisans ultimately responsible for the disruptive, intrusive, violent, and intimidatory policing of their areas by Fascist militias and German troops.

The partisan bands' commanders and political leadership were likely to take a broader view of the crucial interaction between the individual bands and the local people. They recognized the importance of good relations between bands and people, but often took what they saw as the real objectives of the armed struggle as the deciding factor in weighing up the gains and losses of any partisan initiative. Was the death of a German soldier worth the ten, or twenty, civilians killed by the Germans in reprisal? It might be, when the partisans' attack on German soldiers demonstrated to the occupier the resistance's strength and effectiveness, and increased the occupier's fears of an enemy capable of striking at them, anywhere. This kind of hit-and-run guerrilla warfare was fought in the mind as well as by the body, and the constant sniping at German targets gave the partisans a psychological edge on their opponents, who could never be sure that they would defeat them.

The fact that the bands usually contained local men and often operated in the areas from where the partisans came, might well have eased their reception locally, but only heightened the dilemma of the level and kind of activity they should undertake. Any reprisals their actions provoked would directly put at risk their own families and friends. This meant that as far as possible, each action undertaken by the bands had to be proportional to both the aims of the action and to the likely impact on the local population. One can quite see that such calculations of risk would sometimes induce inaction and inhibit any meaningful resistance activity altogether. Inertia, of course, invalidated the whole point of there being an armed resistance, which was to make life difficult for the occupier. Two modes of survival, that of the local community and that of the band, somehow had to be made to harmonize.

A rule of thumb for all partisan commanders was that the band should not be like the Fascists and the Germans in the way it behaved and in the way it treated the local population. Food and shelter should be paid for, or in some way compensated for, by offering protection or safe passage for the transit of goods, for example. The band should not steal from, or prey on, the local people. So, in the words of Cirio, the *nom de guerre* of the Garibaldi commander in the Valsesia valley of Novara province, west of Milan, the execution of some of his partisans for theft and rape ('banditry') was not primarily an 'act of justice, but a political gesture publicized with posters throughout the valley'.[23]

But it was very difficult to develop a modus operandi which covered the partisans in most circumstances, and in most areas. The complicated and, it must be said, sometimes tragic interactions between partisans, police, and local people, and what a band's presence could mean for a small community where everybody knew each other's business, are best conveyed by an example. In Caltignana, again in the province of Novara, the municipal doctor Sebastiano Russo was killed in December 1944 by a group of partisans who were trying to extort from him a confession that he was a Fascist. He was, in fact, a Fascist Party member, since it was a requirement of him exercising his profession. But he had, apparently, been the only doctor to tell the provincial prefect, who had instructed doctors not to help injured partisans, that he would not treat people on the basis of their political activities. His daughter, the local chemist, had supplied medicines to sick and wounded partisans. The Decima Mas were responsible for policing the area, and they gave Russo's daughter a pass allowing her to recover her father's body and investigate his death. The local partisan command then attempted to hijack the search for the doctor's killers, and the daughter, on their suggestion, enticed the partisans responsible to a local restaurant where they were arrested by their fellow partisans, tried by a partisan tribunal, and sentenced to death. The execution was to be public, because it was now clear that the partisan command wanted to discipline the errant partisans itself and regarded the real crime as being the discrediting of the band in the eyes of the local people, 'more than any propaganda of the enemy', as the tribunal judgment put it.[24] But there was a sting in the tail of the story. The execution did not take place, and the 'guilty' partisans were effectively allowed to leave the area because of the *omertà* (silent connivance) of the other band members, who felt that their comrades should not be punished for something they had done on the basis of false and malicious information about the doctor supplied by a local person. To them, the guilt lay with the informer, not the partisans.

The incident revealed a great deal, starting with the individual civil disobedience of the doctor and his daughter, whose professional integrity led them to resist in a social realm outside the immediate orbit of armed resistance. The war, the civil war, and the choices they imposed, made it impossible for these two professionals to sit out the conflict and await its end. The existence of the informer indicated a community divided against itself, and who knows what personal or professional grudge, or, indeed, political conviction, lay behind the decision to inform on the doctor to the partisans. What mattered to the partisan commander was the band's standing with the local population, crucial for its survival and, indeed, for his evident desire not only to police his own men but also to police the locality. The unravelling of the case showed a shift in the balance of forces in the area, with the partisans rather than the Fascist police acting as law and order. Finally, there was the group solidarity of the partisan band. Its attitude to the killings was determined by ties of comradeship and, beyond this, by a concern for the functioning and survival of the band, whose cohesion was threatened by the informer, a member of the local community they had to rely on.

The life of a partisan band was an unnatural one, even though living off the countryside, as for the evacuees, brought them closer to the natural world. Partisans were fugitives, outlaws, obliged by the nature of their existence to develop a group cohesion and an internal discipline and morality with its own self-justifying logic of survival. The policemen or troops the bands might have captured in an ambush were both a boon and a liability. They could be used in prisoner exchanges. But they consumed the often precarious material resources of the band and became a real danger and burden when the band was being harassed by Fascist and German round-ups. They could not be released, because they would inform on their whereabouts, and they could not be looked after or protected on the run. So, during anti-partisan sweeps, they were usually killed. Even new recruits to the bands threatened their cohesion and survival: more mouths to feed, more men to find weapons for, more men whose loyalties and intentions were, as yet, untested and unproven.

Urban partisans lived a particularly unnatural existence, largely dictated by the environment in which they operated. They had to work alone, or in small cells, and always clandestinely, in order to remain undetected in a crowded place. They were, literally, the archetypal lone assassins, targeting local Fascists and their collaborators, spies and informers, German troops. A member of GAP said that his enforced isolation made him the 'jailor of myself'.[25]

Identities had to be disguised or changed. Most partisans, men and women, adopted or were made to adopt *noms de guerre*, both to save themselves and the others from detection and to dignify and mark a new kind of existence which was essentially alien and abnormal. Gina Negrini, on joining the Garibaldi brigade, was told by her commander, 'from this moment on, you're a soldier. Your name, just forget it. We'll call you Tito.'[26] Tolmina Guazzaloca, a courier for the regional partisan command of Emilia-Romagna, described her experience as a partisan as being 'outside life', in the sense of having to abandon the attachments and emotions of a normal existence. Adalgia Gallerani died alone in a hospital in Bologna after being injured by a bomb, unwilling to call in her friends and family, who were from the deep south in Calabria, because she wanted to retain her false name and identity and not compromise her fellow partisans.

Women were natural or perfect resisters, since they could use their gender and social gender stereotyping to disguise and protect the resistance's clandestine activities. The role played by women in the resistance was equivalent to the very visible presence traditionally given to Italian women in popular protests and demonstrations. Their position at the head of a procession immediately disarmed and disorientated the police or troops sent out to contain or repress the protest. During the war and occupation, women could go to places and move around with a freedom not available to men, because their femininity apparently ruled out the possibility of certain kinds of action or behaviour, and eased the way with men in authority, using 'flirtatiousness as a form of self-defence'.[27] This was why women were often used as couriers for partisan groups. In Bologna, and in most Italian cities, official permission was required, from 1941, to move around on a bicycle, but the ban did not apply to women. One partisan aborted a child she was carrying because she was afraid that once fully pregnant, she would not be allowed to keep and use her bike. Young female partisans were meant to make the most of being a woman in a man's world. But even here, doing so could distort perceptions and normal contacts and relationships. Ena Frazzoni, initially 'Nicoletta', then 'Bianca', who became the partisans' liaison with the Allies, wondered whether being eyed up in the streets of Bologna was a matter of suspicion or simply the casual admiration of passers-by.

The unnaturalness of being a partisan has been emphasized as a way of gauging the extent to which people were changed by their participation in resistance activity. A lot of weight, and a lot of hopes, were placed on the Resistance's capacity to shape a new and better post-war Italian society. For the Action Party, especially, and indeed for the PCI, involvement in resistance was seen at the time as an educative and formative experience which would help to create the citizens of a post-war democratic polity. They thought that the resistance experience was essential in remoulding young men and women who had been educated and brought up under Fascism and whose entry to the bands was usually circumstantial rather than political.

The partisans would not have needed telling by the anti-Fascist political parties that they were fighting to defeat fascism, in the shape of the RSI and the Nazi occupier. Who their enemies were, was clear enough from the daily conditions and dangers of partisan life. It would be safe to say that whatever Fascism was in them at the start, the partisan experience would have forced it out of them. The partisans, in other words, would have actually experienced the armed resistance as a civil war and a war of national liberation. Whether they experienced it as a class war might well have depended on a range of other factors, including social, occupational, and family background and previous levels of politicization, as well as what their individual bands actually got up to. Even though the initial choice to join might have been made under a form of compulsion, the feeling of being and acting as a group and developing the kind of solidarities which put group before individual inter-ests, would have been formed organically as an outcome of participating in the band. But if these were civic virtues, the attributes which enabled an individual to live in a society, then, arguably, they were developed in the SAF, as well. The partisans had to live a kind of military existence, abiding by codes of conduct which were functional to the survival of the band. One wonders just how transferable to post-war civilian society were the values and ways of such necessarily sealed-off micro-worlds as the partisan bands, and whether, indeed, the bulk of the partisans themselves saw the modes of operation of the band as ones appropriate to a peacetime society.

The women partisans were a particular case. The roles they performed in and for the bands were often as gender-stereotypical and as auxiliary as those of the members of SAF. The model that was cascaded down to other partisan bands by the partisan leadership was that of the Garibaldi brigade which in August 1944 had a group of thirty-eight women working for it, mainly the mothers, wives, and sisters of the male partisans, who did shifts of washing, ironing, mending and making clothing and bedding under the watchful supervision of a male partisan who was a tailor by trade. These were the usual social and sexual hierarchies of everyday working life relocated to the partisan community of the mountains. The weekly medical checks for sexually transmitted diseases would not necessarily have happened back home, but they would have happened in the military barracks or garrison.

Women partisans in the Communist Garibaldi formations were not normally allowed to take part in the triumphal march-pasts after liberation, though female comrades in other non- or party-affiliated bands were. If they did participate, their presence was often disguised or passed off as nurses. This move, apparently, was to protect the seriousness of the bands against any ironic popular comment. The women's sense of independence and self-worth might well have survived such an humiliation. But, clearly, this was a source of great resentment for some women resisters (though not all). A female courier was, if not exactly happy, then eventually understanding of the decision to make her part of the audience rather than the play, during her own formation's post-liberation procession in Turin. If the public had seen her marching alongside her male comrades, they would have thought she was a *puttana* (prostitute), which, by her account, was the word used in the crowd when the women partisans of the autonomous bands passed by. Society, it would appear, was as unchanging as the bands. Annunciata Cesani, one of the group who attacked the work supervisor in Osteriola, was abruptly returned to the familiar world of the patriarchal family when told by her father after the liberation, 'Adesso basta! That's enough, now! You've been gallivanting around enough!'[28]

It should be clear from the swelling of the ranks of the partisan bands in the summer of 1944 that organized, armed resistance could not have existed without the kind of individual and collective acts of civil disobedience, of the refusal to comply with German and RSI demands, which were, in fact, the most characteristic and prevalent forms of popular resistance to Fascism and the German occupation. These unorganized popular choices to resist were, in at least two ways, much more difficult choices to make than that of becoming a partisan. People had to make these choices very much on their own or within the family, because the usual guides to behaviour in difficult circumstances, like the Catholic Church, were absent or deficient. Catholics, of course, believed in peace and harmony under God among all men and women. War and conflict were considered unnatural when it was human beings' Christian propensity to live at peace with others. The Church's official teaching could only be to regret and condemn all violence, whoever perpetrated it, and to care indiscriminately for the victims of violence and suffering. 'Prayer, prudence, charity'[29] was the guidance issued by the Tuscan bishops to their parish priests, in April 1944, as if there was not a war on at all. Catholics also believed in giving due deference to 'the things which are Caesar's'. The Church never officially recognized the RSI as the legitimate government of Italy, to the Fascists' great resentment. But it was prepared to urge or advise Catholics to obey its de facto authority, as long as the essentials of good order and the protection of religion were secured. Even the Germans were to be obeyed, on this count.

The problem with the Church's stance of neutrality, its apparently even-handed rejection of all violence, Fascist, German, or partisan, was that it neutered its ability to influence people's choices about what to do and how to behave. When everything and everybody was at war, with the Germans, with each other, the Church effectively recognized the impotence which followed inescapably from the logic of its position of not taking sides. The bishop of Cremona's advice to fugitives, in late September 1943, might as well have been the advice to the Italian people throughout the period of German occupation: 'I would say to them that they clearly consider the dangers of one or the other way, and do what they want.'[30]

The Catholic Church's official wringing, and washing, of its hands, had, to be fair, a strangely liberating effect on parish priests, because if ordinary Catholics were left to their own devices, so were the priests. Pastoral concern for one's flock could be interpreted and expressed in all kinds of ways in a wartime situation, and we often find priests reinforcing their positions in local communities and even assuming something of a leadership role. Even if not directly implicated in resistance activity, and many of them were, they were the people sought out by fugitives of all kinds wandering in strange territory, the go-betweens in prisoner exchanges, even truces, between Fascists, Germans, and partisans, the organizers of temporary ceasefires to allow the retrieval and burial of people killed in either the civil war or the Allied war.

The other reason for the difficulty of the choices facing civilian resisters was that they lived, and continued to live, in real society, usually unarmed if not exactly defenceless, which meant that they and the people close to them had to bear the immediate consequences and implications of the choices they made. The partisans withdrew from real society to arm themselves and form their own kind of society with its own norms and outlook, and the consequences of their actions were often borne not by themselves but by the inhabitants of real society. Only the women of the partisan bands straddled both partisan and real society. In the brilliant phrase of Paolo Pezzino, one of the historians of civilian massacres in wartime Italy, civil resistance was 'the capacity to resist with one's own framework of solidarity',[31]—personal and collective resourcefulness, in other words. The illuminating force of this categorization of what constituted most popular resistance in German-occupied Italy can be indicated by thinking about the calculation of what risks were worth taking for survival, in all senses, which lay behind the popular demonstration of thousands of women outside the German military command in the Tuscan town of Carrara, in July 1944. The province of Massa-Carrara, on the western extremity of the Gothic Line, was a war zone for nine months. The protest was against the German order for the entire population of the town to evacuate inland to Sala Baganza, across the mountains in the neighbouring province of Parma. In the face of this desperate collective effort to preserve themselves as a community, the Germans decided to abandon their plans for evacuation.

One of the most impressive and extensive acts of unarmed, unorganized popular resistance was the help given by Italian peasants and their families to the Allied POWs who walked out of their camps during the hiatus of the armistice of 8 September 1943. The Allied screening commission set up for the purpose received nearly 100,000 applications for paid acknowledgement of services to Allied prisoners, and although not all were granted, the figure showed the extent of the phenomenon. It also revealed something of the motivation for providing help, which was, in part, anyway, seen by the peasants as a deal. Escaping POWs were a source of labour in the countryside when labour was short, and shelter, protection, and subsistence was all the payment they required. All escapes of POWs were, in some sense, arranged deals. The fishermen off the Adriatic coast from Torre di Palme agreed to take British officers in their boats to landing points to the south, behind Allied lines, on condition that their fishing areas would be spared Allied air raids. A young woman from Varese, north of Milan near the Swiss border, became part of an escape chain for Allied POWs, on the understanding that her husband, an Italian POW of the British in a camp in India, was released. For the peasants, a very welcome inversion of the usual power relationships in the countryside was occurring: they had something to offer, which was desperately needed, and could negotiate the price from a position of some strength. It corresponded to the great wartime shift in town and country relations, when the superior town folk became dependent for survival on what the inferior country folk provided, whether a supply of food or shelter, or both.

In this way, the peasants' resistance was self-contained, in alignment with the values and imperatives of their own peasant world, as Pezzino's definition suggests. The elderly peasant woman, betrayed to the Germans for sheltering Allied POWs in her village near L'Aquila in south central Italy, told her captors that 'I did not help them because they are British but because I am a Christian [*meaning* a human being] and they, too, are Christians.'[32] Peasants lived needy, precarious lives themselves and saw themselves as prey to external, alien, usually urban, forces. Their hearts, and minds, went out to fellow strugglers, in trouble with and being pursued by authority. They experienced a tremendous sense of their value and worth in helping, with all the attendant risks, young men who were completely helpless and dependent on them, strangers with no idea of where they were and where they were going, and who were endlessly grateful for the shelter they were given. Peasant women, wives and daughters, were charmed by such polite helplessness, when their own men, husbands and brothers, treated them indifferently and unkindly. No wonder some of them formed, or imagined, sentimental attachments with the good-looking exotic young soldiers to whom they brought food on a daily basis.

There was a dark side to this rural idyll of peasant families making outsiders, honorary insiders. Perhaps two-thirds of the 50,000 escaping POWs were recaptured. Even though many of them, in effect, would have given themselves up, because they were unable to manage living rough and being constantly on the move, such hunger and disorientation reflected the lack of a welcome in the countryside. What was worse, over 300 POWs were murdered, and more would have been handed over to the RSI police by local people, when there were rewards on offer and the fear of detection and reprisal if they protected them. In some cases, the better deal was to shop the stranger who had chanced into their area. Some local men in the region of the Marches became bounty hunters, tracking down and killing escaped POWs. They were never actually tried and punished for their crimes after the war, because the local population closed ranks and refused to testify against them, even though everybody knew whom they were. The same distrust of authority and the same concern to protect the fugitive from authority, which had saved some Allied servicemen during the war, now saved the perpetrators of crimes against them. The only thing that can make sense of such contradictory behaviour, sometimes protecting, sometimes pursuing, was a peasant culture of survival above all else and of a visceral and rooted dislike of outside authority.

As one might expect of people struggling to survive in wartime conditions, averting or minimizing danger to themselves was what guided their behaviour. As German troops embarked on the clearance of central Italy in the summer of 1944, peasants in the Appennines to the south of Cesena, in Emilia, improvised patrols of their own to head off German and RSI expeditions sweeping the area for partisans, advising them to go back because the area they were approaching was a partisan zone and they would surely be attacked. Such approaches could be categorized as resistance, since the peasants were attempting to divert the Germans and Fascists from where partisans were operating, and also as collaboration, since they were, of course, warning them of the presence of partisan bands. The categories are, in fact, made redundant by their behaviour: they simply wanted to keep both sides out of their locality. In the same Emilian mountains, Garibaldi bands complained of the 'peasant's mentality'[33] which saw them being chased away by local people threatening to denounce them to the Germans.

Industrial worker evacuees from Terni, resuming contact from late 1943 with the surrounding countryside from which their parents had migrated for urban employment, and now working for the Todt organization building defensive fortifications, stole supplies from their German employers, on this occasion, shoes, for barter with the peasants of their places of evacuation. In fact, these entrepreneurial evacuees developed a system of domestic manufacture and exchange with their peasant hosts, which allowed them to continue to view their country cousins with some condescension. The urban evacuees bartered what were luxuries to the peasants, stolen shoes, traded salt, ersatz tobacco, black market soap which they made from shoe polish, in return for what was essential for them, food. The acts of collaboration—working for the Germans—and of resistance—stealing from the Germans and deserting their jobs—were incidental to what mattered: the struggle to survive in an alien rural environment.

One of these trader evacuees, an ex-industrial worker born in Terni, dealt in cigarettes picked up in Civitavecchia, the nearest port up the coast from Rome. He traded with everybody in his evacuee village, and both Fascists and partisans regularly bought cigarettes from him and used him as a source of gossip and information on the other. He remembered:

> We were all friends, the partisans as much as the Fascists; we were all from Terni, I knew them well . . . well, they gave me the money, asking if I had seen anybody around. Not today . . . Afterwards, the Fascists came to buy cigarettes, asking if I had seen the partisans. Well, they passed through yesterday. Be careful, I say . . . They were all my friends.[34]

This man was not being neutral or *attendista*, in the sense of not having anything to do with either side. He was dealing with both sides, and what bridged the differences between them, trader, Fascists, and partisans, were, apparently, being friends and being from Terni. But, of course, what really bridged them was the trade in cigarettes, and this trade brought the trader survival in more than one sense. He received money for his sales, and also earned the protection of both sides. Neither side wanted to risk losing an informer and his cigarettes. The playing of both sides might be regarded as an exemplary personal resourcefulness in extraordinarily difficult circumstances, or as shallow, non-committal opportunism in a country riven by civil war. It is impossible to judge this man's behaviour by any polarized measure of collaboration or resistance, when the only point of what he was doing was to survive, which justified itself.

# 8

# Continuing the Wars, and the Second Fall of Mussolini, April 1945

I N 1990, an Italian called Giuseppe Bonfanti, 66 years old, returned to Italy from Brazil, where he had emigrated after the war. The purpose of his visit was to kill another elderly man, 68-year-old Giuseppe Oppici. It was not a tidy killing. If it had happened forty-five years earlier, Bonfanti would undoubtedly have used his gun. As it was, he killed Oppici with a pickaxe in an alley in Salina, the birthplace of both men. The reason, and justification, for the killing was that in November 1944 Oppici was among a group of Fascists on a reprisal expedition who burned down the partisan Bonfanti's house and slaughtered his livestock. 'I came back just to kill him,' said Bonfanti; 'finally I made him pay.'[1]

In Piacenza d'Adige, during the German occupation, the Germans and Fascist police had paraded through the village local men they had arrested or picked up in the course of a round-up of partisans in the area, before busing them off to prison and, for some, execution. This was how Silvano Trambaiolo, then 10 years old, remembered things once the Germans had left and the Allies had arrived, in April 1945:

> Early one evening, I was with my mother in the vegetable garden, where we were planting the new season's tomato seedlings, when we suddenly froze at the sound of repeated bursts of a machine gun firing, breaking the evening stillness. The ominous sound was coming from the banks of the Adige, less than three hundred yards away. Neither of us said a word. We both realised immediately that so-called justice was being done. We knew all five of the people (amongst them a woman and her old father) who at that moment were being shot in anger by other people whom we also knew very well, and whom

at that time we wished we didn't know. For, whatever the rights and wrongs, both executioners and victims were still very much part of the *paese*.

The explanation for the killings was that

not long after the arrival of the allied troops, village people who had lost relatives at the hands of the *Repubblichini* (the Fascist Republic's men) couldn't wait to take their revenge on the *paesani* (village people) who had supported the *Repubblichini* all along. The latter, naturally, had fled the village at the first signs of the German army's imminent collapse.[2]

The recording of the child's memory practically coincided with the old man's belated act of revenge. Bonfanti enacted what Trambaiolo remembered. Time, of course, separated the two incidents. Bonfanti had gone on fighting the war, in his head, for over forty years, finally deciding to finish the war before it was too late.

Italy was a violent and lawless place, north and south, before, during, and after the final liberation of the country by Allied troops in late April 1945 and the end to fighting in the war in Italy on 2 May 1945. That the Allied liberation of Italy between 1943 and 1945 did not end Italy's wars, was in many ways because wartime social and economic conditions persisted into the post-liberation and post-war periods—and, in some areas, worsened. Many factories had closed or were operating below capacity because of the shortage of fuel and raw materials. With the end to war contracts and wartime demand, industrial unemployment rose, and the general pool of labour expanded as demobilized soldiers and partisans returned to civilian life, and internees and deported workers were repatriated. Inflation moved northwards with Allied occupation and reunification of the south with the north in the summer of 1945.

The partisans had urged the peasants to evade the *ammassi* in the summer and autumn of 1944 as their patriotic duty to resist Fascist and German requisitioning. Even though the Fascists and Germans had gone, peasants, everywhere, went on bypassing the requisitioning system, in order to sell on the free market, because the terms of trade and exchange between country and town remained as favourable to them as they were in wartime. Black marketeering and contraband continued to be a way to survive for whole communities. For example, the people of Isola del Liri, just south of Rome, were liberated early in 1944. Their local paper mills were abandoned and idle. They used the redundant paper supplies to manufacture cigarettes, with 'imported' tobacco. People worked from their homes, in an improvised cottage industry, carefully faking the labels on the packs to resemble those produced by the state monopoly. This illegal manufacturing and trading enterprise lasted well into 1946, protected from the finance police by a maverick socialist provisional mayor who thought that his people should be allowed to carry on while it was their only source of livelihood. Enterprising criminal commerce such as this always found consumers at a time when normal trade and communication were disrupted by wartime damage to the infrastructure.

Many buildings were destroyed or damaged, and evacuees came back to ruined towns and cities. Sometimes, if their houses and apartments were still standing, they found them occupied by the homeless. People moving in the opposite direction had similar experiences. In September 1945, the prefect of Bologna ordered the city's thousands of refugees from the surrounding countryside to return to their villages, and since the villages were where the fighting had taken place, nothing much was left standing for the returning population. Overcrowding in scarce accommodation was common, and as a result, the incongruous social interactions of wartime continued. For instance, in the Tuscan industrial port city of Livorno, where 70 per cent of buildings were destroyed, a wealthy middle-class Jewish lawyer had to share his apartment with a young woman who had become a prostitute and a black marketeer.

Much of the immediate post-war crime wave of thefts and robberies was to do with survival in severely straitened economic circumstances. Still-armed ex-partisans held up cars and lorries on the open road, to steal whatever packages or supplies they were carrying. Shops were raided for food and clothing, sometimes by a few armed individuals, sometimes by a mob of hungry and desperate people. In Serra San Bruno, in the southern province of Catanzaro, hand grenades were lobbed from the crowd against the *carabinieri* attempting to put a stop to a mass break-in of the local bakery. Some of the post-war violent crime was connected to the black market, with groups of ex-partisans being commissioned to steal and supply foodstuffs to illegal traders, often located in neighbouring provinces. In the region of Emilia, some gangs came to specialize in the theft of certain prized local products, like parmesan cheese.

What characterized the crime wave were the use of weapons and the willingness to be violent. There were plenty of weapons, especially handguns, in circulation. The police, sometimes admittedly in rather a panicky way, reported to their superiors that the disbanding and disarming partisans in the spring and summer of 1945 were handing over their heavy weaponry, but not their pistols. One provincial police chief estimated that perhaps a quarter of all partisan-held weapons were still at large. Retreating Germans and advancing Allied soldiers abandoned weapons as the battle fronts passed, though when civilians recovered or found them, many would have been damaged or unmaintained. Ammunition was a problem. But Allied war depots were often casually guarded, and some of the post-war's most infamous criminal gangs kept themselves going by raids on Allied military supplies and vehicles.

Peasants were agitated and agitating, throughout the country. In the south and islands, they took possession of uncultivated land, in part encouraged, in part inhibited, by the government decrees on land reform issued by the communist Minister of Agriculture, Fausto Gullo, in late 1944. In areas of Calabria and Basilicata, some entire peasant communities had become self-administering enclaves; it took a combined Allied and *carabinieri* military operation to dismantle the peasant 'republic' of Caulonia in Reggio Calabria province in the spring and summer of 1945. Allied troops also supported the rather more traditional agents of agrarian repression in the south, the *carabinieri* and the landowners' armed roughnecks, in ejecting peasants from the land they had occupied in other parts of the region. In some cases, the peasants fought back, staging a violent popular demonstration against the *carabinieri* in Bocchigliero, in Cosenza province, in May 1945, because of the decision to prosecute two hundred of them for occupations which under the Gullo decrees could be taken as illegal.

In the centre and north, the rumbling agrarian dispute of 1945–6 was over the revision of sharecropping contracts, with peasant tenants and their union, Federterra, claiming—and their landlords resisting—a more than half share of farm production for themselves. The experience of war definitely gave an edge to these post-war and post-liberation contractural confrontations and land occupations in the countryside. The peasants' agitation was, of course, driven by a traditional and long-standing land hunger and concern to run and dispose of their holdings as they wished. But it was also now a matter of getting war-damaged land and fields which had been fallow during the war, back under cultivation. A major complaint of peasant tenants against the landowners was the latter's reluctance to proceed with and pay for the rehabilitation of land made uncultivable as a result of the war.

The mood had changed, too, as an outcome of the war. In the Ciocaro area of southern Lazio, the big local landowner, an aristocrat and ex-Fascist Party leader, had withdrawn to Rome for the duration of the war, leaving his property and livestock to be stewarded by the peasants, an onerous task when the Germans were in occupation, without any of the compensating paternalistic welfare and support in hard times expected of the traditional seigneur. Now, with the Germans gone, the count returned and claimed the renewal of the pre-war contract for the division of the produce between farmer and proprietor, as if he had never been away. The peasants were no longer prepared to defer to their absentee master. The count's land agent and factotum was driven to distraction by the obstinate negotiating position of one peasant woman. 'My God! Now even Concetta starts talking about the law!',[3] he grumbled to her, incredulous at her self-assertiveness and her use of the Gullo decree as leverage against his boss.

The interview with an ex-peasant from the Tuscan sharecropping village of Castagneto Carducci, revealed how an already rather cussed individual, who had avoided following the local men into the *fascio* headed by his aristocratic landowner some years earlier, employed his war experience to break for good the bonds of social deference. The man had been a soldier interned by the Germans after the armistice, and on his return from Germany at the end of the war, had been criticized by the estate manager for not paying the usual respects to the count. The man recalled, retorting to the manager (and the account was probably embellished in the retelling),

> Look, I am just a poor guy who went to war for his country of which, look as I might, not even a very small part belongs to me. Ok? I see, on the other hand, that [the] Count . . . who has lived in hiding and who has done all sorts of things, is still enjoying a nice piece of his homeland . . . Well, if I were the Count . . . shouldn't I go to greet these peasants who went to war to defend his country and risked everything so that he could find his homeland as it was before?[4]

The quite calculated play on the 'ownership' of 'his' country (the count's or the peasant's?) shows how the landowner's complicity with Fascism and his wartime 'hiding' had put him at such a disadvantage in seeking to resume customary social relationships after the war. The returning peasant soldier, and his village, voted for the Communist Party in 1946. It must be said, however, that this man's sense of independence was only finally secured when he moved to an industrial factory job shortly after. The count refused to renew the agricultural contracts of his more recalcitrant peasant farmers, and attempted to replace them with more amenable peasant families from the south, who turned out not to be compliant at all, in time acclimatizing to the radical political climate of their new surroundings.

There was a general sense in which wartime lawlessness contributed to the lawlessness of the post-war. Things had to be decided by violence in the final months of German occupation and nominal RSI control, as the civil war nastily intensified. The Nazi version of law and order in the towns and cities of the north was inherently anarchical and deregulated. Their occupation gave free rein to private Fascist militias and armed gangs who operated simultaneously as policemen and lawbreakers. The people they arrested—or rather captured—and interrogated and tortured in their own prisons, usually private houses, could be partisans or citizens kidnapped for ransom. Some of the ex-partisan gangs who terrorized their neighbourhoods in the immediate aftermath of the war showed precisely the same blend of political criminality. One of several similar incidents was the raid on Gaggio Montano, a small place in the mountains near Bologna, in November 1945, by a group of armed men, nearly all of them ex-Garibaldi partisans and Communist Party members, who blocked off the village at both ends, imprisoned the local *carabinieri*, shot and killed five people, and robbed the bank as well as private residences. By their own account at the trial, the expedition was to raise funds for the support of the families of ex-partisans on the run for 'crimes' committed during the period of liberation.

More mundanely, people who might not have regarded themselves as resisters, but certainly saw themselves as survivors, were accustomed to behaving illegally in their daily lives and, indeed, had to, in order to survive. The recourse to the black market was the most evident sign of widespread, popular criminality. It was, perhaps, not so much that people were brutalized by the experience of war; rather, that acting illegally and resolving problems by direct, often violent, action, constituted customary and necessary behaviour in wartime, and would continue in the post-war period, also, since conditions remained the same. Surviving war and occupation was not necessarily good training for post-war democratic citizenship.

As was the case in many countries emerging from a war, the poorly resourced, disorganized, and demoralized state of the police forces was another reason for the post-liberation and post-war crime wave. Inadequate and low-level policing gave a kind of immunity to violent crime, and increased feelings of insecurity. Not only were the police ineffective; the courts and the public administration were not working properly, either. There was a general institutional hiatus. People sensed that the state had ceased to function, which apparently gave a licence to crime and enabled people to dispense their own forms of rough justice.

One of the explanations for the demoralization and disorganization of the police and the state bureaucracy was the purges (and investigations which might lead to purging) of officials for their previous service under the Fascist regime and during the German occupation. Such purges of 'Fascist' personnel and office holders were initially pursued with some vigour by the Allied Military Government in the liberated south. But they were stalled, and often reversed, by the king's government under Badoglio once the control of liberated territory passed to an Italian administration. In the liberated north, the anti-Fascist Resistance government of Parri removed or suspended thousands of police officers, as new CLN-nominated police chiefs and prefects began investigating their own staff. The idea was to replace them with army officers and, especially, with ex-partisans, in a now typical transitional strategy to domesticate and channel the violent energies of the country's freedom fighters.

Some prefects, who were responsible to the central government for settling down the disorder which they were reporting on, were sensible enough to realize that the immediate post-war lawlessness would probably be a passing phenomenon, an unavoidable side-effect of the transition from war to peace-time conditions and from one political system to another. But most of them saw the post-war volatility as a straight law and order issue, to be repressed rather than understood. They also drew easy connections between post-war social and economic unrest; the very visible presence of the PCI, unions, and communist ex-partisans; and a subversive revolutionary design, assuming that the troubles were inspired and driven by an insurrectionary communist movement.

Such perceptions were reflected back at them by Parri's government, which had communists and socialists holding the key ministries of Justice and the Interior and therefore responsible for running the judicial and policing system. Post-war lawlessness, and the need to handle it, was probably the major reason for the overall failure, indeed reversal, of the purges of a state bureaucracy complicit with Fascism and Nazi-Fascism. The parties of the left, particularly the PCI, could not afford to condone popular illegality when the political price to pay might well be the breakdown of the wartime anti-Fascist unity with conservative forces, the continuation of which seemed to be the best way of establishing themselves in post-war democratic national politics. Many communist ex-partisans and party members might well have believed that Soviet tanks would not stop at the Yugoslav frontier. But the PCI's national leadership knew that Italy, on one of the European borders between the fighting forces of the anti-Nazi alliance, would be under Anglo-American, not Soviet Russian, control, and that the most they could hope and work for was a progressive democratic republican system of government.

The career civil servants fought back, exploiting the deliberate self-limitation of wartime and post-war anti-Fascist governments. They lobbied successfully to the Allied Military Government, who were very willing to listen, and to the Italian central government, who should have known better, to the effect that only their technical, professional expertise could get to grips with the country's crime epidemic and threat of revolutionary subversion, which was beyond the incompetent, inexperienced and politically partial policing of an improvised ex-partisan force. Indeed, to the career police and civil service, the ex-partisans, now policemen, were a major cause of the country's post-war problems, not part of their solution.

As a result of the civil servants' fight-back, files closed on purge investigations, suspended police officers were recalled to duty, senior civil servants and policemen who had made their careers under Fascism and continued them under Nazi occupation, returned to replace the CLN-nominated liberation officials. Life was made very difficult for the ex-partisans who wanted and intended to stay in the police. Some communist ex-partisans, their anti-Fascist records now once again being used against them, were just sacked. Others were induced to seek compensated resignation by being constantly moved around the country from post to post, often in the south and the islands, long regarded as places to park unsatisfactory and uncongenial officials. In a dangerously volatile internal situation post-war, and an equally uncertain international situation, with both Italy's north-western and north-eastern borders under threat, the old state bureaucracy would have appeared to the Italian government as a really important nationalizing and normalizing institution, one which both embodied and could help to bring about national integration.

The continuation of Pavone's three wars was clearly discernible in 1945. But the Resistance as a patriotic war of national liberation took on a rather different dimension on Italy's contested northern frontiers. In the north-west, since both France and northern Italy were under Nazi occupation, the Franco-Italian border had effectively ceased to exist for both French and Italian resistance movements. Partisans sought refuge in each other's territory, and supplied and reinforced each other across the border, in the common struggle against German occupation. Cross-border cooperation between national resistance movements ended dramatically in late April 1945, at the point when it seemed to be at its closest.

On the pretext that their help was needed to ensure that German troops withdrew from Italy, the Free French provisional government under Charles de Gaulle sent both regular army forces and partisans into Aosta, a French-speaking Alpine region on the Italian side of the border. Italian partisans in French territory were disarmed and offered the equally uncongenial choices of internment and forced labour or enlistment in the French Foreign Legion, not very different from what the Germans offered after the September 1943 armistice. These moves were belated revenge for the Fascist Italian invasion of France in June 1940. France, in de Gaulle's view, was still at war with Italy, and was not a party to, and therefore not bound by, the 1943 armistice and the Italian changing of sides. It was clear de Gaulle intended to treat Italy as a defeated enemy country which had not managed to fight and resist its way back into the Allied camp. He wanted to get French forces and French equivalents of the CLNs into Italian territory. Their presence was to be a prelude to a permanent adjustment of the frontier in France's favour, exploiting and promoting residual regional separatism in Aosta, and a way of ensuring that France had a say in the post-war peace settlement and any redistribution by the victors of Axis territory and resources.

In response, the Allied military government in north-western Italy postponed the planned and agreed disarmament and disbanding of Italian partisans, and allowed them to retain their weapons and patrols on the Franco-Italian border. Clashes between previously cooperating Italian and French partisan groups only encouraged and justified a larger French military presence in Italy. By late May 1945, French troops were in the Ligurian riviera, and behaving as if they were the administration of north-west Italy, rather than the Allied Military Government or the Italian government. This very tense situation could only be resolved internationally. In a clear demonstration of where the real power now lay in liberated western Europe, French forces withdrew from Italy in the course of June and July 1945, when the Americans threatened to cut off aid to de Gaulle's army in France unless they did so.

The situation on Italy's north-eastern border had even greater national and international ramifications. After the September 1943 armistice, the Germans had occupied Italian-annexed and Italian-occupied territory in the Balkans. They had then, also, de facto, annexed the north-eastern border regions of Venezia Giulia and the Alto Adige and Trentino, and parts of the Yugoslav Dalmatian coast. These German annexations were a body blow to Mussolini who had claimed that his Fascist Republic could represent Italy and the national interest from within the Axis. The Italian Dalmatian enclave of Zara, after being occupied by the Germans and heavily bombed by the Allies, was taken over by Tito's Slav forces in late October 1944. In a practice to be followed throughout liberated Yugoslav territory, a Slav civil administration was set up there. The late 1944 dual power deal arranged between Tito and General Alexander, the commander of Allied forces, was that on liberation from German occupation, an Allied military government would be established in Istria and Venezia Giulia, overarching a Yugoslav civil administration.

Tito also incorporated those Italian ex-soldiers prepared to make the move, into the Yugoslav forces fighting against German occupation. Later, he involved both Italian communist Garibaldi formations and autonomous partisan groups in the liberation of Yugoslav territory, as a way of utilizing and at the same time controlling them as a military force. Italian partisans, both communist and apolitical, were part of the Slovene Ninth Corps occupying the border city of Trieste, early in May 1945.

In the Pola area, on the Istrian peninsula, the Slav partisans' capture and killing of 'Fascists'—Italian civilian and military officials and public employees, whose task had been both to administer and to Italianize—probably began immediately after the armistice, before the Germans and the Fascist Republic were able to take over. The killings resumed after Slav forces entered Pola on 2 May 1945 during the interregnum before the setting up of the Allied military government in June 1945. Fiume was liberated on 3 May, though liberation was not how it was seen by the resident Italian population. The Italian leaders of a revived autonomist movement which wanted to restore Fiume to its free city status of 1920, were immediately killed by Slav partisans. The Slav administration thereafter constantly and threateningly asked the unanswerable question of the Italians, which was why Fiume had not risen up against German occupation before or during the Slav taking of the city.

Trieste also went through a temporary period of Slav occupation, or rather joint Allied (New Zealand forces) and Slav occupation, running from the withdrawal of the Germans in early May 1945 to the establishment of the AMG on 12 June. These were the 'forty days of terror'[5] recalled by an Italian female pharmacist. Along with other professional people in the city, she became a target both for the Slav partisans who wanted to make use of her pharmaceutical skills and supplies, and then for the AMG, which as it did in other liberated parts of Italy, instituted an investigation of her

'Fascist' past. People like her participated in the pro-Italian and anti-Slav demonstrations in Trieste on 6 May. Her sentiments may have resembled those of the Italian woman who remembered the occupying Slav partisans as being 'dirty, ragged, or in uniforms stolen from Italian soldiers'. Some of them raided and ransacked her family's house, and put a gun to her head, 'breath stinking of wine'.[6] These bitter memories lack any proper depth and perspective. All that the woman had to offer was a dubious historical and cultural explanation for such behaviour, apparently characteristic of 'Asiatic' Slavs made uncivilized by centuries of Ottoman rule.

The *foibe* (deep natural chasms) at Monrupino and Basovizza, just outside the city, were used to kill or dump Italians taken in the Slav round-ups. The *foibe* killings were group murders of a gruesomely economical kind: prisoners were tied together, stood on the edges of the ditches, and the ones on the end, shot; as they fell, their momentum dragged the others over and down. Other captured Italians were imprisoned in camps further east in Slav-held territory.

In Trieste, and throughout Venezia Giulia, the war between Slavs and Italians for control of the frontier, was also a national and civil war among Italians. Communist Garibaldi partisan formations fought turf wars with the autonomous bands, who had started up in late 1943 and were particularly strong in the region. In Friuli, the head of the British mission to the Italian resistance pulled out of one operation to parachute in special forces troops to help the local partisans, because while the autonomous groups backed the expedition, the Garibaldi command did not. What was at stake here was the operational independence of the partisans, which for the Garibaldini was undermined by the autonomous bands' acceptance of an auxiliary role to Allied operations, and the balance among the various partisan formations, which the autonomous bands could move in their favour by securing access to Allied support.

In such a sensitive and contested border area, however, the conflict between the bands could become very destructive and reflect significant political divisions. In February 1945, in an incident at Porzûs, resurrected in the 1990s to demonstrate the PCI's anti-national stance then and now, a Garibaldi partisan group set on and killed twenty men belonging to the Osoppo autonomous formations, part of a rumbling conflict between the two, embittered by the national issue. The Osoppo, like the pro-Italian non-communist anti-Fascist elements of the Trieste CLN, and the Allies, wanted Venezia Giulia to remain Italian. The Garibaldi partisans and PCI in the region backed the pro-Yugoslav provisional administration set up temporarily in Trieste in May and June 1945, and the incorporation of Venezia Giulia into a Communist Yugoslavia.

It was, and is, of course, possible to idealize both positions. The Osoppo were patriotically defending the national borders, and, indeed, the borders of western civilization, against an internationalist and subversive communist tyranny rolling inexorably westwards. The Garibaldi were redeeming a brutal Italian annexation and occupation of Yugoslavia by recognizing the right to nationhood of all free peoples in a Europe liberated from Nazi tyranny. By conceding to the Yugoslavs on the north-eastern frontier, a free Italy could remove a long-standing cause of Italo-Yugoslav conflict and so contribute to post-war international harmony and reconciliation.

The difficulties of being even-handed in such situations were exemplified by the tortuous journey home to Italy at the end of the war of a group of men rounded up by the Germans and deported to factory work in Berlin, in November 1944, where they were treated as the traitorous 'soldiers of Badoglio'. From victims, and traitors, they soon became perpetrators. Liberated and then imprisoned by the Russians entering Berlin from the east, these Italian deportees were marched with other Italians into Soviet-occupied Poland, and thence transported by train through Russian-occupied Czechoslovakia and Hungary to a prison in Belgrade, the capital of a new Communist Yugoslavia. To their Slav captors, these Italians were 'soldiers of Mussolini',[7] as were the group of Italian partisans imprisoned with them for refusing to continue fighting with the Slav forces once the war was formally over. The Italians were released and repatriated in July 1945.

Again, as in north-west Italy, the border dispute could only be settled by international agreement among the main players. General Alexander negotiated a demarcation line with Tito, which, running near the Trieste city centre, meant Yugoslav troops left the city exclusively to the AMG in June 1945. The international peace treaty of February 1947 extended the respective gains and losses of the demarcation line. To Yugoslavia went all of Istria and Dalmatia, and over half of the provinces of Gorizia and Trieste, which remained Italian—just. These agreements prompted the acceleration of the departure of Italians from Italian Yugoslavia. Perhaps 350,000 'giuliano-dalmati' Italians left what they regarded as their homeland for resettlement in mainland Italy, some leaving in late 1945 and early 1946, the rest taking up an option to leave in the early 1950s. In a sense, the national and civil war never ended for these Italians. Disembarking at the Adriatic port of Ancona, they were barracked by communist workers as Fascists, and on arrival at the refugee camps in La Spezia, on the opposite Ligurian coast, were condemned by the local PCI as Giulian bandits.[8] They continued to see themselves as 'exiles in their own country',[9] unwanted in both Italy and Yugoslavia. Many, in fact, emigrated. They were not really forgotten, as they endlessly complained, but rather exploited politically in post-war Italian political struggles. The fate of the Dalmatian and Istrian refugees was used in an anti-communist vein by the Christian Democrats in the infamous cold war local and national elections of 1947 and 1948. Their cause has been all but revived and the case of the lost territories reopened, again in a nationalist and anti-communist vein, by the Berlusconi governments of the 1990s, which included, of course, the National Alliance, the neo-Fascist heir, once removed, of the Fascist regime and Republic which annexed and occupied the old Yugoslavia.

On 6 July 1945, nearly a year after the Allied liberation of this part of Romagna, in east central Italy, a group of ex-partisans raided the country house of Countess Beatrice Manzoni, near Lugo, in the province of Ravenna. They shot and killed the countess, her three adult sons, a maid, and the dog. Robbery was not the motive, though it occurred. The countess's sons were or had been Fascists, and backed the Fascist Republic. But if that was sufficient reason to kill them, these killings should have taken place much earlier, at a point during or shortly after liberation. The Manzonis were the big local landowners, and had been and still were the most powerful family in the area. They had rejected demands from their tenants to put right the wartime damage to the land they farmed, and in the widespread post-liberation regional conflict over the revision of sharecropping contracts, had refused to agree to Federterra's claim for the peasants to have a 60 per cent share of the produce. The killings were carried out by ex-partisans, but they had the feel of a peasant rising against the family held responsible for decades of social and economic oppression and dependence. The villagers ransacked the family's villa after the killings.

This incident in a continuing class and civil war had a wider historical setting than the war. The regions of Emilia and Romagna were marked by a bitter and often violent class conflict between large landholders and landless labourers and sharecroppers, both represented by the same socialist peasant leagues, since the emergence of a capitalist agriculture on reclaimed and improved land in the late nineteenth century. This class war was particularly intense in the first post-war, the 'red two years' of 1919–20, and was resolved then and effectively for the next twenty years by Fascist paramilitary squads which violently smashed the socialist peasants' unions and restored contractural conditions in favour of the employers. The partisans of the area, many of them landless labourers and sharecroppers, inserted themselves into the endemic class struggles of the countryside, much as the Fascists had done over twenty years earlier.

These and other similar killings and attacks on landholders would have appeared logical to their perpetrators and those who benefited from their violent resolution of class war. If it was justifiable for the Fascists to use violent means to secure the employers' socio-economic interests in the early 1920s, then there could be no argument with partisan and ex-partisan violence to defend the agricultural proletariat in the late 1940s. What had happened between the two post-wars was hardly incidental. When partisans attacked the local pillars of the propertied classes, they were killing the capitalist roots of Fascism and eradicating Fascism for good.

The ex-partisans who actually killed the Manzoni family were not tried and convicted for their deaths, since there was a rush to judgement which said much about the class war mentality of the post-war police and judiciary. Those responsible confessed to the crime from the safe distance of a hiding place outside the country. The PCI, in cases of this kind, usually connived at, if did not actually arrange, the safe passage of communist ex-partisans under police investigation and charge, to countries in Soviet Eastern Europe. The police did have some other ex-partisans in custody, and in a race to get a conviction, the court tried them for the murders and also convicted in their absence those who had admitted to the killings, for the offence of making false confessions.

Both sets of ex-partisans, those wrongly convicted of murder and those wrongly convicted of false confessions, belonged to the communist Garibaldi formations and were PCI members in a region which had voted strongly for the PCI in the post-war elections. The communist vote was the result of the area's agricultural working-class revolutionary tradition and of the spread of communist-led armed resistance to the Germans and the Fascist Republic. What the killings and the trial revealed was that a significant minority of communist ex-partisans in the region had decided not to demobilize after liberation and the end of the war, but to retain their weapons for use in a revolutionary class war, and to commit thefts and robberies against people and property in order to fund the revolution.

The PCI had its men in the Parri government, including the national party leader, Palmiro Togliatti, who was minister of justice at the time when these class war killings by communist ex-partisans were occurring. The situation was perceived to be particularly serious in the province of Reggio

Emilia, where communist ex-partisans were also targeting local leaders of non-communist anti-Fascist parties and groups (the PCI's partners in national government) for assassination. Togliatti himself was obliged to make a visit to Reggio Emilia, giving both a public and a secret speech. The latter effectively required regional and provincial PCI leaders to get control of their members and ensure that they kept to the party line of the democratic rather than the social revolution, and hence, the resolution of social conflict by democratic not violent means.

The issue was real enough, too, in other areas where there was a relatively high incidence of post-war killings. In Milan, the so-called Volante rossa (Red Flying Squad), a group of communist ex-partisans probably enjoying a measure of protection and support from the local PCI section, were killing Fascists, or rather ex-Fascists, as class enemies well into the late 1940s. They did so in a public and demonstrative way, as if they were trying to set an example and raise a revolutionary class consciousness among the city's workers.

That the PCI's democratic strategy prevailed over the revolutionary one, but not without a struggle with some of its own membership, can be gauged from the four-way split in a group of ex-partisans from the plains around Bologna who went on killing Fascists in the class war until mid-May 1945, when they were instructed by the PCI regional leader to disarm. Most of the group either accepted the PCI's official line on the democratic way, or disbanded to ordinary civilian life saying that they were disillusioned with politics. A few of them decided to disobey their party's directives and to continue with revolutionary violence, while a few, again, turned to violent crime for personal gain, with no pretence that their violence was still political, though they used the weapons and operational practices of the partisan band.

The PCI's stance on post-war violence reflected a broader position on the democratic rather than the revolutionary potential of the armed wartime resistance for the post-war period. One of the effects of the Party's line was that it removed the political gloss or justification for many acts of violence by communist ex-partisans, and allowed them to be treated as common crimes, something seized on by the PCI's political opponents in the late 1940s.

The end to the civil war of 1943 to 1945 was hardly likely to coincide with the end of the military war. The ferocity of the war between Fascists and anti-Fascists in the final months of German occupation in a place like Bologna, ensured that a revengeful settling of accounts was bound to occur. German and Fascist violence was very fresh in people's minds. In

Bologna, and in Emilia generally, in the days shortly before liberation, withdrawing German troops and Fascist militiamen murdered and, in some places, displayed the bodies of partisans whom they were holding prisoner. They also killed civilians in the same kind of murderous retreat they had followed throughout the war in Italy.

In some cases, the killings of Fascists and collaborators with the Germans were official, even legal. Prior agreements had been reached by the CLNAI with the Italian government and the Allies over the transition of power from the Fascist Republic to the Allied military government during the period of the final liberation of the country in April 1945. These agreements, which were broadly kept to by all sides, were very important for determining what would happen on the final defeat of German forces in Italy and immediately afterwards. They also conveyed what impact the armed resistance would have, or be allowed to have, on the shape of post-war Italy.

The Allied command were surprised, and perhaps even shocked, to find that when their troops entered Florence in August 1944, the Germans had already been pushed out of the city and that the local CLN were effectively administering it, with the partisans as the police force. If nothing else, this act of self-liberation and then self-government rather pre-empted the plans the Allied Military Government (AMG) had for the running of the city and other liberated territory. The Florence experience of a popular liberation rising finally brought home to the Allies the need to take the Italian armed resistance seriously. Events in Greece increased Allied preoccupations with the resistance, since here, after the German occupation had ended, the communist partisan formations had attempted a coup against the AMG and the Greek government in December 1944, precipitating a civil war which lasted well into 1949. The Allies wanted to avoid a repetition of these events in Italy, and the emergence, therefore, of an armed communist force capable of becoming militarily and politically independent of the Italian government and the Allied occupying armies and administration. The prospect of an armed rising by the resistance, in which communist Garibaldi formations were the strongest component, was also anathema to the conservative establishment forces in Italian life, including the Catholic Church and the monarchy. They were hoping to complete a successful passage from complicity and cooperation with the Fascist regime to a non-Fascist, but also non-communist, post-Fascist era. The moderate and conservative non-communist anti-Fascist elements in the Italian government and the CLNs felt the same concerns, for the same reasons.

The Allies could scarcely deny to the armed resistance some sense that anti-Fascist Italians had liberated themselves from Fascism and German occupation. The increasing size and strength of the resistance movement by late 1944, and, as Florence had shown, its capacity for independent action, meant that the Allies would have faced serious problems in preventing some kind of resistance-led popular rising against the Fascists and the Nazis, if they had wanted to. The agreements made between the Allies, the CLNAI, and the Italian government were, then, a kind of trade-off between the interests and aspirations of all three players. At the time, and retrospectively, there were some on the political left who thought that the Resistance should be and was capable of determining the kind of Italy which would emerge from the war. They rather unrealistically saw the agreements as a capitulation of the Resistance leadership to the government and the Allies, an act of excessive self-limitation.

The CLNAI, in effect, made parallel agreements with the Italian government and the Allies. The Rome government was to recognize the CLNAI as the clandestine provisional government in German-occupied northern Italy and as its fully empowered agent to effect the transition from Fascism and Nazi occupation to Allied military administration. In return, the CLNAI acknow-ledged that its powers to act in northern Italy were ones delegated to it by the Italian government. In other words, the CLNAI recognized that the govern-ment in Rome was the legitimate government of the country. The Allies agreed to fund and support the CLNAI's clandestine government and its military arm of the resistance, implicitly accepting that its own final military offensives might well be preceded or accompanied by partisan-led popular uprisings, and recog-nized that the CLNAI would be the interim, transitional authority during and after the liberation. In return, the armed resistance was to become an army at the command of General Alexander, who would set the military strategy and targets of the partisan formations. Once the CLNAI had passed power and authority to the AMG, the partisans were to disarm and disband. The agreements amounted to the CLNAI exchanging much of its operational independence and clout for both Allied and governmental recognition of its legitimacy, its right to exist, and its primary role in the transfer of power from the Fascist Republic and German occupation.

As things turned out, the agreements satisfied the Allies' main concern, which was to secure actual control of the country as soon as possible after the German military defeat. The CLNAI, and through it the local CLNs, were to exercise full emergency powers in the course of the liberation, and were to transfer these powers to the AMG as soon as the Allies were in a position to assume them. The position was retrospectively formalized in the various post-war government amnesties. The summary killings of Fascists and collaborators were legal or open to amnesty if committed up to the formal end of the war in Europe on 8 May 1945; the discretionary period was later extended to 31 July 1945.

The CLNAI's recommendations to the regional and local CLNs on what should happen at liberation in April 1945 attempted to grade Fascists and their retribution. Mussolini and national Fascist Party leaders were to be captured and treated as traitors and war criminals, which meant a death sentence. Members of the Black Brigades, the Decima Mas, and other Fascist militias were also war criminals and to be executed summarily. Saboteurs, looters, rapists, and thieves were liable to be killed by partisans, if caught in the act. Members of the Fascist Republic's armed forces should be arrested and interned, for eventual trial before special war tribunals.

CLNs and partisan commands had sometimes already tried and passed sentence on leading Fascists, and during and immediately after the liberation, carried out these sentences. This helps to explain the relatively systematic way in which the partisans killed the Fascists and collaborators they could find and capture during the liberation. They were not usually executed in public, but formally, either individually or in small groups, in prisons and barracks which the partisans had taken over, after rapid and impromptu trials and sentencing. Some CLNs preferred that a more transparent and legal procedure was followed, that Fascists and collaborators would be invited to surrender to the partisans, who would arrest them, imprison them, and then bring them for trial before special courts set up for the purpose. Most of the killings of Fascists, however, occurred in what was effectively an emergency period during and immediately after the liberation of towns and cities, when the CLNs exercised their full transitional powers through their military force, the partisans.

One should say that the post-liberation killings of Fascists and collaborators by the armed resistance occurred in every country which had been under German occupation. Much of the post-war violence in Italy was not documented or investigated, which meant that figures for the number of post-war killings were intrinsically unreliable. This has allowed neo-Fascists and Fascist apologists to invent pretty much what they wanted in order to convey the impression of a barbarous and uncontrolled bloodbath. The wildest figures produced by neo-Fascist writers were of 300,000 people

13. A young woman is marched through Milan by armed partisans who have branded her as a Fascist by painting 'M' for Mussolini on her head shortly after liberation, April 1945.

14. Fascists are summarily executed by partisans during the liberation of Milan, April 1945.

killed in April 1945 alone. On the basis of prefects' reports from around the country, the Interior Ministry in 1946 came up with a figure of approximately 9,000 Fascists killed on or around liberation in April and May 1945. This figure was not made public, and quite why the Christian Democrat Interior Minister, Mario Scelba, mentioned a figure of 1,732 during a parliamentary debate on a law against post-war neo-Fascism in June 1952, was, and still is, mystifying. Probably of wider political significance was the fact that Christian Democrat-dominated governments had not made public the results of the Interior's 1946 inquiry, which created the vacuum then filled by the wild and unsubstantiated estimates of those with every interest (especially Fascists and neo-Fascists) in portraying a blood-soaked aftermath to the war.

The leeway between the popular and partisan insurrections which allowed their temporary takeover of towns and cities, and the arrival of Allied troops and the handover to Allied control and administration, varied from place to place. Unusually, because of a last-minute breakdown in communication between the Allied troops and the partisans, Bologna was simultaneously liberated by Polish forces entering the outskirts of the city on the morning of 21 April, and the partisans occupying the city centre districts. Here, the partisans' round-up and killing of the mainly middle and lower rank Fascists who remained in the city, took place over 21 and 22 April, when Allied troops were already present. The Allies insisted that the partisans in Bologna disarm and disband by 25 April. Also, exceptionally, Allied troops did not enter Turin until 5 May. Usually, partisan and CLN emergency transitional rule lasted for a few days. So in the Emilian towns of Modena and Reggio Emilia, the partisans had a free hand from 21 to 23–4 April, when Allied troops entered and took over.

It was clear that in some instances, Allied officers practically acknowledged the right of partisans to exercise a summary justice against Fascists and enabled them to do so. Colonel John Stevens, the Allied liaison officer with the Turin partisans, reportedly told Franco Antonicelli, the president of the regional Piedmontese CLN, 'listen, president, clear things up in two, three days, but on the third day, I no longer want to see dead on the streets'.[10] The officer obviously did not want nor expect a bloodbath, but his words were still more an invitation to act than a warning not to do so. In and around Reggio Emilia, too, the Allied military commanders were prepared to look the other way, as long as their military operations were not affected by the enactment of partisan justice. Here, the partisans' round-ups of Fascists went on undisturbed

15. Italian partisans pose on a tank with the first Allied troops to arrive in Turin, May 1945.

16. Armed urban partisans of the communist GAP formations fighting to liberate Turin on 25 April 1945; notice the Nazi-Fascist wall slogans.

for a couple of weeks after liberation—one reason, anyway, for the relatively high number of killings in the province during and after April 1945.

Where the military fighting continued for longer than expected, the partisans were still needed by the Allies as a military force, and were permitted to hang on to and use their weapons for that much longer. This happened in the Emilian city of Parma, which was liberated by the partisans on 25 April. American, Brazilian, and partisan forces then cooperated in the round-up of large numbers of retreating German troops as fighting continued in the province until 30 April, leaving the partisans to disarm in a public ceremony on 9 May. It made a difference how long the Allies took to enforce the agreed disarming and disbanding of partisan formations. Piacenza, to the north-west of Parma, on the way to Milan, was liberated on 28 April and the partisans handed in their arms on 5 May, by which time some important local Fascist figures had been located and shot, including the prefect and the provincial chief of the Fascist Republican Party.

There were other factors to account for the killings of Fascists beyond the official period of liberation and emergency powers. In many areas, the partisans continued to operate after liberation as policemen—usually with the agreement of the Allies and the CLNs—in the absence, inadequacy, or incrimination for Fascist pasts of the regular career police forces. In this policing role, they went on hunting down, arresting, interrogating, and sometimes killing Fascists. A group of partisans were acquitted of the kidnapping, maltreatment, and killing of eight people in a place near Bologna between 23 April and 15 May 1945. This was not only because no bodies were found. They had, on the orders of their commanders, acted as policemen until the local *carabinieri* resumed their duties and even beyond, and those they had arrested (and presumably disposed of) were known Fascists, men of the GNR and the Black Brigades.

The Fascists themselves often took time to be located, since many of them had withdrawn further north as liberation occurred, and only returned—or, rather, were returned—when their places of refuge were liberated. Emilian recruits to the GNR were killed once the local partisans had liberated their training camp and barracks at Treviso, in Venetia, some 130 km away from Bologna. At Concordia di Modena, in the middle of May 1945, partisan police stopped a convoy of vehicles organized by a Catholic charity to transfer people who, because of the war, were resident in the north of the country, to their homes further south. At their checkpoint, the partisans discovered in the lorries armed Fascists and Republican soldiers with false papers, some of whom were sifted out and later shot, while the convoy was allowed to proceed.

Not all the post-liberation partisan killings of Fascists were so authorized. At a prison near Cesena, an area liberated long before, seventeen Fascist prisoners were killed during the night of 8–9 May 1945 by masked ex-partisans who managed to bluff their way in. Because of the general breakdown in policing and security, the country's prisons were very porous and unsafe places, vulnerable both to break-outs and break-ins. The San Vittore prison in Milan saw a kind of civil war on a miniature scale, but all the more intense because of the prison's overcrowding and insecurity. The Fascists imprisoned there were kept in a separate wing. But the many prison riots which broke out during 1945 and 1946 were an opportunity for the ex-partisans in jail for robbery and armed violence—for their unwillingness, in other words, to stop the war—to move in on them and beat them up. Fascist and anti-Fascist prisoners wore their colours, black and red, and chanted their wartime songs at each other. The two groups, nevertheless, cooperated with each other and with the ordinary criminals and black marketeers in riots against the prison system and conditions. The most notorious post-war criminal gangs crossed the political divide, and gang leaders were ex-partisans and ex-Fascist militiamen who had first met in prison.

Perhaps 40,000 Fascists were in prisons across the country in 1946. Such a large political prison population might indicate that after the initial liberation period of summary killings, Fascists were being treated differently, that is, arrested and imprisoned for trial, rather than being shot. But it was hardly a case of them being in prison for their own safety. Some of the most dramatic collective civil war killings of the post-war period were the outcome of break-ins by ex-partisans, clearly affronted by the state's protection of Fascists and determined to complete unfinished business. The most serious massacre took place at the prison in Schio, an industrial town north of Vicenza, in Venetia, during the night of 5–6 July 1945, a few months after liberation. The raid on the prison was as planned and methodical as the authorized killings during liberation itself, though it all ended in chaos. The masked ex-partisan raiders started to work through the prisoners, to comb out those who 'deserved' to be killed. Realizing what was going on, the prisoners panicked and refused to be sorted out into groups, inducing the ex-partisans to fire indiscriminately on what had become a general mêlée, killing fifty-four prisoners, including thirteen women.

Another manifestation of the civil war in the post-war, and another category of post-war killings, was acts of popular retribution which often did not involve armed partisans. The incident at Piacenza d'Adige probably belonged here. It was a targeted, precise affair, involving the people directly hurt by the actions of those being shot. But retribution could also be a collective, community matter. When, in late May 1945, the Fascists held responsible for the last-ditch torture and killing of partisan prisoners in Imola just before the liberation, were returned to the area for trial, the truck carrying them was stopped by a crowd of hundreds of people who chased away the *carabinieri* and ex-partisan escort and lynched most of the prisoners.

These were angry and yet calculated measures of revenge for past misde-meanours, suffering, and abuses of power, with elements of family vendetta thrown in. They were likely to go unpunished, because as the memory of the Piacenza d'Adige events imply, the *omertà* of the local community would have protected the killers who were dispensing what locals would have seen, or justified, as rough justice. It was in its own way significant that people did not want nor intend to leave the punishment of Fascists in their own localities to the police and judicial authorities. People came to see that summary punish-ment of this kind justified itself. One of the factors inducing the ex-partisans in Schio to act was a build-up of anger and tension in the population. The people felt that the restraint they and the local CLN had shown up to this point in waiting for legal punishment of Fascists, was being exploited by the AMG and conservative political forces who did not want to proceed against Fascists at all.

Certainly, the Schio prison killings justified the AMG's dismantling, with local Christian Democrat party support, of the post-liberation apparatus of purge and control held by the CLN in a town which was a militantly anti-Fascist island in a largely rural and conservative Catholic regional sea. The September 1945 trial of the ex-partisans arrested for the killings became a cold war rather than a civil war event. It was one of a series of 'trials of the resistance' which occurred in the late 1940s and into the early 1950s, where the communist armed resistance was generally indicted for its violence and specifically for extending it into the post-war period, murdering in this case, 'innocent' prisoners, as part of an allegedly deliberate strategy to foment disorder and revolution. These political judgements on ex-partisan violence were more difficult to resist, when it was clear that some of the ex-partisans responsible were in hiding in Communist Yugoslavia.

Fascists who were not killed, but arrested and tried, for their Fascist and wartime activities, generally avoided what their victims would have regarded as justice. In Reggio Emilia province, where the number of revenge killings was high, there were over four hundred Fascists killed after the liberation in the months of April, May, and June 1945. The first trials of Fascists took place in June, and of the 240 dealt with in the province's courts over the summer of 1945, fifty received the death penalty, of whom six were executed, and the rest were eventually amnestied in 1946.

Settling the accounts of the past was a way of the community closing ranks in order to face the future, which was one reason why people were not prepared to wait for their revenge. The death of the Fascist dictator Mussolini fell in the period of authorized liberation killings of Fascists, and also had significant aspects of popular retribution.

On 18 April 1945, Mussolini moved himself and his government from their dispersed locations on Lake Garda to the city of Milan, perhaps his one serious attempt during the life of the Fascist Republic to become independent of his German ally and minder. The move was, clearly, also, to save his skin—not just because it made Switzerland accessible, though that was important. By moving to Milan, Mussolini was closer to the people with whom or through whom he might be able to negotiate his own safety.

He was aware of the feelers put out by General Karl Wolff, the Waffen SS commander in Italy, to both the Allies and the CLNAI, for a German surrender. It clearly mattered to Mussolini and to his immediate survival whether he would be handed over to the partisans or the Allies, in the event of a German surrender. He hoped to be able to talk to both the Allies and the CLNAI, using the Catholic bishop of Milan, Cardinal Alfredo Schuster, as mediator and facilitator. One of the Fascist leaders accompanying him to Milan was the head of the Fascist Party, Pavolini, who, true to his stance after the 25 July 1943 sacking of Mussolini as prime minister, wanted resistance to the end, a final stand in the Alps, whether the Germans surrendered or not. This was brave and, in a sense, a more honourable exit for Fascists. But it was ruled out for its impracticality. To stand and fight from some mountain stronghold in the Alps required them first to clear the ground of partisans. Mussolini, with Schuster, met CLNAI representatives on 25 April, and told them that he intended to leave the city and seek a surrender to the Allies. If this move had come off, then the Allies would have undoubtedly been obliged to stage an Italian Nuremberg. Mussolini's decision to surrender to the Allies alone was clearly unacceptable to the CLNAI, which wanted Mussolini to give himself up to them.

Mussolini fled from Milan with his faithful, long-standing mistress, Clara Petacci, her brother, and a small group of Fascist leaders, including Pavolini, on a German military convoy heading north. He was disguised in a German coat and helmet, and spectacles. The Nazi SS had orders to take Mussolini to Germany, just as Marshal Pétain had earlier been taken from Vichy France. Mussolini was not in SS hands, but it is possible that the convoy was aiming to reach Germany. The area near the Swiss border which the convoy was passing through, was regularly patrolled by the partisans, and a group of them, from a communist Garibaldi brigade, stopped the lorries near Dongo, on the shores of Lake Como. Mussolini's German disguise was a sensible one, since the partisans were likely to allow passage to German military forces who were clearly intending to leave the country. The partisans were definitely interested in finding any Italians on board. 'Here's Fatso!' shouted one of the partisans. The ex-dictator was disarmed, taken from the back of the lorry, and early in the morning of 28 April was moved to a house in a nearby village. Accounts vary somewhat, but it was probable that on the afternoon of 28 April, he, Clara, and the other Fascists seized at the checkpoint, were shot and killed by a special execution squad of partisans dispatched from Milan by the communist partisan command.

The partisans clearly could not allow Mussolini's story to end here, on a mountainous Alpine frontier. The bodies were taken back to Milan, and dumped before dawn on a nondescript square in the city, Piazzale Loreto. An announcement of his death and whereabouts was made on local radio. The displaying of Mussolini's body and those of the others shot with him, was a quite deliberate act. Only Achille Starace, the ex-head of the Fascist Party for much of the 1930s, a rather sad figure who lived in Milan, was actually killed in the city after Mussolini's death, captured in his slippers by local partisans. His body was displayed with the others.

The square is not today formally marked out as the place of Mussolini's final public showing. It was renamed after the liberation of the city as 'the square of the fifteen martyrs', to commemorate the shooting and display of fifteen hostages by the Fascist GNR in August 1944. Displaying Mussolini's body here was, then, both a specific and general reprisal and retribution for Fascist killings done in his name. The Milanese partisan leadership wanted to demonstrate tangibly to the Italian people that Mussolini and with him, Fascism, were dead, and that he had been killed not by the Allies, but by anti-Fascist Italians. Photographs of the displayed bodies were circulated

17. The bodies of Mussolini and his mistress, Clara Petacci (near left) are strung up in Piazzale Loreto, Milan, in April 1945.

throughout the country and appeared in newspapers and as wall posters. After Mussolini's dismissal by the king in July 1943, people had defaced and overturned statues of Mussolini and other visible signs of the Fascist regime's ubiquitous presence, in a symbolic premature celebration of the passing of the dictator and his system. Now the Milanese public were given the opportunity to note and mark the real passing of the dictator. One of the PCI's Milanese leaders at the time of Piazzale Loreto said in an interview many years later that the display of Mussolini's body was 'necessary', if distasteful, since it allowed the anti-Fascist resistance to show that it had defeated Fascism, and to convey to the Italian people that with the passing of the old Fascist order, a new anti-Fascist era was opening up.[11]

The bodies soon attracted a large crowd, replenishing itself throughout the day. Partisans acted as crowd controllers, and it was their decision to hang Mussolini and the others, upside down, from the metal framework of a petrol station. This was done to enable people to see the bodies, and to put a stop to the personal and symbolic attacks on Mussolini's body—ironically, the hanging up of the bodies was meant to spare them further humiliation, not to prolong it. Looking carefully at the photographs of the scene, it is noticeable that Clara's skirt has been carefully arranged around and between her legs and not allowed to swing about her face.

The popular emotions reportedly on display in the square were strong ones: celebration, anger, contempt, even shame and nausea at the public degradation of the bodies. There were reports of people kicking Mussolini's body, even firing shots into the body (killing him again). Clearly, most of the crowd were personally affected and damaged in some way by the war for which Mussolini was responsible. One could say that the public display was a way of destroying the mystique and charisma of the Duce. But these had disappeared for most Italians much earlier in the war.

The final impression to take from the gruesome scene in the square was, rather, the popular denigration of a powerful leader, now as impotent as the people he once had power over. Perhaps the display and the crowd's reaction to the display were best seen as popular carnival, during which there was a cathartic and cruel inversion of real-life roles and status. When ordinary Milanese women attempted to place a dead mouse, the lowest kind of animal, in Mussolini's mouth, or placed a piece of cheap low-grade black bread near his hands, they were saying that he was now as poor and contemptible as he had made them. They were celebrating, temporarily, a victory of the powerless over the powerful. Their presence at this public display of Mussolini's corpse, and the vicarious involvement of many other Italians who saw the photographs when they were circulated throughout the country, was as intended, a way of cathartically liberating themselves from Mussolini. But the popular rituals of contempt which were on show did not suggest that they thought that the order of things would change in real life, once the carnival was over.

# Conclusion: Italy's War

How should Italians remember the war? How it actually was, is the too obvious answer.

It is very difficult to measure the extent and the quality of popular consent and support for Mussolini and the Fascist regime, since as a totalitarian system, Fascism sought to mobilize a particularly active and committed kind of consent, resembling the fervour of the religious zealot, but did so in an essentially repressive framework. However, it can be broadly accepted that the Italian people were behind Mussolini's decision to go to war in June 1940, on the understanding that it would be short and victorious. War was at the core of Fascism, as a means of completing and testing the Fascistization of Italians and of securing the *spazio vitale* (living space) of empire. Many anti-Fascists had by 1940 come to the conclusion that, given the regime's basically firm hold on the country and its efficient repression of dissent and opposition, the only hope for getting rid of Mussolini would come with the gamble of war. War was welcomed by both Fascists and anti-Fascists, the one in order to strengthen the regime, the other to weaken it. It was, then, entirely fitting that Mussolini should fall as a result of failing the only test that he, as a Fascist, wanted to be judged by.

The war, not short and victorious but prolonged and precarious, drained away popular support from Mussolini, even among Fascism's natural constituency in the nationalistic middle classes. But Mussolini was not overthrown by the people, nor by the anti-Fascists. He was toppled by overlapping palace coups, planned and executed by Fascism's own disaffected elite and by the monarchy, backed by the other fellow-travelling conservative institutions of Italian life, including the military and civilian state bureaucracy, the Catholic Church, and big business. The loss of popular support for Mussolini and the war created a hollowness around the dictator, which enabled the Fascist and conservative elites to move against him in the knowledge that his removal was unlikely to be resisted or lamented.

Mussolini's fall from power at the hands of the king was not definitive. There was no democratic anti-Fascist succession, but rather a military monarchical government which wanted to manage the transition with Italy's conservative institutions intact, and so restrained anti-Fascist forces re-emerging in the country on Mussolini's fall from power. Anti-Fascism was, in a very real sense, released into action as a result of the armistice of September 1943, arguably the real watershed of Italy's war and of Italy's twentieth century. The armistice and the botched changing of sides pro-longed the war still further; opened up the country to invasion, occupation, and division by Nazi Germany and the Allied powers; led to the destruction by death, disbandment, and internment of Italy's armies; and discredited the monarchy and the military as national institutions, nearly but not quite to the point of extinction. Thereafter, Italians, increasingly confused about where they were and would be, and where they felt they belonged, participated in a struggle for survival in worsening wartime conditions. It was a struggle for personal and family survival, but also one to determine not so much the survival of the nation, as the kind of nation it would be after the war.

Organized and active resistance to, and collaboration with, German occu-pation, was bound to be a minority affair. In the first place, this was for the banal geographical reason that much of the south of the country was spared the worst of German occupation or experienced it for a relatively short period of time. Such a reprieve has almost been held against the south and southerners, and inhibited the south's full incorporation into the post-war nation, perpetuating that apartness which had been there since the political and territorial unification of the country in the late nineteenth century. Mussolini never really solved the 'southern problem', and neither, really, did the war. Some southern Italians entered the reconstituted regular army units which fought alongside the Allies, but not enough to create the sense that the south had contributed to the liberation of the nation from Nazi-Fascism. These regular soldiers would have developed little of the voluntarist spirit and élan, and hence, the committed drive behind a cause, of those partisans who made their own choices to resist, whatever the circumstances which impelled those choices.

In the second place, the dangers and risks involved in becoming an active resister or collaborator were so great that they were ones to be avoided, if possible. Being a partisan meant being an outlaw, and exposing one's family and friends to the reprisals of one's Fascist and German opponents. It involved being hunted down by quite ruthless enemies, on an uncertain terrain of popular support, tolerance, or hostility. What kind of reception it was usually depended on how partisans conducted themselves in the communities and localities where they operated. To be a Fascist militiaman meant facing similar physical danger in the near-certainty of defeat, which was only likely to enhance one's sense of desperation and recourse to violence. It also meant taking action against one's fellow countrymen in the service of a foreign occupier, and living a life of violence which was as isolating as that of the partisan.

But the recognition that organized resistance and collaboration was a matter for large numbers of people who were, nevertheless, significant minorities in the population at large, does not leave the field to a silent majority of apathetic, indifferent Italians who could only wait for the war to end and to see which side won. Everybody knew who was going to win. Nobody could realistically expect to sit out the war. The grey area between collaboration and resistance was constantly being eroded by the effects and demands of, and choices imposed by, the war. The great, submerged phenomenon of the war in Italy was existential collaboration and resistance, the outcome of unorganized, uncongenial, but unavoidable individual day-to-day responses to war and occupation. Sometimes, these choices had no pattern or consequence for the next choice, and were driven by what was elemental to all Italians at war, survival. Sometimes, one choice, taken in one set of circumstances, set in train others, and made others more difficult to avoid. The young woman joining the Fascist women's auxiliary organization for a job, was involved in the purpose and rationale of the organization simply by working for it. Everywhere, in conditions of war and occupation, the society of the majority was drawn into the society of the committed minorities. The female courier for the resistance could only continue to live at home and give herself the disguise of normality which protected her clandestine activity, if she could depend on the complicit silence and ignorance of her neighbours when Nazi soldiers or Fascist police came knocking. There could be few out-and-out fence-sitters, in such circumstances.

Resistance, collaboration, survival, then, fragment into a collage of individual actions, responses, and choices. So it is possible to say that Italians behaved both badly and well during the war. Some peasants handed over Allied POWs to the Germans, others protected them. Some Romans denounced their Jewish neighbours to the Germans during their occupation of the city in 1943–4, and for reasons of personal and material gain as much as ideological anti-semitism; others did all they could to protect them from discovery and round-up. Some soldiers participated in the awful attempted pacification and counter-insurgency campaigns in occupied Yugoslavia and Greece. Others, internees imprisoned in Germany, refused to sign up for the Fascist Republic's army, even though it was the best ticket home. Some people changed as a result of the war experience; others did not. Some women were undoubtedly empowered by their involvement in the resistance or in evacuation, or in post-liberation reconstruction. But one always has the sense that Italian society as a whole would have to change more fundamentally before that wartime self-confidence made any real difference to their lives. These changes arguably came later, during the so-called economic miracle of the 1950s.

There were huge international constraints on what would happen in Italy as a result of the war. One of the unavoidable consequences of defeat and occupation was that the country's future would be largely determined by those powers which had defeated and occupied Italy. The American and British governments were likely, at most, to allow a democratic parliamentary system to emerge in Italy, as elsewhere in liberated western Europe. But they were demonstrably unwilling to allow a social revolution in Italy, especially when Italy was on the border between Allied and Soviet armies at the end of the war.

Now that we can understand that most Italians who resisted German occu-pation did so for existential reasons—or a mix of existential, ideological, and other reasons—surely we can begin to see that this was bound to limit the impact of the armed resistance as a force for change. What could realistically be expected as an outcome of the Resistance was what was realized, the transition from a Fascist dictatorship to an anti-Fascist democratic parliamentary Republic. The various resistance formations, whatever their formal political affiliation or lack of it, were unified by their common initiative to remove the Germans from Italy and to defeat Mussolini's Fascist Republic. They were never unified by anything much more than this, and certainly the idea of the war against Nazi-Fascism becoming a revolutionary war, divided rather than united them.

The Italian people, finally, settled accounts with a monarchy which was complicit with the Fascist regime and had ceased to be a credible and worthy embodiment and symbol of the nation, as a result of the September 1943 armistice. We have to remind ourselves that if the king's intention had been realized in overthrowing Mussolini in July 1943, then the Fascist regime would not eventually have been succeeded by a democratic republic. The needs of post-war national survival and reconstruction after what Churchill called 'the hot rake of war', were one reason, or justification, why Italy's socially and politically progressive democratic post-war constitution was administered and implemented by a largely unreconstructed state bureaucracy and judiciary inherited from twenty years of a Fascist regime. Once again, it is necessary to distinguish the impacts of the great discontinuity of war, which always appear to be more significant that they actually were, from the passage of mere time.

There is a strand of post-war Italian remembering of the war which emerges persistently in both public and private memories. This concerns the way that Italians have attempted to portray themselves as victims. The ubiquity of the continuing sense of victimhood can be shown by a rather grotesque contemporary happening. For the first time, on 10 February 2005, orchestrated by the government under its prime minister, Silvio Berlusconi, the monopolistic media entrepreneur and owner of Milan soccer club, there was a newly minted national day of remembrance. This was to mark the wartime and immediate post-war ethnic cleansing of anything between 6,000 and 15,000 Italians by Yugoslav partisans on Italy's then (and even now) contested north-eastern frontiers. Some of the victims were pushed, dead and alive, into the natural chasms or deep ditches of the area, called *foibe*. To commemorate what was near enough the sixtieth anniversary of these murders, tricoloured ribbons and special stamps were issued; a RAI state television fictional documentary attracted over ten million viewers; and Italy's Foreign Minister, Gianfranco Fini, the leader of the National Alliance—Berlusconi's coalition partner and heir to the post-war neo-Fascist movement, the MSI (in turn, the heir of the rump Fascist Republic of 1943–5)—attended a military ceremony in Trieste, where some of the killings occurred. The ceremonies of commemoration were also deliberately staged to coincide with the anniversary of the post-war peace treaty of February 1947, which confirmed the transfer of Italian Slav territory to Yugoslavia. They came barely a week after the world's commemoration of the liberation of the most notorious of the Nazi death camps, at Auschwitz.

There was something very serious happening here, as Berlusconi was only too keen to remind Italians: 'If we look back to the twentieth century we see pages of history we'd prefer to forget. But we cannot and should not forget.'[1] However, it all depends on what Italy and its politicians choose to remember, and to forget. This new day of national mourning, 10 February, presented as Italy's home-grown holocaust with Italians cast as the victims of a totalitarian ideology, was a very political move. It was a deliberate attempt to challenge the usual emphasis on people being the victims of Nazi and Fascist atrocities, and to portray Italians as the victims of communism. The commemoration threw the Italian left on the defensive, confirmed Berlusconi's anti-communist credentials, and broke explicitly with what the post-war nationalist right has always regarded as a predominantly left-wing cultural bias in appropriating and disseminating the Resistance myths of Italy's wartime experience.

The pervasive and lasting image of victimhood reflected some of the reality of the experience of Italians at war, after the armistice and changing of sides of September 1943. The German disbanding of Italian armies and their intern-ment in Germany, the experience of a brutal and exploitative Nazi occupation of central and northern Italy, made the Italians as much the victims of Nazi oppression as the other occupied peoples of a Nazi-dominated Europe. Being victims, and remembering themselves as victims, allowed Italians to remember the years 1943 to 1945, rather than the years of the Fascist war between 1940 and 1943, when Italians were perpetrators rather than victims, invading and occupying the USSR and Balkan countries in ways which emulated the brutal Nazi systems of occupation.

Memories of being victims were, and remain, strong and emotional among Italians. But, like many memories, what they have in emotional depth they lack in perspective and context. If one chooses to remember the *foibe* killings, then one should, also, remember the forced Italianization campaigns of the Fascist regime in annexed Yugoslav territory before the war and the brutal Italian occupation of Yugoslav lands conquered (by the Germans) during the war itself. This is a very harsh judgement, but a nation which continues to see itself solely as victims is probably incapable of properly coming to terms with its Fascist and wartime past.

The 1980s saw a real flowering of social history in Italy, and historians started to apply anthropological, sociological, and psychological concepts to the his-torical study of modern society and culture. There was something of a boom in studies of the Fascist period and the war which were based on oral and written personal memories. It was the optimum time to interview men and women in their sixties and seventies about their Fascist and wartime adolescence and early adulthood. Some people, of course, prefer, and choose, not to remember at all, and most people remember selectively. People's memories are not necessarily the best guide to what actually happened. They do, however, reveal a person's culture or mentality, their way of looking at the world. Older people, when they remember, often recall events and happenings which occurred at this old child, young adult stage of their lives, since they regard them, justifiably, as first-time life-forming experiences which determined the kind of people they were to become. The landscape of wartime remembering was transformed by the collection and analysis of the memories of groups of veterans of Fascist Italy's military campaigns in the USSR and of Italian military occupation of the Balkans, of men and women ex-partisans, of women who joined the Fascist Republic's female organizations and who sheltered escaping Allied POWs, of evacuees driven out of the countryside by the bombing of their towns and cities.

The more or less officially sanctioned memory of a unified national patriotic and popular resistance fragmented into a variety of actual memories which were not monolithic, but often conflicted with each other, revealing a multitude of different takes on what happened during the war. One of the sources which I have used extensively in this book is an anthology of personal testimonies of civilians during the war, called *Fronte italiano—c'ero anch'io* (The Italian Front—I was there, too). It belongs to this outpouring of personal memories in the 1980s, and contains the personal stories of some of the groups just mentioned, and others besides, including Italians who lived in Italian-annexed and occupied parts of Yugoslavia. The theme of the anthology is Italians as victims. But I have used the book, nevertheless, partly because nobody else seems to have used it, and mainly because the personal stories are so full that they can be read against the grain of the book as a whole. The book, despite itself, reveals Italians behaving as anything but victims.

It should be clear that history was, and is, politics in post-war Italy, and that approaches to the Fascist and wartime experience have been modified according to changing political alignments and developments. The February 2005 *foibe* commemoration was a politically motivated public recovery of a previously relatively neglected wartime atrocity. It was an invented commemoration, not in the sense that the events were fictional, but in terms of the importance now being attached to them. The ceremonies represented a kind of culmination of a really significant shift in Italy's and Italians' perspective on their uncongenial Fascist and wartime past. This sea change occurred in the late 1980s and early 1990s, coinciding with, and to some extent impelled by, the end of cold war politics internationally and internally and of communism as an international force, and the apparent collapse and reformation of Italy's post-war party-political system in the wake of corruption scandals involving an entire political class. The fall of the first Italian Republic led to the coalition in government of Berlusconi's amorphous political movement originally called Forza Italia (Come on, Italy) after one of the more polite soccer slogans, the separatist and anti-south Northern League, and the so-called post-Fascist National Alliance.

Berlusconi's political initiative of the 10 February celebrations, a quite deliberate attempt to reopen the Yugoslav issue on both national and international fronts, has its intellectual equivalent in a revamped conservative nationalist revisionist reading of Italy's Fascist and wartime past by a school of 'anti-anti-Fascist'[2] historians. The school's treatment of the degree of popular consent, or rather consensus, for the Fascist regime in the 1930s, its attempt to dilute the meaning and significance of the wartime armed resistance and to upgrade those of the wartime Republican Fascists, portraying them as the active minorities fighting for the soul of the nation over the largely inert and wait-and-see popular majority, point to a deeply divided national society during and since the war and contested national identities. Similar things happened in Yugoslavia at about the same time. As the country de-federated into independent statelets, the new states put out readings of the wartime experience which differed from and challenged the dominant myth of a 'Yugoslav' anti-German and anti-Italian resistance, which accompanied the communist refoundation of Yugoslavia in 1945. The perceived contemporary crisis of national identity in Italy, precipitated by the collapse of its political system and the undermining of the historical myth sustaining it, finds its attempted resolution in Berlusconi's revival of a nationalistic nationalism which seeks to reopen the old national wounds on the north-eastern frontier. But although often politically driven, these conservative revisionist historians, together with the ground-breaking work on the resistance mentality, or mentalities, of the anti-Fascist historian Claudio Pavone, have from very different ideological perspectives, generated a much more nuanced and ambiguous treatment of Italy's wartime experience. Their approaches probably bring us closer to the reality of Italians' lives than the straightforward story of a popular, national anti-Fascist crusade.

One final comment. Politicians of Italy's post-war political parties, both those who were the mainstays of the first Republic and those who created, or reinvented, themselves on its ruins in the 1990s, have used history and memory of the war to make political points and delegitimize their opponents. This use, or misuse, of history has forced some scrupulous Italian historians into their professional shells. They do not want their work to legitimize or discredit anybody. Sometimes, they take their professional detachment to the point of saying that their history serves no public purpose at all. But clearly it does. The recent historical reconstructions and analyses of, say, the German massacres of Italian civilians across Tuscany in 1944, reveal the dynamics of a triangular relationship of Germans, partisans, and people, and bring us closer to the complex and ambiguous interactions of wartime existence in Italy. These histories make a properly historical use of people's recollections of past traumas, contextualizing them and so deepening the often shallow perspective of memory. Even in the late 1990s, it appeared unlikely that Italy's politicians would be either willing or able to help Italians to take account of their country's Fascist and wartime past. Italy's professional historians seem rather more capable than its politicians of enabling Italians to tell themselves proper stories.

# Notes

## Preface

1. Uwe Schmidt, of the overseas TV service in Berlin, in a conversation with Anna Funder for her book, *Stasiland: Stories from behind the Wall* (London: Granta Books, 2004), 14.
2. Epigraph to the autobiography of Gabriel García Márquez, *Living to Tell the Tale* (London: Cape, 2003).

## Introduction: Remembering the Second World War in Italy

1. See e.g. P. Burrin, *Living with Defeat: France under the German Occupation* (London: Arnold, 1996); R. O. Paxton, *Vichy France: Old Guard and New Order, 1940–1944* (London: Barrie and Jenkins, 1972); J. F. Sweets, *Choices in Vichy France: The French under Nazi Occupation* (New York: Oxford University Press, 1986); M. L. Smith, 'Neither Resistance nor Collaboration: Historians and the Problem of the *Nederlandse Unie*', *History*, 72 (1987).
2. See G. Bedeschi (ed.), *Fronte italiano—c'ero anch'io: La popolazione in guerra* (Milan: Mursia, 1987), 9; L. Ceva and G. Rochat, 'Italy', in I. C. B. Dear and M. R. D. Foot (eds.), *The Oxford Companion to the Second World War* (Oxford: Oxford University Press, 1995), 595; J. M. Winter, 'Demography of the War', ibid. 290.
3. A local Nazi Party briefing written in late 1943 or 1944, in J. Noakes (ed.), *Nazism, 1919–1945: A Documentary Reader*, iv. *The German Home Front in World War II* (Exeter: Exeter University Press, 1998), 91–7.
4. *New Statesman*, 1 May 1999.
5. Quoted in F. Focardi and L. Klinkhammer, 'The Question of Fascist Italy's War Crimes: The Construction of a Self-Acquitting Myth (1943–1948)', *Journal of Modern Italian Studies*, 9/3 (2004), 342.
6. Quoted in R. Ben-Ghiat, 'Liberation: Italian Cinema and the Fascist Past, 1945–50', in R. J. B. Bosworth and P. Dogliani (eds.), *Italian Fascism: History, Memory and Representation* (London: Macmillan, 1999), 84.
7. See *Guardian*, 11 Jan. 2006.

## 1. The First Fall of Mussolini, July 1943

1. Dino Grandi, *25 luglio: Quarant'anni dopo*, ed. R. De Felice (Bologna: il Mulino, 1983), 268.
2. Quoted in G. B. Guerri, *Galeazzo Ciano: Una vita, 1903–1944* (Milan: Bompiani, 1979), 562.

3. Giuseppe Bottai, *Diario, 1935–1944*, ed. G. B. Guerri (Milan: Rizzoli, 1982), 415.
4. Dino Grandi, *25 luglio*, 286.
5. Entry for 2 Aug. 1943: Bottai, *Diario*, 422.
6. Entry for 23 Aug. 1943: ibid. 431.
7. Dino Grandi, *25 luglio*, 266.
8. 'Pay attention, gentlemen!', ibid. 264.
9. Ibid.
10. Ibid. 268.
11. Mussolini's speech to the Fascist Party national congress, June 1925, in *Opera omnia di Benito Mussolini*, ed. E. and D. Susmel, xxi (Florence: La Fenice, 1952), 362.
12. Dino Grandi, *25 luglio*, 266.
13. Entry for 17 Jan. 1941: Bottai, *Diario*, 246.
14. Entry for 23 Jan. 1943: ibid. 357.
15. Entries for 23 July and 14 Oct. 1941: ibid. 278, 287.
16. Quoted in Guerri, *Ciano*, 527.
17. Quoted in Dino Grandi, *25 luglio*, 26.
18. Entry for 12 Nov. 1941: Bottai, *Diario*, 289.
19. Entry for 13 Nov. 1942: ibid. 334.
20. Entry for 13 July 1943: ibid. 388.
21. Farinacci to Grandi, 23 July 1943, in Dino Grandi, *25 luglio*, 243.
22. Quoted ibid. 61.
23. Quoted in O. Chadwick, 'Bastianini and the Weakening of the Fascist Will to Fight the Second World War', in T. C. W. Blanning and D. Cannadine (eds.), *History and Biography: Essays in Honour of Derek Beales* (Cambridge: Cambridge University Press, 1996), 234.
24. D. Alfieri, *Due dittatori di fronte* (Milan: Rizzoli, 1948), 315.
25. Quoted in Guerri, *Ciano*, 558.
26. Dino Grandi, *25 luglio*, 242.
27. Quoted in Guerri, *Ciano*, 636.
28. Hitler conference, 26 July 1943, in F. Gilbert (ed.), *Hitler Directs his War* (New York: Award Books, 1950), 57.
29. Hitler conference, 25 July 1943: ibid. 48, 50.
30. Hitler conference, 26 July 1943: ibid. 57, 60.
31. Entry for 24 Nov. 1942: V. Klemperer, *To the Bitter End: The Diaries of Victor Klemperer, 1942–1945* (London: Phoenix, 2000), 207.
32. Entry for 1 Jan. 1944: ibid. 349.
33. *The Goebbels Diaries*, ed. L. P. Lochner (London: Hamish Hamilton, 1948), 331.
34. J. Noakes (ed.), *Nazism, 1919–1945: A Documentary Reader*, iv. *The German Home Front in World War II* (Exeter: Exeter University Press, 1998), 549.
35. Hitler conference, 26 July 1943: Gilbert (ed.), *Hitler*, 57.

## 2.  Fascist Italy at War, 1940–1943: Propaganda and Reality

1. Quoted in L. Ceva, 'Italia e Grecia, 1940–1941: Una guerra a parte', in B. Micheletti and P. P. Poggio (eds.), *L'Italia in guerra, 1940–1945* (Brescia: Annali della Fondazione 'Luigi Micheletti', 1990–1), 215–16.

2. D. Gagliani, 'La guerra in periferia: Cittadini e poteri in un comune appenninico', in Micheletti and Poggio (eds.), *L'Italia in guerra*, 904.

3. Quoted in P. Cavallo, *Italiani in guerra: Sentimenti e immagini dal 1940 al 1943* (Bologna: il Mulino, 1997), 79.

4. Quoted ibid. 243.

5. Quoted in A. Lepre, *Le illusioni, la paura, la rabbia: Il fronte interno italiano, 1940–1943* (Naples: Edizioni Scientifiche Italiane, 1989), 29.

6. From a 1940 pamplet, quoted in Cavallo, *Italiani in guerra*, 114.

7. Quoted ibid. 115.

8. From a poem used in a theatrical work staged in 1943, quoted ibid. 125.

9. Quoted in M. Isnenghi, *Le guerre degli italiani: Parole, immagini, ricordi, 1848–1945* (Bologna: il Mulino, 2005), 285.

10. Quoted in G. Vaccarino, 'L'occupazione italiana in Grecia', in Micheletti and Poggio (eds.), *L'Italia in guerra*, 240.

11. 'Me ne frego' ('I don't give a damn') was one of the slogans used by paramilitary Fascist squadrists in the early 1920s.

12. Quoted in Gagliani, 'La guerra in periferia', 906–7, 909.

13. The phrase was Palmiro Togliatti's, the Italian Communist Party leader in exile in the USSR, in a 'Radio Milano-Libertà' broadcast of 12 Dec. 1941, quoted in Cavallo, *Italiani in guerra*, 186.

14. Quoted ibid. 128.

15. Quoted in Gagliani, 'La guerra in periferia', 910.

16. The phrase was used in articles in Mussolini's newspaper, *Il Popolo d'Italia*, in the spring of 1943, and quoted in M. Di Giovanni, 'I volontari paracadutisti tra miti bellici e guerra reale', in Micheletti and Poggio (eds.), *L'Italia in guerra*, 998.

17. Quoted in Isnenghi, *Le guerre degli italiani*, 287.

18. Quoted in R. De Felice, *Mussolini l'alleato, i. L'Italia in guerra, 1940–1943, 2. Crisi e agonia del regime* (Turin: Einaudi, 1996), 734.

19. Quoted ibid, 1. *Dalla guerra 'breve' alla guerra lunga* (Turin: Einaudi, 1996), 173.

20. Quoted in D. Stefanutto, 'La morte celata: Miti e immagini della morte in guerra', in Micheletti and Poggio (eds.), *L'Italia in guerra*, 940.

21. Quoted in De Felice, *Mussolini l'alleato*, i/2. *Crisi e agonia del regime*, 1309.

22. Quoted in Cavallo, *Italiani in guerra*, 264.

23. Quoted in M. Mafai, *Pane nero: Donne e vita quotidiana nella seconda guerra mondiale* (Milan: Mondadori, 1987), 63.

24. Quoted in Cavallo, *Italiani in guerra*, 184.

25. Quoted ibid.

26. Quoted ibid. 185.

27. Quoted in A. Bendotti, G. Bertacchi, M. Pelliccioli, and E. Valtulina, ' "Ho fatto la Grecia, l'Albania, la Yugoslavia ..." : Il disagio della memoria', in Micheletti and Poggio (eds.), *L'Italia in guerra*, 289.

28. See T. Sala, 'Guerra e amministrazione in Yugoslavia, 1941–1943: Un'ipotesi coloniale', ibid. 91; and also, 'La politica italiana nei Balcani', in F. Ferratini Tosi, G. Grassi, and M. Legnani (eds.), *L'Italia nella seconda guerra mondiale e nella Resistenza* (Milan: Franco Angeli, 1988), 91.

29. Quoted in T. Ferenc, 'Gli italiani in Slovenia, 1941–1943', ibid. 162.

30. Quoted in Isnenghi, *Le guerre degli italiani*, 304–6.

31. Quoted by Claudio Pavone in his 'Introduction' to 'The Hidden Pages of Contemporary Italian History: War Crimes, War Guilt, Collective Memory', *Journal of Modern Italian Studies*, 9/3 (2004), 274.

32. See A. Bendotti et al., ' "Ho fatto la Grecia" ', 296, 298.

33. Qoted in Mafai, *Pane nero*, 96.

34. Quoted in Lepre, *Le illusioni, la paura, la rabbia*, 100.

35. Quoted in M. Legnani, 'Guerra e governo delle risorse: Strategie economiche e soggetti sociali nell'Italia, 1940–1943', in Micheletti and Poggio (eds.), *L'Italia in guerra*, 360.

36. Quoted in De Felice, *Mussolini l'alleato, i/2. Crisi e agonia del regime*, 1063.

37. Quoted in Mafai, *Pane nero*, 87.

38. Quoted in Cavallo, *Italiani in guerra*, 236–7.

39. Quoted ibid. 86.

40. Quoted in Lepre, *Le illusioni, la paura, la rabbia*, 85.

41. Quoted ibid. 86.

42. Quoted in Cavallo, *Italiani in guerra*, 62.

43. Quoted ibid. 356.

3.   *Fascist Italy at War, 1940–1943: Collapse of the Home Front*

1. Quoted in P. Cavallo, *Italiani in guerra: Sentimenti e immagini dal 1940 al 1943* (Bologna: il Mulino, 1997), 266.

2. Quoted ibid. 106–7.

3. Quoted in M. Mafai, *Pane nero: Donne e vita quotidiana nella seconda guerra mondiale* (Milan: Mondadori, 1987), 123.

4. Quoted in Cavallo, *Italiani in guerra*, 303.

5. Quoted in G. De Luna, 'Torino in guerra: La ricerca di un'esistenza collettiva', in B. Micheletti and P. P. Poggio (eds.), *L'Italia in guerra, 1940–1945* (Brescia: Annali della Fondazione 'Luigi Micheletti', 1990–1), 899.

6. See P. Sorcinelli, 'War in the Mental Hospitals: Psychiatry and Clinical Files (1940–1952)', *Journal of Modern Italian Studies*, 10/4 (2005), 449.

7. Documentary appendix to R. De Felice, *Mussolini, l'alleato*, i. *L'Italia in guerra, 1940–1943*, 2. *Crisi e agonia del regime* (Turin: Einaudi, 1996), 1515.

8. Quoted in E. Ragionieri, 'La storia politica e sociale', *Storia d'Italia*, iv/3. *Dall'Unità ad oggi* (Turin: Einaudi, 1976), 2322.

9. Quoted in De Felice, *Mussolini l'alleato*, i/2. *Crisi e agonia del regime*, 949.

10. Quoted ibid. 955.

11. For the text of Mussolini's speech, see *Opera Omnia di Benito Mussolini*, ed. E. and D. Susmel, xxxi (Florence: La Fenice, 1963–4), 128–32.

12. Quoted in Cavallo, *Italiani in guerra*, 273.

13. Quoted ibid. 272.

14. Quoted in N. Gallerano, 'Gli italiani in guerra, 1940–1943: Appunti per una ricerca', in F. Ferratini Tosi, G. Grassi, and M. Legnani (eds.), *L'Italia nella seconda guerra mondiale e nella Resistenza* (Milan: Franco Angeli, 1988), 320.

15. Quoted in E. Agarossi, *A Nation Collapses: The Italian Surrender of September 1943* (Cambridge: Cambridge University Press, 2000), 45.

16. Quoted in Cavallo, *Italiani in guerra*, 278.

17. Quoted ibid. 330.

18. Quoted ibid. 383.

## 4.  *The Forty-Five Days, July to September 1943*

1. D. Mack-Smith, 'The Italian Armistice of 1943', *Rivista: Journal of the British Anglo-Italian Society*, 332 (1989), 2.

2. Quoted in E. Agarossi, *A Nation Collapses: The Italian Surrender of September 1943* (Cambridge: Cambridge University Press, 2000), 88.

3. Quoted ibid. 97.

## 5.  *The Armistice, September 1943*

1. Quoted in M. Franzinelli, 'L'8 settembre', in M. Isnenghi (ed.), *I luoghi della memoria: Personaggi e date dell'Italia unita* (Bari: Laterza, 1997), 243.

2. G. Bedeschi (ed.), *Fronte italiano—c'ero anch'io: La popolazione in guerra* (Milan: Mursia, 1987), 112.

3. Ibid. 137.

4. Ibid. 567.

5. Ibid. 590.

6. Quoted in R. De Felice, *Mussolini l'alleato*, i. *L'Italia in guerra, 1940–1943*, 2. *Crisi e agonia del regime* (Turin: Einaudi, 1996), 1310.

7. Bedeschi (ed.), *C'ero anch'io*, 685–6, 689.

8. Quoted in C. Pavone, *Una guerra civile: Saggio storico sulla moralità nella Resistenza* (Turin: Bollati Boringhieri, 2003), 15.

9. Bedeschi (ed.), *C'ero anch'io*, 543.

10. Quoted in Franzinelli, 'L'8 settembre', 248.
11. Quoted ibid.
12. Quoted in M. Isenghi, *Le guerre degli Italiani: Parole, immagini, ricordi, 1848–1945* (Bologna: il Mulino, 2005), 259.
13. Quoted in Franzinelli, 'L'8 settembre', 248.
14. Bedeschi (ed.), *C'ero anch'io*, 52–3.
15. Ibid. 149.
16. Ibid. 271.
17. Ibid. 309.
18. Quoted in M. Di Giovanni, ' "Eroi" contro la nazione, "vincitori" senza memoria: I paracadutisti della RSI e del regno del sud', in M. Legnani and F. Vendramini (eds.), *Guerra, guerra di liberazione, guerra civile* (Milan: Franco Angeli, 1990), 366. Some of the captain's men returned to their regiment, awaiting the arrival of the Allies, a sign of the indecisiveness and difficult choices of the times.
19. Bedeschi (ed.), *C'ero anch'io*, 275.
20. Ibid.
21. N. Revelli, 'La ritirata di Russia', in M. Isenghi (ed.), *I luoghi della memoria: Strutture ed eventi dell'Italia unita* (Bari: Laterza, 1997), 374.
22. Quoted in A. Bendotti et al., ' "Ho fatto la Grecia, l'Albania, la Yugoslavia ..." : Il disagio della memoria', in B. Micheletti and P. P. Poggio (eds.), *L'Italia in guerra, 1940–1943* (Brescia: Annali della Fondazione 'Luigi Micheletti', 1990–1), 303.
23. Bedeschi (ed.), *C'ero anch'io*, 115.
24. Ibid. 324.
25. Ibid. 322.
26. Ibid. 562.
27. Ibid. 555.
28. N. Lewis, *Naples '44* (London: Eland Books, 1983), 15.
29. Bedeschi (ed.), *C'ero anch'io*, 569.
30. Quoted in Franzinelli, 'L'8 settembre', 246.
31. Bedeschi (ed.), *C'ero anch'io*, 70–2.
32. Ibid. 592.
33. Ibid. 287.
34. Ibid. 31.
35. S. Trambaiolo, 'The Child and the She-Wolf: Memories of a Fascist Childhood', in J. Milfull (ed.), *The Attractions of Fascism: Social Psychology and Aesthetics of the 'Triumph of the Right'* (New York and Oxford: Berg, 1990), 13, 15.
36. Quoted in Pavone, *Una guerra civile*, 41.

6.  *The Invasion and Occupation of Italy, and the Kingdom of the South,*
    *1943–1945*

    1.  Quoted in R. Absalom, 'Ex-prigionieri alleati e assistenza popolare nella zona
        della linea gotica, 1943–1944', in G. Rochat, E. Santarelli, and P. Sorcinelli
        (eds.), *Linea gotica, 1944: Eserciti, popolazioni, partigiani* (Milan: Franco Angeli,
        1986), 454, 468.
    2.  Quoted in Field Marshal Lord Carver, *The War in Italy, 1943–1945* (London:
        Pan Books, 2002), 80.
    3.  Quoted ibid. 251.
    4.  G. Bedeschi (ed.), *Fronte italiano—c'ero anch'io: La popolazione in guerra* (Milan:
        Mursia, 1987), 31.
    5.  Ibid. 535.
    6.  Quoted in P. Salvetti, '*Il Risorgimento* di Napoli (4 ottobre 1943–4 giugno
        1944)', in N. Gallerano (ed.), *L'altro dopoguerra: Roma e il Sud, 1943–1945*
        (Milan: Franco Angeli, 1985), 497–8.
    7.  Quoted in G. Chianese, 'Ceti poplari e comportamenti quotidiani a Napoli',
        ibid. 279.
    8.  N. Lewis, *Naples '44* (London: Eland Books, 1983), 171.
    9.  Ibid. 115.
    10. Ibid. 43.
    11. Ibid. 192–3.
    12. Quoted in D. W. Ellwood, *Rebuilding Europe: Western Europe, America and*
        *Postwar Reconstruction* (London: Longman, 1992), 227.
    13. Quoted in L. Piccioni, 'Roma e gli alleati: Solo il primo gradino di un lungo
        dopoguerra', in Gallerano (ed.), *L'altro dopoguerra*, 195.
    14. Quoted in S. Adorno, 'Lo sfollamento a Pesarò', in Rochat et al. (eds.), *Linea*
        *gotica*, 293.
    15. Quoted in S. Lotti, 'Donne nella guerra: Strategie di sopravvivenza tra persis-
        tenze e mutamenti', ibid. 327.
    16. Ibid. 325.
    17. Ibid.
    18. Quoted in A. Portelli, 'Assolutamente niente: L'esperienza degli sfollati a
        Terni', in Gallerano (ed.), *L'altro dopoguerra*, 137.
    19. Bedeschi, (ed.), *C'ero anch'io*, 421.
    20. Ibid. 239.
    21. Lotti, 'Donne nella guerra', 333.
    22. Quoted in A. C. Federici, 'Il passaggio del fronte attraverso le relazioni dei
        parroci della diocesi di Fano', in Rochat et al. (eds.), *Linea gotica*, 364.
    23. Ibid. 366.
    24. Bedeschi (ed.), *C'ero anch'io*, 421.
    25. Ibid. 455.
    26. Ibid. 456.
    27. Quoted in G. Bocca, *La Repubblica di Mussolini* (Bari: Laterza, 1977), 57.

28. This appeared in the first edition of the newspaper *L'uomo qualunque*, quoted in E. Forcella, 'Introduzione: Lo Stato nascente e la società esistente', in Gallerano (ed.), *L'altro dopoguerra*, 23.

## 7. The Other Two Italies, and their Three Wars, 1943–1945

1. See the intervention of Walchiria Terradura, in G. Rochat, E. Santarelli, and P. Sorcinelli (eds.), *Linea gotica, 1944: Eserciti, popolazioni, partigiani* (Milan: Franco Angeli, 1986), 673.

2. Quoted in C. Pavone, 'Le tre guerre: Patriottica, civile e di classe', in M. Legnani and F. Vendramini (eds.), *Guerra, guerra di liberazione, guerra civile* (Milan: Franco Angeli, 1990), 28.

3. Quoted in C. Pavone, *Una guerra civile: Saggio storico sulla moralità nella Resistenza* (Turin: Bollati Boringhieri, 2003), 440.

4. Ibid. 441.

5. Quoted in P. Morgan, *Italian Fascism, 1915–1945* (2nd edn., Basingstoke: Palgrave Macmillan, 2004), 220.

6. Quoted in M. Di Giovanni, ' "Eroi" contra la nazione, "vincitori" senza memoria: I paracadutisti della RSI e del regno del Sud', in Legnani and Vendramini (eds.), *Guerra, guerra di liberazione*, 365.

7. Quoted in E. Sarzi Amadé, 'Delazione e rappresaglia come strumento della "guerra civile" ', ibid. 347.

8. Quoted in P. Corsini and P. P. Poggio, 'La guerra civile nei notiziari della GNR e nella propaganda della RSI', ibid. 272.

9. C. Mazzantini, *A cercar la bella morte* (Milan: Mondadori, 1986).

10. Quoted in Di Giovanni, ' "Eroi" contra la nazione', 386.

11. See M. Mafai, *Pane nero: Donne e vita quotidiana nella seconda guerra mondiale* (Milan: Mondadori, 1987), 260.

12. Pavone, *Una guerra civile*.

13. Quoted in M. Valdinosi, 'Il fronte è vicino: Popolazione cesenate e avanzata alleata', in Rochat et al. (eds.), *Linea gotica*, 396–7.

14. Quoted in Pavone, *Una guerra civile*, 361, 363.

15. Quoted ibid. 396.

16. Quoted in L. Mariani, 'Memorie e scritture delle donne', in B. Dalla Casa and A. Preti (eds.), *Bologna in guerra, 1940–1945* (Milan: Franco Angeli, 1995), 445.

17. Quoted in D. Borioli, 'La percezione del nemico: I partigiani di fronte al nazifascismo', in Legnani and Vendramini (eds.), *Guerra, guerra di liberazione*, 135.

18. Quoted in S. Carli Ballola and L. Casali, 'Alla ricerca del consenso: La stampa fascista e antifascista nel 1943–1944', in Rochat et al. (eds.), *Linea gotica*, 544–5.

19. Quoted in M. Isenghi, *Le guerre degli Italiani: Parole, immagini, ricordi, 1848–1945* (Bologna: il Mulino, 2005), 126.

20. Quoted in S. Morgan, 'The Schio Killings: A Case Study of Partisan Violence in Postwar Italy', *Modern Italy*, 5/2 (2000), 153.
21. Quoted in S. Lotti, 'Donne nella guerra: Strategie di sopravvivenza tra persistenze e mutamenti', in Rochat et al. (eds.), *Linea gotica*, 330.
22. G. Bedeschi (ed.), *Fronte italiano—c'ero anch'io: La popolazione in guerra* (Milan: Mursia, 1987), 513–14.
23. Quoted in C. Bermani, 'Giustizia partigiana e guerra di popolo in Valsesia', in Legnani and Vendramini (eds.), *Guerra, guerra di liberazione*, 168.
24. Quoted ibid. 180.
25. Quoted in Pavone, *Una guerra civile*, 501.
26. Quoted in Mariani, 'Memorie e scritture delle donne', 441.
27. See ibid. 442–3.
28. Quoted ibid. 446.
29. Quoted in S. Tramontin, 'I documenti collettivi dei vescovi nella primavera-estate del 1944', in Legnani and Vendramini (eds.), *Guerra, guerra di liberazione*, 418.
30. Quoted in F. Traniello, 'Il mondo cattolico italiano nella seconda guerra mondiale', in F. Ferratini Tosi, G. Grassi, and M. Legnani (eds.), *L'Italia nella seconda guerra mondiale e nella Resistenza* (Milan: Franco Angeli, 1988), 356.
31. See P. Pezzino, 'The German Military Occupation of Italy and the War against Civilians', paper given at Association for the Study of Modern Italy conference, *Italy at war, 1935–2005*, Edinburgh, November 2005, 13.
32. Quoted in R. Absalom, 'Allied Escapers and the *Contadini* in Occupied Italy (1943–1945)', *Journal of Modern Italian Studies*, 10/4 (2005), 422.
33. Quoted in Pavone, *Una guerra civile*, 482.
34. Quoted in A. Portelli, 'Assolutamente niente: L'esperienza degli sfollati a Terni', in N. Gallerano (ed.), *L'altro dopoguerra: Roma e il Sud, 1943–1945* (Milan: Franco Angeli, 1985), 142.

*Chapter 8. Continuing the Wars, and the Second Fall of Mussolini, April 1945*

1. Quoted in P. Sorcinelli, 'War in the Mental Hospitals: Psychiatry and Clinical Files (1940–1952)', *Journal of Modern Italian Studies*, 10/4 (2005), 457.
2. See S. Trambaiolo, 'The Child and the She-Wolf: Memories of a Fascist Childhood', in J. Milfull (ed.), *The Attractions of Fascism: Social Psychology and Aesthetics of the 'Triumph of the Right'* (New York and Oxford: Berg, 1990), 19–20.
3. Quoted in A. Martini, 'Tra tedeschi e alleati: Vita quotidiana, aspettative e comportamenti sociali fra Roma e Cassino (1943–1946)', in N. Gallerano (ed.), *L'altro dopoguerra: Roma e il Sud, 1943–1945* (Milan: Franco Angeli, 1985), 248.

4. Quoted in C. Sonetti, 'The Family in Tuscany between Fascism and the Cold War', in J. Dunnage (ed.), *After the War: Violence, Justice, Continuity and Renewal in Italian Society* (Market Harborough: Troubadour, 1999), 83.

5. G. Bedeschi (ed.), *Fronte italiano—c'ero anch'io: La popolazione in guerra* (Milan: Mursia, 1987), 95.

6. Ibid. 88–9.

7. Ibid. 389–90.

8. Ibid. 105–6.

9. Ibid. 122, 212.

10. Quoted in N. S. Onofri, *Il triangolo rosso (1943–1947)* (Rome: Sapere 2000, 1994), 32.

11. See M. Dondi, 'Piazzale Loreto', in M. Isenghi (ed.), *I luoghi della memoria: Simboli e miti dell'Italia unita* (Bari: Laterza, 1998), 497.

## Conclusion: Italy's War

1. See *Guardian*, 11 Feb. 2005.

2. The phrase comes from M. Knox, 'The Fascist Regime, its Foreign Policy and its Wars: An Anti-Anti-Fascist Orthodoxy?', *Contemporary European History*, 4 (1995).

# Select Bibliography

*Biographies of Mussolini*

Bosworth, R. J. B., *Mussolini* (London: Arnold, 2003).

Clark, M., *Mussolini* (Harlow: Pearson Education, 2005).


*Fall of Mussolini and Fascist Regime*

Alfieri, D., *Due dittatori di fronte* (Milan: Rizzoli, 1948).

Battaglia, R., 'Un aspetto inedito della crisi del '43: L'attegiamento di alcuni gruppi del capitale finanaziario', *Il Movimento di Liberazione in Italia*, 34–5 (1955).

Bottai, Giuseppe, *Diario, 1935–1944*, ed. G. B. Guerri (Milan: Rizzoli, 1982).

Chadwick, O., 'Bastianini and the Weakening of the Fascist Will to Fight the Second World War', in T. C. W. Blanning and D. Cannadine (eds.), *History and Biography: Essays in Honour of Derek Beales* (Cambridge: Cambridge University Press, 1996).

Cherubini, G. et al. (eds.), *Storia della società italiana, 22. La dittatura fascista* (Milan: Teti, 1983).

Ciano, G., *Diario, 1937–1943*, ed. R. De Felice (Milan: Rizzoli, 1980).

Colarizi, S., *L'opinione degli italiani sotto il regime, 1929–1943* (Bari: Laterza, 1991).

Deakin, F. W., *The Brutal Friendship: Mussolini, Hitler and the Fall of Italian Fascism* (London: Phoenix Press, 2000).

Ganapini, G., 'I cattolici nella crisi del 1943: Il caso di Milano', *Il Movimento di Liberazione in Italia*, 109 (1972).

Grandi, Dino, *25 luglio: Quarant'anni dopo*, ed. R. De Felice (Bologna: il Mulino, 1983).

Guerri, G. B. (ed.), *Rapporto al Duce: Il testo stenografico inedito dei colloqui tra i federali e Mussolini nel 1942* (Milan: Bompiani, 1978).

—— *Galeazzo Ciano: Una vita, 1903–1944* (Milan: Bompiani, 1979).

Kallis, A. A., ' "A question of loyalty": *Mussolinismo* and the Collapse of the Italian Fascist Regime in 1943', *Journal of Modern Italian Studies*, 6/1 (2001).

Martinelli, R., 'Il Partito Nazionale Fascista in Toscana, 1939–1943', *Italia Contemporanea*, 158 (1985).

Rogari, S., 'L'opinione pubblica in Toscana di fronte alla guerra (1939–1943)', *Nuova Antologia*, 557 (1987).

Ventura, A. (ed.), *Sulla crisi del regime fascista, 1938–1943: La società italiana dal 'consenso' alla Resistenza* (Venice: Marsilio, 1996).

## Italy at War

Abse, T., 'Italy', in J. Noakes (ed.), *The Civilians in War: The Home Front in Europe, Japan and the USA in World War Two* (Exeter: Exeter University Press, 1992).

Bertolo, G. (ed.), *Operai e contadini nella crisi italiana del 1943–1944* (Milan: Feltrinelli, 1974).

Candeloro, G., *Storia dell'Italia moderna*, x. *La seconda guerra mondiale, il crollo del fascismo, la Resistenza* (Milan: Feltrinelli, 1984).

Carver, Field Marshal Lord, *The War in Italy, 1943–1945* (London: Pan, 2002).

Cavallo, P., *Italiani in guerra: Sentimenti e immagini dal 1940 al 1943* (Bologna: il Mulino, 1997).

Colarizi, S., *La seconda guerra mondiale e la Repubblica, 1938–1958* (Turin: UTET, 1984).

Collotti, E., and Sala, T., *L'Italia nell'Europa dannubiana durante la seconda guerra mondiale* (Milan: INSMLI, 1967).

—— —— and Vaccarino, G., *Le potenze dell'Asse e la Yugoslavia: Saggi e documenti, 1941–1943* (Milan: Feltrinelli, 1974).

Dalla Casa, B., and Preti, A. (eds.), *Bologna in guerra, 1940–1945* (Milan: Franco Angeli, 1995).

Dear, I. C. B., and Foot, M. R. D. (eds.), *The Oxford Companion to the Second World War* (Oxford: Oxford University Press, 1995).

De Felice, R. (ed.), *L'Italia fra tedeschi e alleati: La politica estera fascista e la seconda guerra mondiale* (Bologna: il Mulino, 1973).

—— *Mussolini l'alleato*, i. *L'Italia in guerra, 1940–1943*: 1. *Dalla guerra 'breve' alla guerra lunga*; 2. *Crisi e agonia del regime*; ii. *La guerra civile, 1943–1945* (Turin: Einaudi, 1996–7).

Di Nolfo, E., Raniero, R. H., and Vigezzi, B. (eds.), *L'Italia e la politica di potenza in Europa (1938–1940)* (Milan: Marzorati, 1986).

Ferratini Tosi, F., Grassi, G., and Legnani, M. (eds.), *L'Italia nella seconda guerra mondiale e nella Resistenza* (Milan: Franco Angeli, 1988).

Fondazione 'Luigi Micheletti' (ed.), *1940–1943, L'Italia in guerra: Immagini e temi della propaganda fascista* (Brescia: Fondazione 'Luigi Micheletti', 1989).

Gallerano, N., 'Il fronte interno attraverso i rapporti delle autorità (1942–1943)', *Il Movimento di Liberazione in Italia*, 109 (1972).

Gribaudi, G., *Tra bombe alleate e violenze naziste: Napoli e il fronte meridionale, 1940–1944* (Turin: Bollati Boringhieri, 2005).

Knox, M., *Mussolini Unleashed, 1939–1941: Politics and Strategy in Fascist Italy's Last War* (Cambridge: Cambridge University Press, 1982).

—— 'The Italian Armed Forces, 1940–1943', in A. Millet and W. Murray (eds.), *Military Effectiveness*, iii. *The Second World War* (London: Unwin Hyman, 1990).

Lamb, R., *War in Italy, 1943–1945* (London: John Murray, 1993).

Legnani, M., and Vendramini, F. (eds.), *Guerra, guerra di liberazione, guerra civile* (Milan: Franco Angeli, 1990).

Lepre, A., *Le illusioni, la paura, la rabbia: Il fronte interno italiano, 1940–1943* (Naples: Edizioni Scientifiche Italiane, 1989).

Mafai, M., *Pane nero: Donne e vita quotidiana nella seconda guerra mondiale* (Milan: Mondadori, 1987).

Malgeri, F., *La chiesa italiana e la guerra, 1940–1945* (Rome: Studium, 1980).

Micheletti, B., and Poggio, P. P. (eds.), *L'Italia in guerra, 1940–1945* (Brescia: Annali della Fondazione 'Luigi Micheletti', 1990–1).

'The Never-Ending Liberation', whole issue of *Journal of Modern Italian Studies*, 10/4 (2005).

Ragionieri, E., 'La storia politica e sociale', *Storia d'Italia*, iv/3. *Dall' Unità ad oggi* (Turin: Einaudi, 1976).

Rainero, R. H., and Biagini, A. (eds.), *L'Italia in guerra: Il primo anno, 1940* (Rome: Stabilmento Grafico Militare, 1991); *Il secondo anno, 1941*; *Il terzo anno, 1942*; *Il quarto anno, 1943* (Gaeta: Stabilmento Grafico Militare, 1992–4).

Rizzi, L., *Lo sguardo del potere: La censura militare in Italia nella seconda guerra mondiale* (Milan: Rizzoli, 1984).

Sala, T., 'Guerriglia e controguerriglia in Yugoslavia nella propaganda per le truppe occupanti italiane (1941–1943)', *Il Movimento di Liberazione in Italia*, 108 (1972).

Secchia, P. (ed.), *Enciclopedia dell'antifascismo e della resistenza* (Milan: La Pietra, 1968).

Vinci, A. (ed.), *Trieste in guerra: Gli anni 1938–1943* (Trieste: Istituto Regionale per la Storia del Movimento di Liberazione nel Friuli-Venezia Giulia, 1992).

## The Forty-Five Days and the Armistice

Agarossi, E., *A Nation Collapses: The Italian Surrender of September 1943* (Cambridge: Cambridge University Press, 2000).

Istituto Nazionale per la Storia del Movimento di Liberazione in Italia (ed.), *L'Italia dei quarantacinque giorni* (Milan: INSMLI, 1969).

Mack-Smith, D., 'The Italian Armistice of 1943', *Rivista: Journal of the British Anglo-Italian Society*, 332 (1989).

Pinzani, C., 'L'8 settembre: Elementi ed ipotesi per un giudizio storico', *Studi Storici*, 13/2 (1972).

Rochat, G., and Pieri, P., *Pietro Badoglio* (Turin: UTET, 1974).

Von Plehwe, F. K., *The End of an Alliance: Rome's Defection from the Axis in 1943* (London: Dent, 1971).

Zangrandi, R., *L'Italia tradita: 8 settembre, 1943* (Milan: Mursia, 1971).

## Occupation, Collaboration, and Resistance

Absalom, R., *A Strange Alliance: Aspects of Escape and Survival in Italy, 1943–1945* (Florence: Leo S. Olschki, 1991).

—— (ed.), *Gli alleati e la ricostruzione in Toscana (1944–1945)* (Florence: Leo S. Olschki, 2001).

—— (ed.), *Perugia liberata: Documenti anglo-americani sull'occupazione alleata di Perugia (1944–1945)* (Florence: Leo S. Olschki, 2001).

Agarossi, E., 'La situazione politica ed economica dell'Italia nel periodo 1944–1945', *Quaderni dell'Istituto Romano per la Storia d'Italia dal Fascismo alla Resistenza*, 2 (1971).

Arbizzani, L. (ed.), *Al di qua e al di là della Linea Gotica, 1944–1945: Aspetti sociali, politici e militari in Toscana e in Emilia-Romagna* (Bologna and Florence: Regioni Emilia-Romagna e Toscana, 1993).

Battini, M., and Pezzino, P., *Guerra ai civili: Occupazione tedesca e politica del massacro, Toscana, 1944* (Venice: Marsilio, 1997).

'Behind Enemy Lines in World War Two: The Resistance and the OSS in Italy', whole issue of *Journal of Modern Italian Studies*, 4/1 (1999).

Bocca, G., *La Repubblica di Mussolini* (Bari: Laterza, 1977).

Collotti, E., *L'amministrazione tedesca dell'Italia occupata* (Milan: Lerici, 1963).

Conti, G., 'La RSI e l'attività del fascismo clandestino nell'Italia liberata dal settembre 1943 all'aprile 1945', *Storia Contemporanea*, 10/4–5 (1979).

Cooke, P. (ed.), *The Italian Resistance: An Anthology* (Manchester: Manchester University Press, 1997).

Ellwood, D. W., *Italy, 1943–1945* (Leicester: Leicester University Press, 1985).

Foot, J., 'The Tale of San Vittore: Prisons, Politics, Crime and Fascism in Milan, 1943–1946', *Modern Italy*, 3/1 (1998).

Fraddosio, M., 'La donna e la guerra—Aspetti della militanza femminile nel fascismo: Dalla mobilitazione civile alle origini Saf della Repubblica Sociale Italiana', *Storia contemporanea*, 20/6 (1989).

Gallerano, N., 'L'influenza dell'amministrazione militare alleata sulla riorganizzazione dello stato italiano (1942–1943)', *Italia contemporanea*, 115 (1974).

—— (ed.), *L'altro dopoguerra: Roma e il Sud, 1943–1945* (Milan: Franco Angeli, 1985).

—— 'A Neglected Chapter in Italy's Transition from Fascism to the Republic: The Kingdom of the South', *Journal of Modern Italian Studies*, 1/3 (1996).

Ganapini, L., *La repubblica delle camicie nere* (Milan: Garzanti, 1999).

Goebbels, *The Goebbels Diaries*, ed. L. P. Lochner (London: Hamish Hamilton, 1948).

Gribaudi, G. (ed.), *Terra bruciata: Le stragi naziste sul fronte meridionale* (Naples: l'ancora del mediterraneo, 2003).

Imbriani, A. M., *Vento del Sud: Moderati, reazionari, qualunquisti (1943–1948)* (Bologna: il Mulino, 1996).

Istituto Storico della Resistenza in Toscana, *Toscana occupata: Rapporti delle Militärkommandanturen, 1943–1944* (Florence: Leo S. Olschki, 1997).

Klinkhammer, L., *L'occupazione tedesca in Italia, 1943–1945* (Turin: Bollati Boringhieri, 1993).

Lepre, A., *La storia della Repubblica di Mussolini* (Milan: Mondadori, 2000).

Lewis, N., *Naples '44* (London: Eland Books, 1983).

Micheletti, B. (ed.), *La guerra partigiana in Italia e in Europa* (Brescia: Fondazione 'Luigi Micheletti', 1986).

Pavone, C., 'Caratteri e eredità della "zona grigia" ', *Passato e Presente*, 43 (1998).

—— *Una guerra civile: Saggio storico sulla moralità nella Resistenza* (Turin: Bollati Boringhieri, 2003).

Peli, S., *La Resistenza in Italia: Storia e critica* (Turin: Einaudi, 2004).

Pezzino, P., *Anatomia di un massacro: Controversie sopra una strage tedesca* (Bologna: il Mulino, 1997).

Poggio, P. P. (ed.), *La Repubblica Sociale Italiana, 1943–1945* (Brescia: Annali della Fondazione 'Luigi Micheletti', 1986).

Quazza, G., *Resistenza e storia d'Italia* (Milan: Feltrinelli, 1976).

'Resistance and its Representation', issue of *Modern Italy*, 5/2 (2000).

Rochat, G., Santarelli, E., and Sorcinelli, P. (eds.), *Linea gotica, 1944: Eserciti, popolazioni, partigiani* (Milan: Franco Angeli, 1986).

Valdevit, G., 'Gli Alleati e la Venezia Giulia, 1941–1945', *Italia contemporanea*, 142 (1981).

Verdina, N. (ed.), *Riservato a Mussolini: Notiziari giornalieri della Guardia Nazionale Repubblicana, novembre 1943–giugno 1944* (Milan: Feltrinelli, 1974).

Zucotti, S., *Italians and the Holocaust. Persecution, Rescue and Survival* (New York: Basic Books, 1987).

## From War into Post-War

Crainz, G., 'Il conflitto e la memoria. "Guerra civile" e "triangolo della morte" ', *Meridiana*, 13 (1992).

Dondi, M., *La lunga liberazione: Giustizia e violenza nel dopoguerra italiano* (Rome: Edizioni Riuniti, 2004).

Duggan, C., 'Italy in the Cold War Years and the Legacy of Fascism', in C. Duggan and C. Wagstaff (eds.), *Italy in the Cold War: Politics, Culture and Society, 1948–1958* (Oxford: Berg, 1995).

Dunnage, J. (ed.), *After the War: Violence, Justice, Continuity and Renewal in Italian Society* (Market Harborough: Troubadour, 1999).

Millar, E. A. (ed.), *The Legacy of Fascism* (Glasgow: Glasgow University Press, 1989).

Onofri, N. S., *Il triangolo rosso (1943–1947)* (Rome: Sapere 2000, 1994).

Petacco, A., *A Tragedy Revealed: The Story of Italians from Istria, Dalmatia, and Venezia Giulia, 1943–1956* (Toronto: University of Toronto Press, 2005).

Sluga, G., *The Problem of Trieste and the Italo-Yugoslav Border: Difference, Identity and Sovereignty in Twentieth Century Europe* (New York: SUNY Press, 2001).

Storchi, M., *Combattere si può, vincere bisogna: La scelta della violenza tra resistenza e dopoguerra (Reggio Emilia, 1943–1946)* (Venice: Marsilio, 1998).

Valdevit, G., *Foibe* (Venice: Marsilio, 1997).

Woller, H., *I conti con il fascismo: L'epurazione in Italia, 1943–48* (Bologna: il Mulino, 1997).

Woolf, S. J. (ed.), *The Rebirth of Italy, 1943–1950* (London: Longman, 1972).

## Memory, Memories, and Representation

Baldissara, L., and Pezzino, P. (eds.), *Crimini e memorie di guerra: Violenze contro le popolazioni e politiche del ricordo* ( Naples: l'ancora del mediterraneo, 2004).

Bartram, G., Slawinski, M., and Steel, D. (eds.), *Reconstructing the Past. Representations of the Fascist Era in Post-War European Culture* (Keele: Keele University Press, 1996).

Bedeschi, G. (ed.), *Fronte italiano—c'ero anch'io: La popolazione in guerra* (Milan: Mursia, 1987).

Bendotti, A., Bertacchi, G., Pelliccioli, M., and Valtulina, E. (eds.), *Prigionieri in Germania: La memoria degli internati militari* (Bergamo: Il filo di Arianna, 1990).

Bosworth, R. J. B., and Dogliani, P. (eds.), *Italian Fascism: History, Memory and Representation* (London: Macmillan, 1999).

Bravo, A., and Bruzzone, A. M., *In guerra senza armi: Storie di donne, 1940–1945* (Bari: Laterza, 1995).

—— and Jalla, D. (eds.), *Una misura onesta: Gli scritti di memoria della deportazione dall'Italia, 1944–1993* (Milan: Franco Angeli, 1994).

Contini, G., *La memoria divisa* (Milan: Rizzoli, 1997).

Crainz, G., *Il dolore e l'esilio: L'Istria e le memorie divise d'Europa* (Rome: Donzelli, 2005).

Draaisma, D., *Why Life Speeds Up As You Get Older: How Memory Shapes Our Past* (Cambridge: Cambridge University Press, 2005).

Focardi, F., *La guerra della memoria: La Resistenza nel dibattio politico italiano dal 1945 a oggi* (Bari: Laterza, 2005).

Franzinelli, M., *Le stragi nascoste—L'armadio della vergogna: Impunità e rimozione dei crimini di guerra nazifascisti, 1943–2001* (Milan: Mondadori, 2002).

Galli della Loggia, E., *La morte della patria: La crisi dell'idea della nazione tra Resistenza, antifascismo e Repubblica* (Bari: Laterza, 1996).

'The Hidden Pages of Contemporary Italian History: War Crimes, War Guilt, Collective Memory', whole issue of *Journal of Modern Italian Studies*, 9/3 (2004).

Isnenghi, M. (ed.), *I luoghi della memoria: Personaggi e date dell'Italia unita* (Bari: Laterza, 1997).

—— (ed.), *I luoghi della memoria: Strutture ed eventi dell'Italia unita* (Bari: Laterza, 1997).

—— (ed.), *I luoghi della memoria: Simboli e miti dell'Italia unita* (Bari: Laterza, 1998).

—— *Le guerre degli italiani: Parole, immagini, ricordi, 1848–1945* (Bologna: il Mulino, 2005).

Levy, C., 'Historians and the First Republic', in S. Berger, M. Donovan, and K. Passmore (eds.), *Writing National Histories: Western Europe since 1800* (London: Routledge, 1999).

Peitsch, H., Burdett, C., and Gorrara, C. (eds.), *European Memories of the Second World War* (New York: Berg, 1999).

'Perspectives and Debates', *Journal of Modern Italian Studies*, 6/3 (2001).

Revelli, N., *La guerra dei poveri* (Turin: Einaudi, 1982).

—— *La strada del davai* (Turin: Einaudi, 1966).

Trambaiolo, S., 'The Child and the She-Wolf: Memories of a Fascist Childhood', in J. Milfull (ed.), *The Attractions of Fascism: Social Psychology and Aesthetics of the 'Triumph of the Right'* (New York and Oxford: Berg, 1990).

Willson, P. R., 'Saints and Heroines: Re-Writing the History of Italian Women in the Resistance', in T. Kirk and A. McElligot (eds.), *Opposing Fascism: Community, Authority and Resistance in Europe* (Cambridge: Cambridge University Press, 1999).

# Acknowledgements

Acknowledgement is made to the following for permission to reproduce illustrations: Alinari Archives, Florence: 14; Archivio dell'Istituto Piemontese per la storia della Resistenza e della Società contemporanea, Turin: 9, 10, 16; Archivio di Stato del Cantone Ticino-Svizzera, Fondo fotografico Christian Schiefer: 17; Bundesarchiv, Koblenz (Bild101I-316-1200): 12; Concessione dell'Archivio Storico della Città di Torino, Gazzetta del Popolo, Archivio Fotografico: 5; Hulton Archive/Getty Images: 18; Imperial War Museum: (NA16084) 11, (K5731) 13, (IA66354) 15, (NA10378) 4; Istituto Luce, Rome: 1,6; Istituto Luce, Rome/Alinari Archives, Florence: 2,7,8; Studio Patellani/Corbis: 3.

# Index

Note: page references in *italic* indicate maps and illustrations.